A Silence After Trumpets

*The Story
of*
Sarah Buchanan Preston

Sarah Buchanan Preston, 1858, in Paris

A Silence After Trumpets

*The Story
of*
Sarah Buchanan Preston

By
Frances Herman Jackson
and
Mary McNease Kinard

THE REPRINT COMPANY, PUBLISHERS
Spartanburg, South Carolina
1998

Copyright © 1998 by Frances Herman Jackson and Mary McNease Kinard
All rights reserved

An original publication, 1998
The Reprint Company, Publishers
Spartanburg, South Carolina 29304

ISBN 0-87152-518-6
Library of Congress Catalog Card Number 98-42516
Manufactured in the United States of America

Photographs of Sarah Buchanan Preston, cover and frontispiece, courtesy of Mrs. Gordon H. Mann

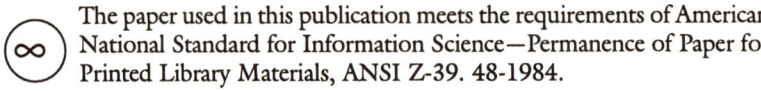 The paper used in this publication meets the requirements of American National Standard for Information Science—Permanence of Paper for Printed Library Materials, ANSI Z-39. 48-1984.

Library of Congress Cataloging-in-Publication Data

Jackson, Frances Herman
    A silence after trumpets : the story of Sarah Buchanan Preston / by Frances Herman Jackson and Mary McNease Kinard.
       p.   cm.
    Includes bibliographical references.
    ISBN 0-87152-518-6
    1. Preston, Sarah Buchanan, 1842-1880—Fiction. 2. Columbia (S.C.)—History—Civil War, 1861-1865—Fiction. 3. Richmond (Va.)—History—Civil War, 1861-1865—Fiction. 4. Hood, John Bell, 1831-1879—Fiction. 5. Hampton family—Fiction. I. Kinard, Mary McNease. II. Title.
PS3560.A21537S55   1998
813'.54—dc21   98-42516
                                                                 CIP

I have seen glory fade, and I have heard
A silence after trumpets. Fortune wanes,
And triumph falters. The resplendent sword
Of valor rusts. Of grandeur, what remains?
Fame's music sounds, and then the music ends.
Even sweet hope herself declines and dies.
Despite all courage, strength to weakness tends.
There's but one thing that every change defies.

From year to year its beauty and its power
Ascend amid defeats and fading prides.
With all else dying, it will come to flower.
With all else fading, nobly it abides.
Its virtue 'gainst all enemies avails.
If love be truly love, it never fails.

From *Love's Meaning*
by Archibald Rutledge
(Fleming H. Revell Co., 1943)

Contents

	Hampton Family Tree	viii
	Cast of Characters	xi
	Sources	xiii
	Prologue: Columbia 1868	1
I	Columbia, 1854	3
II	Paris 1858	19
III	Columbia 1860	37
IV	Columbia 1861	53
V	Columbia 1862	69
VI	RIchmond and Columbia, 1862-63	77
VII	Richmond 1863	99
VIII	Richmond, 1864	127
IX	Columbia, 1864	155
X	Georgia and Tennessee, 1864	171
XI	Columbia and Richmond, 1865	177
XII	York, 1865	197
	Epilogue	205

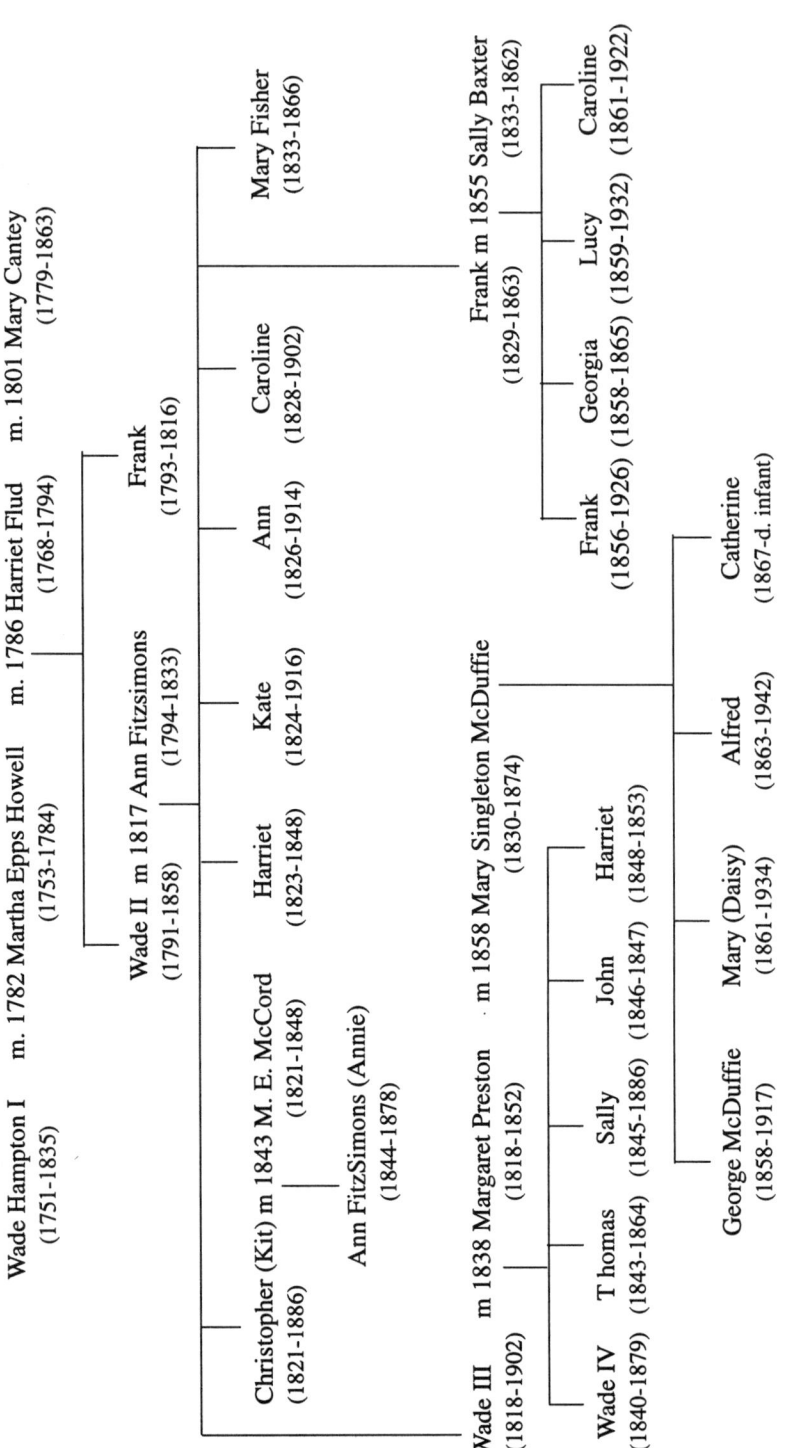

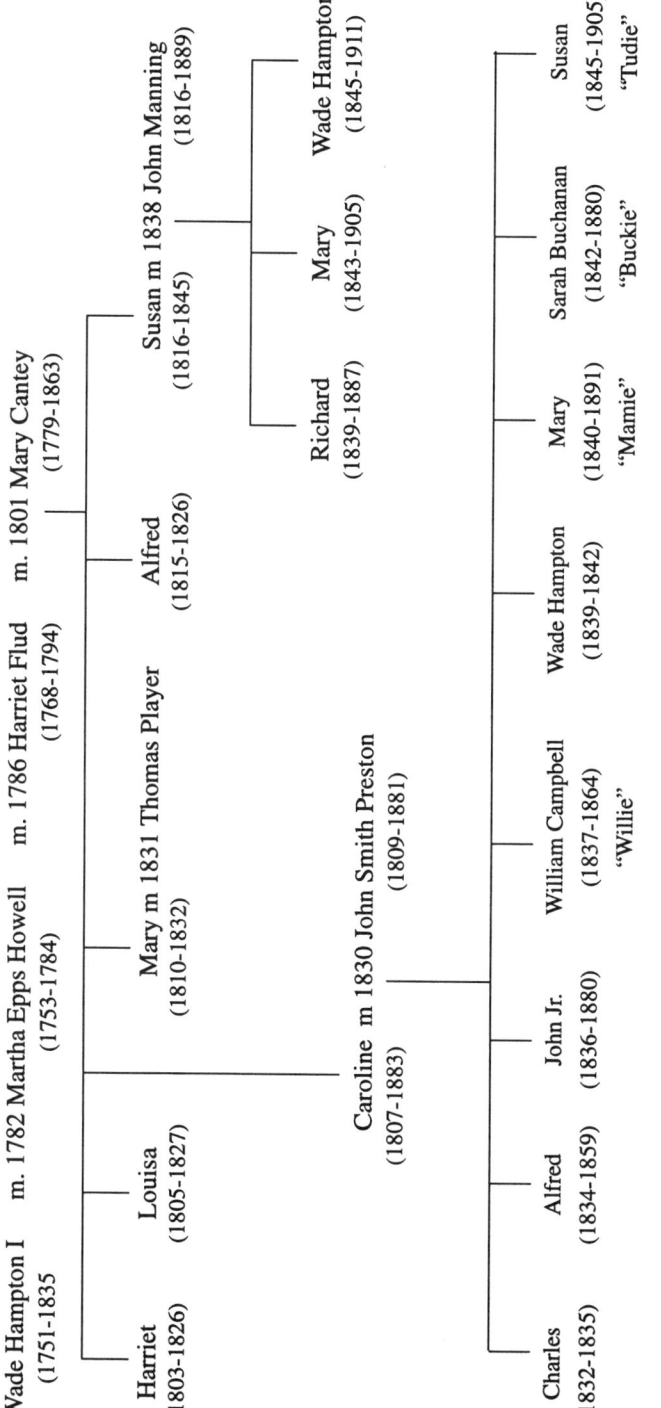

Cast of Characters

Real People

Preston Family

John Smith Preston—father, husband of Caroline, a Virginian
Caroline Hampton Preston—mother, wife of John, daughter of Mary Cantey Hampton and Wade Hampton I
John, Jr.—older son
William (Willie)—younger son and favorite brother
Mary Cantey (Mamie)—oldest daughter
Sarah Buchanan (Buck or Buckie)—middle daughter
Susan Frances (Tudie)—youngest daughter

Hampton Family

Mary Cantey Hampton—Caroline Preston's mother, widow of Wade Hampton I, step-grandmother of Wade III and Frank Hampton, grandmother of Preston children
Wade Hampton III—Caroline Preston's nephew, Civil war general
Frank Hampton—brother of Wade III, husband of Sally Baxter Hampton
Sally Baxter—a New Yorker, wife of Frank
Kate, Ann, Caroline, Mary Fisher—unmarried sisters of Wade III and Frank, known as the "Misses Hampton"

Others

Ransom Calhoun—Charlestonian, cousin of the Prestons
Mary Chesnut—family friend, wife of James Chesnut
Rawlins Lowndes—Charlestonian, aide to Wade III
John Darby—physician and surgeon, from Orangeburg
John Bell Hood (Sam)—Civil War general

Dr. Robert Gibbes—Columbia physician
William, John, and Maria Walker—house slaves belonging to Caroline Preston

Fictional

Jean-Paul Bellanger—a Frenchman, captain in Napoleon III's guard
Edward Gibbes—Charlestonian, nephew of Dr. Gibbes

Special thanks to:
Meynard. Virgina G. THE VENTURERS, Greenville, S.C., Southern Historical Press, Inc. 1981

Sources

Chesnut, Mary Boykin. *A Diary From Dixie*, ed. by Ben Ames Williams. Boston: Houghton Mifflin, c1949.

Coker, Elizabeth Boatwright. *La Belle.* New York: E. P. Dutton, c1959.

Columbia: Capital City of South Carolina 1786-1936, ed. by Helen Kohn Hennig. Columbia, SC: Columbia Sesquicentennial Commission, 1936.

Confederate Receipt Book: A Compilation of Over One Hundred Receipts, Adapted to the Times. Athens, GA: University of Georgia Press, c1960.

Davis, Burke. *Sherman's March.* New York: Random House, c1980.

DeLeon, T. C. (Thomas Cooper). *Four Years in Rebel Capitals: An Inside View of Life in the Southern Confederacy, From Birth to Death, from Original Notes.* Orig. pub. 1892. Reprinted 1975. Spartanburg, SC: The Reprint Company, 1975.

A Divided Heart: Letters of Sally Baxter Hampton, 1853-1862, ed. by Ann Fripp Hampton. Columbia, SC: Phantom Press, Publishers, 1994.

Dowdey, Clifford. *Experiment in Rebellion.* Garden City, NY: Doubleday, 1947.

Dowdey, Clifford. *The Land They Fought For: The Story of the South as the Confederacy, 1832-1865.* Garden City, NY: Doubleday, c1955.

Dyer, John P. *The Gallant Hood.* New York: Konecky & Konecky, c1950.

Graydon, Nell S. *Tales of Columbia.* Columbia, SC: R. L. Bryan, c1981.

Henry, Robert Selph. *The Story of the Confederacy.* Garden City, Garden City Publishing Co., c1931.

Lee, Richard M. *General Lee's City: an Illustrated Guide to the Historic Sites of Confederate Richmond.* McLean, VA: EPM Publications, c1987

Lucas, Marion Brunson. *Sherman and the Burning of Columbia.* College Station, TX: Texas A & M University Press, c1976.

Mary Chesnut's Civil War, ed. by C. Vann Woodward. New Haven: Yale University Press, c1981.

Muhlenfeld, Elisabeth. *Mary Boykin Chesnut: A Biography.* Baton Rouge: Louisiana State University Press, c1981.

O'Connor, Richard. *Hood: Cavalier General.* New York: Prentice-Hall, c1949.

The Paris We Love, ed. by Dore Ogrizek. New York: McGraw-Hill, c1950.

This is a work of fiction. While based on real people, much of the conversation and some of the events are imaginary. The authors, being docents at the Hampton-Preston Mansion in Columbia, have come to know the family very well and really feel that they are telling the story as it happened.

Prologue
Columbia, South Carolina, 1868

On a cold day in late February 1868, the two younger Preston sisters sat in the upstairs parlor of the family home in Columbia, shivering with the cold and discussing the details of Buck's approaching wedding.

"I do hope it's not as cold on the tenth of March as it is today! Firewood and coal are so hard to get since the war, and the house never seems warm," said Tudie. "Why in the world didn't you wait until spring to get married?"

Buck replied, "It seems to me that we have waited quite long enough."

"I suppose you're right, but Mamie's wedding was lovely. September is a good month for the weather. I'm glad you can wear her dress, even if you freeze!"

"Oh, I do wish she and John could be here. It seems so long since we were all together in Paris."

"It's strange for just the two of us to be making plans. You and Mamie and I are all so different, but we usually agree."

"Things don't seem to happen to her like they do to you and to me. Mamie is the steady one. She found John and they loved each other and Papa and Mama were pleased and it all turned out right. I hope now my life will be more like hers. I'm tired of excitement and complications. Perhaps it was all my fault. That's what Willie always said. I can hear him now. 'If you would just make up your mind and stick to it. But no. As soon as you do one thing, you are sorry you didn't do the other.' Well, maybe he would be happy now."

"Don't talk about Willie. It still makes me sadder than anything. Remember that day you and Mamie and Mama and Papa all came back to Columbia from Houmas? You were so angry that Willie wasn't at the house waiting for you."

"You were just a little girl then."

"Yes, but I remember it perfectly."

I
Columbia, 1854

As the train from Augusta pulled into the Columbia station, Buckie Preston, leaning out of the window, said to her older sister, Mamie, "Oh, Mamie, I'm so happy to be back in Columbia, aren't you? Grandmama and Willie and all our friends are here and South Carolina is ever so much nicer than Louisiana! Look, there's Grandmama's carriage now."

Across the station platform, Henry, Mrs. Hampton's coachman, sighed with relief. The train was an hour late and he was tired of waiting. When he saw Buckie, he grinned broadly and waved. Her unusual height, long auburn hair, and violet eyes made her stand out in any crowd. It was hard to believe she was only twelve years old. Henry saw people turning to look at her and called, "Miss Buckie, stay right there. I'll pull the carriage around so you can get in." He turned the two elegant bay horses and drove the carriage over to where the girls now stood.

After he had helped them into the carriage, he went to greet Mr. and Mrs. Preston, who had just descended from the train.

"How are you, Henry? Good to see you again. Been keeping well?"

"Pretty well, sir. Glad to have you and Mrs. Preston back again. You and the young ladies make us all feel better!"

He helped them into the carriage and sent two little Negro boys to collect the trunks and hatboxes and bags which would be brought to the Hampton home later in a wagon. As soon as they were seated, Henry drove away from the depot and down Gervais Street. Columbia, the capital of South Carolina, was a pleasant city of about eight thousand inhabitants in 1854 with wide, tree-lined dirt streets and large handsome houses.

Henry turned left on Pickens Street and down to Walnut Street where he stopped in front of the large family home which had been built in 1818 and bought by Mrs. Preston's father in 1823. It was home not only to the Preston family, but also to Caroline's mother, Mary

Cantey Hampton, and to Mrs. Hampton's three orphan grandchildren, Richard, Lila, and Wade Manning, whose mother, Susan Hampton Manning, had died when little Wade was born, nine years ago.

"Your father made a wise purchase when he bought this house," said John to his wife. "I am surprised he was willing to move, loving Woodlands as he did."

"Oh, it was all Mama. She never did like living at Woodlands and was afraid all the rest of us would die of malaria out there. Papa bought this house to humor her. He always said he paid Mr. Hall an outlandish price. I think it was $35,000. Look, there she is now!"

Mary Cantey Hampton was indeed standing on the porch. Two excited maids hovered in the double doorway behind her. She was a sweet-faced elderly lady dressed in black, as became a widow, with a small lace cap on her soft white hair.

As soon as the carriage stopped, Buckie leaped out and rushed up the steps to kiss her grandmother. "Oh, Grandmama, I am so glad to see you! Where is Willie? May we go out to Millwood tomorrow and see the family? Shall we go to church first so that everyone will know that we are back? Do you think I look older than twelve? I am as tall as Mamie."

Mrs. Hampton held up her hands in despair. "Buckie, Buckie, how can anyone answer you? Let Mamie and your mother and father get out of the carriage. Caroline, my dear, I am so happy to see you at last. Did you have a tiring journey? How did you leave Kit? Were things going well in Louisiana?"

"Grandmama, you ask as many questions as I do."

"Buckie, don't speak in that impudent tone to your grandmother," said Caroline Preston sharply as she came up the steps to the porch.

"You look tired, dear," said Mrs. Hampton, kissing her. "Come on in and sit down, and we will have a nice cool drink while you and John tell me all the news."

As they followed her into the hall where sixteen-foot ceilings gave welcome relief from the June heat, the Prestons' youngest daughter, Tudie, a blonde chubby nine-year old and the three Manning cousins rushed in from the garden. After tumultuous greetings and much hugging and kissing, Caroline said, "Where are the boys?" She wondered why her three sons were not there to greet their parents.

Tudie answered, "They were tired of waiting and decided to go for a ride. They'll probably be back soon."

Buckie said, "But I particularly wanted to see Willie. I've missed him so and have all sorts of things to tell him. He should have known not to go off."

"Well," Tudie retorted, "you'll just have to wait. I'll come and talk to you."

Mrs. Hampton said to the girls, "Mamie, you and Buckie go on up to your rooms. I told Rachel and Susie to take water up so you both could have a nice bath after that hot and dusty train. When your trunks arrive, they can help you unpack and change your clothes."

The girls, with Tudie following, went off up the circular staircase and through the door which led into the newer part of the house, added by the Prestons when they returned from Louisiana in 1848. As they went, Mamie said to her sister, "I'll bet Grandmama sent us off so she could tell Papa and Mama about Uncle Frank's courtship of that lady from New York. I heard them talking about it on the train when they thought we were asleep. They said Aunt Kate and Aunt Ann are not one bit pleased. They always hoped he would marry. . . ."

"You had better hush up, Mamie. You know how Rachel always carries tales to Grandmama. We aren't supposed to know."

John, Caroline and Mrs. Hampton, who had sent one of the maids for lemonade, went into the parlor. The shutters were partly closed and the elegant white marble mantel shone in the half-light. Copies of old masters which had recently arrived from Europe showed up only faintly in their heavy gilt frames. As Caroline sank down on the low yellow velvet sofa, she sighed, "It is good to be home again." Just at that moment, the door burst open and the Preston boys came tumbling into the room to greet their parents.

"Where's Buckie?" asked Willie. His father spoke rather sharply. "Can't you greet your mother and me?"

"Glad you're back, Mama, Papa. Where are the girls?" His mother and grandmother laughed. "They have gone upstairs to change." Willie rushed from the room while the others sat down to talk with their parents.

The next morning, a fine Sunday, nicely cooled from the rain of the night before, John Preston, a tall, distinguished man in his mid-forties with clear hazel eyes, smooth dark-brown hair and a neatly trimmed moustache, dressed in a black suit with a high collar and holding gloves and a top hat, stood on the porch. As he looked past the cast-iron steps which went down both sides of the porch into the garden, he was struck again by the creation of his wife and her mother. The gardens could be enjoyed by all Columbians for the ladies kept the gates wide open and anyone might enter and stroll around. The city block was enclosed on three sides by a brick wall and contained trees of all varieties—giant oaks, magnolias, japonicas, sweet olives and most particularly, the cedars of Lebanon from the Holy Land. Native plants in all their variety mixed with exotic plants brought back by Mrs. Hampton from her travels and gifts from her many friends who shared her passion for horticulture. The superb tall boxwood and privet hedges made living walls to enclose retreats arched over by wisteria and climbing roses, forming cool shelters from the heat of the day.

As John surveyed the garden, he could hear the soft murmur of water splashing in a white marble fountain which stood in the center of a large round pool. Goldfish swam lazily around the fountain base. Rising from its leaf-carved foundation, the fountain resembled a graceful white flower, and the dark-green boxwood hedge surrounding it emphasized its beauty.

Beyond the cedars, toward the rear of the garden were roses in the only sunny space. By the back wall were the hothouses where flowers and fruits were cultivated all year round. Behind this, to one side, was the gardener's cottage.

An English landscape gardener had been brought over to assist in the creation of an English garden in South Carolina. The Cherokee roses climbing on the fence which topped a low wall at the front of the house caught John's eye, but just then he heard the voices of the family behind him and realized that they were ready to leave for church.

John proposed that he and the boys walk the few blocks to Trinity Church as the rain had cut down on the dust, and it had not rained enough to make the streets muddy. There was no need to take two carriages, and Henry could drive Mrs. Hampton, Caroline and the girls. Also, on the way he hoped to meet some of his friends and find out more details about the political situation which his mother-in-law had alluded to yesterday. It seemed as though the abolitionists were causing more trouble in South Carolina than he had read in the New Orleans *Times-Picayune*. The Hamptons and Prestons were not secessionists, but they were among the largest slave holders in the South, and it was certainly a worrisome situation.

When they arrived at the church, whose twin towers and Gothic architecture made it an imposing structure, John hurried over to help his wife and her mother from the carriage. He was, as always, struck by what a handsome woman he had had the good fortune to marry. Caroline was a tall, well-proportioned woman with dark chestnut hair and flashing brown eyes. She had strong features, and a calm, poised manner.

When John and Caroline had met at White Sulphur Springs in Virginia in the summer of 1829, it had been love at first sight. It was the custom of the Hamptons to go to the mountains to escape the heat of Columbia's summers, and the delightful society at the Springs along with the cool air made the long journey worthwhile. John Smith Preston's family was prominent in Southwest Virginia. He had attended Hampden-Sidney College and the University of Virginia and had been a recent graduate of Harvard Law School. After coming home to practise law in Abingdon, he had been pursued by all the local belles as well as by many ladies visiting the Springs. However, once he met Caroline, he was completely entranced. After an ardent courtship, they had married on April 18, 1830 at the family home in Columbia.

As John looked at his wife, he decided she was even more attractive now than when he had first met her. She had an air of distinction and a gracious manner which added to her mature beauty. Her dress of cream muslin patterned with mauve chrysanthemums and white horsehair braid bonnet with ribbons and violets was in the latest fashion, as was her silk shawl.

Mamie, dark-haired like her father, had wide-set eyes, and a fair complexion, a lively expression and an easy out-going manner. She wore a pink-striped dress and a straw bonnet with pink ribbons. Buckie's green plaid dress set off her auburn hair and pale skin. Ladies arriving at church supposed, correctly, that these were from New Orleans.

As the family went up the few steps to church, they were warmly greeted by friends. At the door Mamie and Buck lingered to gossip with their friends, the Thompson girls, but were impatiently hurried on by their mother who could hear the choir going up the steps to take their place in the choir loft. The other children and their grandmother were already settled in the family pew. As the strains of "Holy, Holy, Holy, Lord God Almighty," ended, the Prestons hurriedly took their places and knelt down. Caroline, John and the girls got up from their knees and settled in the pew as Dr. Shand took his place in the chancel.

"The Lord is in his holy temple: let all the earth keep silence before him," he intoned in his deep voice in the well-known opening words for Morning Prayer from the Book of Common Prayer. Caroline sighed.

She had not fully realized until that moment how much she had missed dear familiar Trinity, Columbia and its friendly faces, and her mother and family. Life on the plantation was pleasant in many ways. They usually had guests staying with them whom they lavishly entertained, and Houmas had been decorated the way she and John had planned, but the endless cane fields and the constant care of the many slaves and the lingering smell of sugar being refined sometimes got on her nerves, and John found plantation management more difficult than he had expected. It was a relief to be back at Mrs. Hampton's well-run household with its quiet, polite servants who seemed to work without the constant supervision required even of house slaves on a sugar plantation.

As Dr. Shand began the invitation to the General Confession, Caroline noticed that Buckie's glances, far from being directed toward the altar, were focused on the profile of a handsome young man sitting two pews in front of them. Not only that, but he seemed to be turning around and looking at her. What in the world was going to become of the girl? She was far too attractive at age twelve not to be carefully supervised, and she seemed to be quite aware of her powers. Certainly she would have many admirers and, even now, seemed desirous of receiving men's attention.

Mrs. Hampton was now on her knees for the General Confession, and the rest of the family quickly followed her example. Absolution being pronounced by Dr. Shand, the Lord's Prayer followed and the congregation stood for the Venite and the Creed and knelt again for the prayers. Caroline forced herself to concentrate on the words of the Collects, and did not raise her head until she heard Dr. Shand's voice saying, "The grace of our Lord Jesus Christ, and the love of God, and the fellowship of the Holy Ghost, be with us all evermore," to which she responded with great fervor "Amen!"

Buckie was quite aware of her mother's disapproving glance and the tap of her fan, but she could not help wondering who the young man could be. He was sitting with Mrs. Gibbes but he was certainly not one of her sons, and she could not call to mind any other relative who might be occupying that place. Noticing that he had turned slightly and was observing her, she demurely lowered her eyes to her prayer book. She did not want to again attract her mother's attention, and certainly not her father's, even though she knew she was his favorite. She glanced at him but he seemed deep in thought. Maybe she could persuade him to go for a drive that afternoon, perhaps to Millwood to see Uncle Wade and his new horses. Looking again at her mother, she wondered if she had ever wanted to attract young men's attention and what had been her grandmother's reaction. Mrs. Hampton always seemed much less strict and much more reasonable. Buckie sighed. Both her mother and father were very strict when it came to proper behavior. Their own manners were impeccable and they intended their children's to be also.

Her father had said something the day before about sending all the girls to school. Buckie had heard from her friend Mary Thompson, about a terrible schoolmistress at one school who punished the girls severely for even the most minor infraction of the rules. Maybe he would send her and Lila and Mamie all to Barhamville College. She would like that, if they had to go somewhere before they all went to France. She knew it was the most highly regarded college for young women in the South, but she and Tudie were too young, and she knew that her father would probably want all the girls at the same school, even though Mamie might be old enough to go to Barhamville. Anyway, he had already said that they were to finish their education in Paris, and the very thought of going to France made her willing to put up with anything her father might arrange in Columbia.

While Dr. Shand had been preaching another of his very long sermons, John Preston's thoughts had drifted to politics. He had served in the South Carolina House with Wade Hampton III and another brother-in-law, John L. Manning, father of the three children who now made their home with his own family. Manning had gone on to be elected governor in 1852. Now, in 1854, politics were rapidly becoming a subject of concern to everyone, not only the politicians. Ever since John C. Calhoun's death in 1850 there had been no great steadying force in the state. John Preston hoped with all his heart that he might become such a force. He was a candidate for the post of state senator and anticipated a lively election in the fall. That was why he had come back early from Louisiana.

His eyes wandered upward to the roof of the nave, said to be like that of St. Mary's, Oxford. While Trinity certainly did not compare with the great European cathedrals he had seen, it was very imposing. The walls of grey stone color contrasted with the black oak woodwork. Beautiful colored glass windows cast a flood of rich light on the white marble altar, behind which were four tablets of black marble on which were inscribed the Lord's Prayer, the Apostles' Creed and the Ten Commandments. The floor of the chancel was covered in an elegant velvet tapestry carpet, and in front of the tablets were three Gothic walnut chairs which had been given by his wife.

John's appreciation of the beauty of the church was disturbed by a rustling of prayer books, and he realized that Dr. Shand had completed his sermon, of which he had heard not one word. After the benediction came the final hymn which was one of his favorites, "Jesus shall reign where'er the sun. . . ." As he waited in the pew for his wife and Mrs. Hampton to collect their shawls, reticules and prayer books, he noticed Mrs. Gibbes beckoning to him. Waiting to speak to her, he saw that Buckie had remained with him instead of following her mother and grandmother down the aisle and wondered why. He had not long to wonder.

"Dear Mr. Preston. I cannot wait to tell Dr. Gibbes that you have returned from Louisiana. There are so many matters pertaining to politics which he wishes to discuss with you. He was called to attend a dying patient just as we were getting ready to leave for church. Oh, may I present my nephew, Edward, from Charleston. He thinks he may attend South Carolina College in the fall. He has come to stand the entrance examinations. I know he would be happy to make the acquaintance of Alfred and John, Jr., and Miss Mamie."

"Indeed, Mrs. Gibbes, we should be happy if you and Edward would come to call this afternoon as we shall all be at home. Perhaps Dr. Gibbes will be free to accompany you."

Buckie fumed inwardly at the mention of Mamie, but comforted herself with the look of admiration in the young man's eyes as he bowed politely to her father and to her. She hoped fervently that they would accept her father's invitation and come to call that very afternoon. She had intended to beg him to take them for a drive to see the new sights in town, but that could certainly wait until another day!

❧

Late Sunday afternoon, Dr. and Mrs. Gibbes and Edward arrived at the Hampton townhouse to pay the promised call. Dr. Robert Wilson Gibbes was a prominent Columbia physician who had acquired a large and lucrative practice as the result of a scandal involving another Columbia physician who was forced to leave town because of his indiscretions with the notorious Amelia Boozer. The Gibbes' home at the northeast corner of Sumter and Plain Streets was filled with paintings which rivaled the Prestons' collection. Dr. Gibbes also had a fine library and a scientific collection of fossils and sharks' teeth.

As they got out of the carriage, he said to his wife, Caroline, "I am very glad, indeed, that John Preston is back in Columbia. South Carolina is going to need all her best citizens in the days to come. John's temperament is perhaps a bit too mild, but he is an outstanding orator and his principles are sound."

As he spoke, the door to the mansion was opened by a very dignified slave, William, the butler, who said, "Come right in, Mrs. Gibbes, Dr. Gibbes and young gentleman. Mrs. Hampton and Mr. Preston are in the parlor with the young ladies and gentlemen. Mrs. Preston is attending to one of the maids who is ailing. She will be with you presently."

Dr. and Mrs. Gibbes and Edward entered the parlor. When he saw them, John Preston rose to his feet and greeted them warmly. Mrs. Hampton added her greeting and, after Edward had been presented to her and inquiries made about the health of his parents, his various Charleston relatives, and Mrs. Hampton's other friends, she introduced him to her grandchildren. "Caroline will be here shortly. She was called to see about one of the maids who was indisposed. I do not believe it is anything serious, so Dr. Gibbes, you may rest easy."

As she spoke, Caroline Preston entered the room with the news that all was now well, and happily greeted her guests. As her husband presented her to the Gibbes' nephew, she recognized him as the young man who had looked at Buckie with such flattering glances in church that morning. She also realized that his aunt must have spoken to him about the impropriety of such behavior, as he now turned a bright pink color every time he looked in Buckie's direction. This had not escaped the notice of Mamie and Lila and Tudie, who were giggling softly in the corner. Aware of his discomfiture, Caroline, with her customary tact, suggested that the young people retire to the garden and show Edward the fruit trees which had recently arrived from England. "I will send Abby out there shortly with your tea. You may have it in the summerhouse. Be sure you also show Mr. Gibbes the fountain Mr. Powers gave us—such a delightful man!"

After the young people had left the room, Caroline said to her friends, "I particularly wanted the girls out of the way as John and I want to ask your advice on the matter of the girls' schooling. As you know, we intend to go to Paris in a year or two to finish their education and to put the boys in school in Switzerland, but we are becoming concerned that they may not be adequately prepared for what they may encounter in a French school. I know you, dear Mrs. Gibbes, have been pleased with the education that your daughters have received at the Female Institute, and I have also heard that Dr. Zimmerman's school is quite satisfactory. Mamie might go to Barhamville College, but Buckie, Tudie, and Lila are too young. We would really prefer to send all the girls to the same school."

John Preston added, "Our chief concern is that all the children be able to speak and understand the French language well so that they can profit from their instruction in France."

"But my dear fellow," said Dr. Gibbes, "you and Mrs. Preston speak the language so beautifully that I would imagine you perfectly capable of instructing the children."

"Ah, Dr. Gibbes, I daresay you have found that your own family are the last to follow your medical advice!"

Amid general laughter, Dr. Gibbes had to admit that this was true. "Touché, John," he said, "but let me tell you that I asked Alexander Herbemont his opinion of our girls' French accent. I regard his opinion very highly. As you know, his family are Huguenots and his esteemed father was a native Frenchman and also professor of French at our College. Alexander, himself, you may remember, spent several years as United States consul in Geneva. I digress. When I requested his opinion, he hesitated in responding, and when I begged him to be frank, he admitted that their accent was not, perhaps, the best. That being the case, you might prefer Madame Togno's school to the Female Academy. She, herself, speaks very well, and I understand that she employs an excellent Frenchwoman as a teacher."

"I cannot thank you enough, Dr. Gibbes, for being so frank. We value your opinion above all. Would you care to come into the sitting room with me? I would like to have your opinion on another subject and, I imagine, the ladies have matters to discuss other than politics. We might also have a beverage other than tea!"

With the gentlemen gone, Mrs. Gibbes felt free to ask Mrs. Hampton and Caroline about various rumors she had heard about Millwood and Frank Hampton's courtship of a certain young lady from New York city. She meant to find out, in a delicate way, if the stories she had heard of the Hampton girls' reaction to their brother's choice were true.

The next day, Caroline and her mother determined to drive out to Millwood and hear the truth of the stories which had been told by Mrs. Gibbes. Caroline was eager to see the family again, so they ordered the carriage to be brought quite early. It was a pleasant day and the early morning drive would not be too hot. It was nice to be able to chat freely without John or the children listening to every word, and Caroline and Mrs. Hampton thoroughly enjoyed themselves. The two ladies were in total agreement on most family matters and had missed each other a great deal while the Prestons had been away at Houmas. Also, they knew they could count on the discretion of Henry, Mrs. Hampton's longtime coachman, who had been with the family since birth and was not given to gossip, as were so many of the slaves.

As they arrived at Millwood and drove up the long avenue, they were both remembering how it had looked when built by Mrs. Hampton's stepson and Caroline's half-brother, Wade Hampton II, for his bride from Charleston, Ann Fitzsimons. The house was situated on the highest point of land in the Mill Tract on Garner's Ferry Road. It had been a raised two-story cottage with cabins for the slaves, a kitchen, carriage house, and other necessary buildings close by. In 1838, Wade had decided to renovate the house. When he had finished, in 1843, the cottage had become an imposing Greek revival style mansion. Wings had been added to both sides of the house and twelve columns placed across the front, six two-story columns in the center and three smaller on each side. The wide piazza offered a view of the surrounding countryside.

When the carriage arrived at the steps, a small Negro boy ran up to hold the horses while Henry helped the ladies to descend from the carriage. He then drove the team to a fine stable reserved for the carriage and riding horses, removed from the training stable, which had accommodations for grooms and jockeys.

Mrs. Hampton and Caroline were greeted warmly by Kate Hampton, a dark-haired handsome woman of thirty, the oldest of the four surviving Hampton sisters. "Oh, Grandmama and Aunt Caroline, I can't tell you how happy I am to see you! The girls and the children have just gone out to the stables to inspect a new colt, but they will be back shortly. Do come in and take off your bonnets and refresh yourselves. We must have a good visit and you must stay for lunch and tea."

As she spoke, the ladies entered a large hall which ran the length of the house. Portraits of the Hamptons' famous racehorses decorated the walls. They had been painted at Millwood in the 1840's by a Swiss artist, Edward Troye. At the rear of the hall was a wide staircase which led to the second floor bedrooms. The drawing room to the left was separated from the dining room by wide, folding doors. On the right was the music room and, beyond, Colonel Hampton's office. When opened up, these four rooms provided a large elegant ballroom. Two doors at the rear of the hall opened onto a veranda which ran across the back of the mansion and down the sides of the wings which extended to the back and provided rooms and baths for guests. The large house was home not only to Colonel Hampton and his four unmarried daughters, but also to his widowed sons, when they were not out at the Mississippi and Louisiana plantations and to their children who were being reared at Millwood.

As they went into the drawing room, Caroline Preston said, "Now, Kate, before the others come back from the stable, do tell us the latest news about Frank and Miss Baxter! Mama has met her and says she is most cultivated and charming. Do you think Frank is seriously interested in her?"

"Well, Aunt Caroline, I will tell you what I know. When Miss Baxter arrived in Columbia from Charleston, she had a letter of introduction to Dr. Francis Lieber at the College. The Liebers were quite captivated with her and their son, Oscar, escorted her to many outings, on one of which she met Frank. I declare, I have never seen my brother so smitten with any young lady! She is really quite unusually attractive and fascinating to talk with. She had met a great many people while in Charleston, and her family, I understand, are great friends of Mr. Thackeray, the English novelist. Indeed, it is said that Miss Baxter is the model for one of his heroines."

"I would never have imagined that Frank would be attracted to a literary young lady. I thought his taste ran to rather empty-headed beauties."

"Well, I assure you, Miss Baxter is not empty-headed, and Frank's taste certainly seems to be fixed on her. He sent her a basket of my finest strawberries before she left, and I can imagine what he may have written on the card! He has been pining away ever since she left and, I would not be the least surprised to see urgent business call him to New York City in the very near future."

"Frank is so handsome. At twenty-six he could have his pick of any of the Columbia or Charleston belles. What on earth made him choose a young lady from New York?"

"Well, Caroline," said her mother, "you could have had your choice of the many eligible young men in Columbia and South Carolina. What on earth made you choose a young man from Virginia?"

"John was the most handsome and intelligent and well-educated man I had ever seen!"

"And Miss Baxter is the most handsome, cultivated, and charming young lady that Frank has ever seen!" The ladies all laughed.

"Tell us about your father. What has he been doing?" asked Mrs. Hampton. Kate's father, Wade Hampton II, had been three years old when his mother died. His brother Frank was a baby. Six years later, their father had married Mary Cantey, the step-sister of the boys' mother, Harriet Flud. The boys loved her already, and she brought them up as her own children. They were a very devoted family.

"Why, Grandmama, I thought you knew," said Kate. "He had to go out to Mississippi again, and you know how he hates to go in the summer. Wade and Kit were having a lot of problems at WildWoods with the cotton crop. The new overseer has not been at all satisfactory. I don't know where Papa will look for another. Aunt Caroline, you must have heard about all this while you were at Houmas. Papa says he absolutely *must* increase the income from Walnut Ridge and WildWoods. Expenses have been so high this year. Thank heaven he has given up racing. We still have the stables, but he has not been to the Charleston Meet for three years."

"Is Frank still a member of the Jockey Club?"

"Oh, yes, and Wade also. But Frank has so much to do, with all his duties at Woodlands and both Papa and the boys away, and his courtship of Miss Baxter, that his interest in racing is not quite so intense as it once was."

"Do you have many problems with the children?" asked Caroline. She was thinking of Kit's daughter, Annie, now ten, and Wade's four children left motherless when Margaret Preston Hampton died in 1852. The children all now made their home at Millwood with their aunts. Five orphan children were quite a responsibility.

"They are a joy to us," said Kate. "But I must admit that if it were not for Maum Nelly and her group of nursemaids, I do not believe the girls and I could manage. Ann and Caroline and Mary Fisher and I could certainly not keep up with five lively children, and run the house and servants and entertain all the guests that Papa invites. Sometimes it is a relief to have him go out to Mississippi with Wade and Kit!"

Just then a commotion was heard in the hallway and the children came bursting in, accompanied by Mary Fisher, the youngest Hampton sister.

"Ann and Caroline have gone to see about lunch, but they will join us shortly," she said.

After much hugging and kissing and inquiries about John Preston, Buckie and Mamie, the children were sent off with one of the maids and the ladies, now joined by Ann and Caroline, settled down to a pleasant exchange of family news and gossip before lunch was announced.

Later that afternoon, on their way back to Columbia, Mrs. Hampton and Caroline bemoaned the fact that none of the Hampton girls had married.

"They are all quite remarkably good looking and would make wonderful wives and mothers."

"They certainly have had many opportunities, both here and in Charleston and at the Springs. Remember, that was where you met John and where Wade met Margaret."

"I imagine young Wade and Kit will marry again. And Frank seems determined on matrimony."

"Well, you never know. I would have thought that your brother would have remarried after Ann died, though they do say that he promised her on her deathbed that he never would."

"Well, he has kept his promise, which is more than you could say for most men!"

"It is a good thing, Caroline, that your father never made any such promise!" said Mrs. Hampton, laughing. Since she had been General Hampton's third wife, she had reason for her laughter.

While her mother and grandmother were at Millwood, Buckie managed to see her brother Willie alone, which she had been trying to do ever since they had arrived back in Columbia. Willie was fifteen, three years older than she, tall and athletic, with his mother's chestnut hair, and dark blue eyes. He shared Buckie's love of horses and had rescued her from many childhood scrapes. He was not grown up and superior like Alfred and Jack and had become Buckie's special confidant.

The first thing she asked him was, "Did you take care of Blaze while I was away and ride her every day like you promised?"

"I took care of her, but I didn't ride her *every* day. How could I? What about *my* horse?"

"Oh, Willie, I missed you such a lot. Mama and Papa were always busy so Mamie and I were alone. She doesn't like to ride as much as I do, and besides, it's so hot in Louisiana, and there's nobody else around. All Mamie and I could do was sit around and read. Mamie doesn't mind it as much as I do."

"Well, she doesn't ride as well as you do, and she reads a lot better. Maybe you should try it more."

"Don't give advice like Jack and Alfred. That's why I like to talk to you better than them."

"I'll give you one piece of advice anyway. You'd better not flirt in church anymore. Mama was really upset. I heard her talking to Papa about you."

"I was *not* flirting. I couldn't stop Edward Gibbes from looking at me, could I?"

"Forget it. I didn't mean to make you cross. Let's go for a ride now while Mama and Grandmama are out at Millwood. We can stay as long as we like, but don't tell Mamie and Tudie we're going or they'll want to come too and then we can't talk."

II
Paris, 1858

When the Prestons arrived in Paris in May 1858, the transformation of the city of Napoléon III was proceeding rapidly and no capital in the world had such an exciting atmosphere. As the fiacre carrying Caroline and John Preston, Mamie, and Buckie arrived at the Hôtel Meurice on the rue de Rivoli, Mamie and Buckie could hardly contain their excitement at being at last in the city they had so longed to see. The arcades lined with beautiful shops on one side and on the other the Tuileries gardens were even more magnificent than anything they had imagined.

"Oh, Mama, let's go shopping first and then walk in that beautiful garden over to the river and then. . . ."

"Buckie, Buckie, stop!" said her mother. "I am exhausted after the boat train, and we need to get settled in the hotel and unpack, and I am sure your grandmother must need a good rest. Perhaps your father will take you all for a promenade this evening after we have rested and had dinner."

Just then another carriage carrying Mrs. Hampton and the rest of the family arrived. Porters in the blue and gold livery of the Hôtel Meurice, a favorite hotel of the English gentry and one of the most fashionable in the city, rushed to help them out of the carriages and onto the red carpet which covered the entrance to the hotel under the arcades. Buckie had never seen anything so grand, not even in New Orleans.

"Vous permettez, mademoiselle?" said the doorman as he assisted her out of the carriage. She was thankful that she remembered to say, "Merci, monsieur," and thought that perhaps the boring years at Madame Togno's school had not been entirely wasted.

As they entered the hotel, more porters rushed to help with the luggage, and the concierge appeared, bowing to John Preston, whom he remembered with pleasure as a most excellent client. "We are so pleased to have you and madame with us again, monsieur. I hope it will be for a long stay in our beautiful city. You will find things much changed for the better. Anything we can do to be of assistance, you have only to ask. We have prepared one of our best suites for you, as you requested."

As John followed him to the reception desk to complete the formalities, Caroline and her mother sank gratefully onto a plush velvet sofa in the sumptuous lobby. The soft gaslight chandeliers illuminated the oriental carpets and the beautiful statues and flowers. Fashionably dressed women and their escorts passed to and fro, and Mrs. Hampton murmured to Caroline, "We must visit Monsieur Worth as soon as possible. We can never call on any of our friends in the clothes and bonnets we have brought from Columbia. We should look as though we had stepped out of another century."

"Indeed you are right, Mama. And the girls will all have to have new wardrobes, even if they will have uniforms at school. John will have to take the boys to his tailor before he takes them to their school in Switzerland. And surely Alfred and Jack will have to have proper clothes before setting off on the Grand Tour."

As Mamie and Buckie followed their parents into the hotel, they heard cheers and music coming from the Place de la Concorde, through which they had just passed. They ran back to the entrance of the hotel and saw an escort of cavalry coming along the rue de Rivoli. As the cuirassiers rode by, the girls were entranced with their gleaming white metal helmets with brass crests and black horsehair plumes, scarlet and blue coats, shining steel breastplates, and black kneeboots. All were mounted on matched dappled grey horses, and as they rode by with a clatter of hoofs, cries were heard of "Vive l'Empereur!"

At that moment, the Emperor himself appeared, mounted on a magnificent black charger which he had brought from England. Mamie and Buckie glimpsed gold epaulettes, and a long-bodied, short-legged man with a prominent forehead, brilliant eyes, a long nose, waxed moustaches and a small goatee. He acknowledged the cheers of the crowd and, in that moment, the girls had a glimpse of the air of power and Bonaparte mystique which fired the enthusiasm of the crowd. He was followed by more cavalry.

Buckie's eyes met those of a cuirassier whose stunning good looks were enhanced by his distinctly military bearing. He bowed slightly to her with evident admiration in his shining eyes and smiled.

"Oh, Mamie," she breathed, "did you ever see anyone so good looking? Do you think we will meet any of them while we are here?"

"No," said the practical Mamie, "and if we did, Mama would not allow us to know them. She and Grandmama do not think military men are suitable acquaintances for young ladies. Remember what they said about Cousin Ransom, whom they adore, when he went to West Point?"

"But Napoléon was a military man and he became an Emperor."

"And I heard Grandmama say she didn't care if he were an emperor or not. He was still a parvenu and she would not receive him in her house."

Just then their father appeared saying, "Girls, what ever are you doing? They are waiting to show us to our rooms."

"Oh, Papa, we just saw the Emperor ride by and he was ever so dashing."

"I understand he is an excellent horseman and rides every day in the Bois de Boulogne. Perhaps when we are settled, we may ride there too one day. Right now, we need to go upstairs and try to get unpacked and changed. Your mother and grandmother are fatigued with the journey on the boat train, and it is quite warm today. Nothing like Columbia, but warm for Paris. Perhaps later on this evening the boys and I will take you for a short walk. You know it does not become dark until around ten o'clock since we are so much farther north."

"Not a *short* walk. I want to see everything and not waste a minute. I've heard about Paris all my life, and I want to see it now!" exclaimed Buckie.

Later that same evening, after an elegant dinner in the hotel dining room, rich with painted panels and mirrors which reflected the large chandeliers and the sumptuous table settings, John Preston accompanied Mamie, Buckie, Tudie, and the two younger Manning children on the promised walk. He had decided to allow the older boys a bit of freedom and said they could explore on their own. He particularly cautioned Jack and Alfred, as the two oldest, to be observant and careful and not to venture too far from the hotel. "Remember," he said, "Paris is a great city. It is not Columbia, or even New Orleans, and you may easily become lost or fall into bad company. None of you speak French fluently enough to ask for help or even directions."

The boys smiled knowingly at each other and promised to follow his advice.

"Enjoy yourselves. I advise you to sit in a café and watch the world go by. You may see some very interesting sights." He gave them some money and cautioned them to be back at the hotel by midnight at the latest. He added, "You do not want to worry your mother and grandmother on their first night here."

The ladies had retired after dinner to be rested for their anticipated visit to Monsieur Worth's establishment the next day.

John Preston and his group set off down the rue de Rivoli toward the Place de la Concorde. The soft twilight cast a magic violet glow over the beautiful Tuileries gardens and gaslights illuminated the street as they walked along under the arcades. Realizing that the shop windows were perhaps more alluring to the girls than the magnificent view, he suggested crossing the street before they arrived at the Place and walking along the pebble path inside the garden grillwork.

As they approached one of the world's great squares, John pointed out in the center the Luxor obelisk from Egypt and told them that it had been placed there by Louis-Philippe in the place where the guillotine had stood. Now it was hard to imagine the terrible events which had taken place there just over fifty years ago. Eight large statues depicting eight cities of France stood around the Place and fountains like those in St. Peter's Square in Rome stood on either side of the obelisk. Across the Seine was the National Assembly and, to the right, the rue Royale and the church of the Madeleine. Opposite stretched the avenue des Champs-Elysées, lined with chestnut trees which had recently been the site of an international exposition. Its gas lamps lit up the theaters and restaurants and the throngs of beautifully dressed Parisians full of gaiety and animation.

To the young Prestons and Mannings it was a sight beyond belief, and they longed to cross the Place with its hordes of carriages and see more of this exciting spectacle, but John Preston, feeling quite fatigued himself by now, and realizing that his wife might not approve of certain aspects of the demi-monde which the girls might see, led them instead toward the Pont de la Concorde and the more uplifting view of Notre Dame.

✥

The next day, Caroline and Mrs. Hampton, accompanied by Buckie and Mamie, were in a carriage on their way to the Maison Worth in the Faubourg St-Honoré. Charles Frederick Worth, an Englishman, was the premier couturier in Paris, the capital of haute couture. The Hampton ladies had patronized him before on their several visits to Paris and had sent a note around to his salon to announce their arrival. Worth was known for the elegant style of his clothes, the perfection of his fittings, and the magnificence of the fabrics used in his designs. He said of himself, "I am a great artist. I compose. A costume is a picture."

The new look of wide flowing skirts required enormous amounts of material held out by crinolines and hoops. Worth was the first couturier to present his collection on live mannequins and was the favorite of the Empress Eugénie and the Imperial Court. However, as the Hamptons had known and patronized him before his great fame, they were valued clients.

The ladies had decided that the girls should each have day dresses and one for more formal occasions. As they were still schoolgirls, there would be no ball gowns or extensive wardrobes. Then, they themselves would need several day costumes, evening attire, as well as bonnets, shawls, and all the other accessories. Mrs. Hampton and Caroline looked forward to many pleasant hours of decisions, fittings, and visits to glove makers, perfumers, and all the other establishments on the rue de la Paix and the Faubourg St-Honoré.

As they arrived at the door in their carriage, they saw a strange-looking woman of aristocratic bearing being ushered to her carriage by M. Worth himself.

"Look, Mama," said Buckie, "did you ever see such an ugly woman? She looks just like that little pug dog you used to have."

"Do hush, Buckie," said her mother. "Why do you think no one can understand when you speak in English? Have you no manners? That lady is the Princess Metternich. Her husband is the Austrian ambassador, and she is an intimate of the Empress, so I have been told. It is supposed that she is the one who insisted that the Empress patronize M. Worth and thereby helped him make his name."

As he finished ushering the princess into her carriage, M. Worth turned and saw the Hampton ladies arriving. He greeted them warmly and escorted them up the steps and into a Louis XV salon where, after they had been seated on little gilded chairs and two black-clad vendeuses summoned, he said, "I was so very pleased to receive your note and to know that you were back in Paris. May I offer you some tea, some chocolate?"

"No, indeed, thank you, monsieur, we have just finished breakfast at the hotel."

"These charming young ladies must be your daughters, Mrs. Preston. They are almost as lovely as their mother and grandmother."

"Thank you, M. Worth. You see we came to you and brought the girls the moment we arrived. These are my daughters, Mary Cantey and Sarah Buchanan. They are going to be in school here in Paris and will, of course, wear convent uniforms, but they must have a few dresses for the summer and for some of the social events we will be attending. Now that they are young ladies, they should each have a proper Paris gown."

Just then a vendeuse carrying a beautiful ball gown festooned with garlands of multicolored embroidery, a long corsage with silk roses, and an enormously full skirt with cascading ruffles, passed through the salon.

"Oh, Mama," breathed Buckie, "shall I have a gown like that?"

"Certainly not," answered her mother. "You are only sixteen and a schoolgirl. A dress like that would not be at all suitable! You will have a nice pink silk with sleeves and lace at the neck and perhaps a matching shawl with silk fringe."

M. Worth, seeing Buckie's downcast look, tactfully intervened. "Miss Preston's beautiful auburn hair would be enhanced by a lovely blue-green silk of the shade often worn by the Empress. I will have the new models brought out so that you may choose."

The curtains to the fitting rooms parted and a pretty mannequin appeared in a carriage dress of grey silk in the newest style, two pieces, a jacket and a skirt trimmed with black braid. This was followed by a day dress of yellow lawn and many other models. When Caroline and Mrs. Hampton had made selections of models, a wide range of fabrics from which to choose was brought out.

"I think, M. Worth, that I will wait until later in the week to see the ball gowns," said Caroline. "We have not yet called and left cards nor received invitations, so it is not pressing, and I would prefer that Mr. Preston accompany me so that I might have his advice."

"Certainly, madame," he answered. "That is undoubtedly a wise decision. He will be most interested in the new evening attire, and he has such charming taste."

The ladies were then shown to fitting rooms where fitters waited to take their measurements.

※

When the ladies returned to the hotel, John Preston was waiting for them in the lobby. With him was a gentleman who, though dressed in the latest Paris fashion with a white linen coat, royal blue moiré waistcoat with tan lapels, biscuit-colored trousers, and a natural straw hat in his hand, still stood out as an American in the cosmopolitan crowd.

Buckie forgot completely all her sixteen-year-old dignity and rushed up to hug him.

"Oh, Cousin Ransom, how glad I am to see you! What are you doing here in Paris? How long will you be here? Will you take me to Versailles and to a café?"

Untangling himself from her rather strenuous embrace, Ransom Calhoun smiled broadly. "Still the same Buck. I suppose some day I shall not recognize you when you have become a quiet dignified lady like your mother and grandmother. I think I would prefer you to remain as you are, though you have certainly improved in appearance. You are quite a beauty now."

"Hush, Ransom," said Caroline Preston, "you will turn her head and she will be more impossible than she is now. We are all delighted to see you. John was planning to call at the Embassy and inform you of our arrival. Jack and Willie have talked of little else but seeing you."

"Dear Mrs. Preston, I have come especially to welcome you and Mrs. Hampton and the girls. We heard of your arrival yesterday, and I came as soon as I could. Chargé d'affaires sounds a grand title, but my position consists mostly of running errands for the ambassador, so my time is not entirely my own. However, I wish to be of assistance to you all in any way possible, including taking Miss Sarah Buchanan to a café and to Versailles."

As he spoke, he bowed to Caroline and Mrs. Hampton and greeted them affectionately. "Some of our cousins from Charleston, the Ravenels, are here in Paris also and will be here this afternoon to call on you. Actually, I came to bring you cards to a reception at the Tuileries on Friday of next week. The Emperor and Empress will be giving their final reception of the season before they go to St. Cloud for the summer. They ask the Embassy to invite outstanding citizens who are visiting Paris. I would like to present you all if you will do me the honor."

"How very kind of you, Ransom, to think of us. I am afraid, however, that the girls are too young for such an affair."

"Oh, Mama, Papa," said both girls together, "please, please! The Empress is supposed to be so beautiful and the Tuileries and the Guards!"

"That is very thoughtful of you, Ransom," said John Preston, "and we should be delighted to accept, providing, of course, that M. Worth has the ladies' dresses ready. If Ransom thinks it proper for the girls to go, I think, my dear, that we should bow to his judgment. He has been longer in Paris than we, and has been to many of these affairs. Even if you have to wear your Columbia dresses, you and Mrs. Hampton and the girls will compare favorably to the Empress and the Court beauties."

"What a nice compliment, John," laughed Mrs. Hampton. "I might compare favorably to the Court beauties, and I do appreciate Cousin Ransom's invitation. I do not believe, however, that I would be able to stand so long in a large crush of people, so I am afraid I must forego meeting the Emperor and Empress. But you must tell me all about it."

"If he were a *real* king, I'll bet Grandmama could stand for so long," whispered Mamie to Buckie. "You remember what she said about the Bonapartes being parvenus."

Ransom Calhoun said to Mrs. Preston, "Would you permit me to escort the young ladies to the Louvre this afternoon? I believe they would enjoy seeing the new galleries and watching the artists who work there making copies of the masterpieces."

"Indeed, that is exactly what Dr. Gibbes and I have commissioned young Hiram Powers to do for us here and in Italy," said John. "Are you familiar with his work? He is a friend of young Wade's from Charleston and quite a promising young artist. He wished to study abroad, and we were delighted to make it possible."

That afternoon the girls, Jack, Willie, and Alfred had a guided tour of the Louvre with Ransom Calhoun, and were very impressed by the beautiful paintings and sculpture and the magnificent galleries where they were displayed. They thoroughly enjoyed being with Ransom again as he was always a most entertaining and lively companion.

❧

The following week, as Mamie and Buckie were dressing for the Tuileries reception, they remarked again and again how happy they were that their new Worth dresses had been finished in time. The bluish-green silk set off Buckie's coloring to perfection and her figure, which was already mature for her sixteen years, was molded by the silk and outlined by the white passementerie trimming. Mamie's eyes sparkled as she pulled up the skirt of her dark red silk gown and admired the matching stockings and kid shoes.

"Oh, Mamie," said Buck, "did you ever dream in Columbia that we would have such beautiful dresses and be going to a reception at the Tuileries palace to meet the Emperor Napoléon III and the Empress Eugénie?"

"Never in the world," exclaimed Mamie. "We must thank Cousin

Ransom again. I don't believe for one minute that Mama would have agreed if he had not said that in France young ladies were expected to go about in society and that Paris was not Charleston or Columbia! I think he wants us to see something of the world before we are shut up in that convent school to learn French. He wants us to have something to look forward to when we have finished school! Where are my gloves and fan? Look at Mama and Papa! Don't they look splendid?"

"Come, girls. The carriage has arrived and Ransom is waiting for us."

As their carriage joined the long line of others waiting to deposit their passengers, the girls could hear a band playing *Partant pour la Syrie*, the song composed by the Emperor's mother, Queen Hortense, and which was used now in place of the *Marseillaise*, that song of the Revolution which was now banned. In the gardens they could see cascading fountains.and lackeys in powdered wigs waiting to open carriage doors. A glimpse into the gardens showed gentlemen in formal court dress with ribbons and decorations, and ladies in beautiful off-shoulder gowns with the full crinolines which made them look like great bouquets of flowers. They also wore flowers at the corsage of their gowns and in their hair.

Caroline was shocked to see such low-cut Eugénie style dresses worn in the late afternoon and said to her husband, "John, did you ever see such a display of bosom and it is not yet seven o'clock? I am thankful Mama did not come. I cannot believe that many of these ladies are from the Faubourg St. Germain. I do not see the Ravenels anywhere."

John smiled. "How could you find anyone in such a crowd? There must be five thousand people here. I hope Ransom will look after the girls. It is just as well that your mother decided not to come and that Willie could use her invitation. This way each girl will have an escort."

"*If* the escort remembers his duties. I have no fear of Ransom with Mamie, but I am not at all sure that Willie will not desert Buck if one of those girls flutters her fan at him."

"Well, perhaps fortunately, he does not know enough French to begin a conversation. There is Ransom beckoning to us now."

As they passed into the palace and up the broad stairway to the second-floor reception rooms, they were impressed by the great crystal chandeliers in full blaze and the profusion of flowers in magnificent Sevres urns and bowls. Caroline, mentally comparing the rather gaudy gilded and painted rooms to the elegant Louis XV drawing rooms she had previously visited, felt the whole brilliant display was in rather bad taste. She was not surprised by the stories she had heard that the Court of Napoléon III was being boycotted by the old nobility, and that it was made up primarily of foreigners and the gilded Bohemia and nouveaux riches of Paris. It was said that Parisians did not like Eugénie because she was a foreigner. She was called "l'Espagnole" as Marie Antoinette had been known as "l'Autrichienne." However, with all the pomp and display, there was an atmosphere of gaiety as the chandeliers and gas jets brightened the gold-embroidered court dress of the officers of the Imperial household and the dazzling uniforms of the Hundred Guards. These had been copied from the uniforms of the Grande Armée of Napoléon Ier.

Just as these thoughts were passing through Caroline's mind, the Prestons and Ransom Calhoun arrived in front of the dais where the Emperor and Empress were receiving their guests. Napoléon III wore a general's tunic with orders and crosses, and Eugénie had a pale yellow gown with an enormously full skirt. She was twenty years younger than the Emperor and, at thirty-three, made a striking picture with her blue eyes, red hair, and translucent complexion. She was not wearing the crown diamonds since it was a reception and not a ball. Camellias adorned her small head and around her long graceful neck were matched pearls, and pearl bracelets were on her wrists. The Empress spoke four languages and, as the Prestons were presented to her, she greeted them in English and said she hoped one day to visit the United States of which she had heard so much. They were all enchanted by her gay and easy manner.

As Buckie was being presented to the Emperor, she raised her eyes and met the smiling regard of the handsome cuirassier who had accompanied the Emperor on the day of the Prestons' arrival in Paris. She could see that he had been listening for her name as the liveried footman had announced her. She was thankful that her mother and father had passed on and did not see the admiring look in his eyes and the smile on his face. He moved quickly to her side as Willie was being presented to the Emperor and, before she quite realized what was happening, she found a strong arm leading her into the Salle des Maréchaux where a lavish buffet was spread on long tables heavily laden with silver.

"Mademoiselle Preston, permit me to present myself to you and to fetch you an ice or a glass of champagne. Capitaine Jean-Paul Bellanger of the Emperor's Guards at your service. Have you been long in Paris, mademoiselle?"

Buckie was too overcome by the proximity of the remarkable face with its piercing brown eyes and dark brown sideburns to wonder how he had managed to find her in the crowd. He was even more dashing and attractive than she had remembered from seeing him ride by on the rue de Rivoli. She was not a little pleased by the jealous glances of many of the nearby women. It was a thrill to see that such a charming man who obviously could have had his choice of any woman at the reception had singled her out for his attention. She managed to murmur in a low voice that they had arrived the previous week and were staying at the Hôtel Meurice. She decided it would be better not to mention going to school, and added that they were looking forward to seeing the sights of Paris.

At that moment her other arm was seized by her brother Willie, who, bowing slightly to the officer, said, "Buck, Mama and Papa have been looking everywhere for you. Why didn't you wait for me? Cousin Ransom wants to introduce us to some particular friends of his from the Embassy."

"Au revoir, mademoiselle, et à bientôt," said Jean-Paul bowing to her and to Willie.

"What did he mean by that?" asked Willie, by now in quite a temper. "Buckie, what do you mean going off like that with a man you haven't even been introduced to? Mama and Papa will put you and Mamie in that convent school tomorrow if you don't look out."

"I couldn't very well be rude to him, could I? He was so sweet and polite to take care of me after you disappeared. Mama would certainly expect me to be courteous to a friend of the Emperor."

The next day a bouquet of white rosebuds with a wonderful hothouse fragrance, wrapped in silver foil and dripping with satin ribbons, was delivered to Mademoiselle Sarah Buchanan Preston, Hôtel Meurice, without a card. Buckie had pleaded with Willie not to say anything to her parents about her adventure and he, thinking of the many favors Buckie had done for him in the past, had remained silent. The bouquet was a great mystery to the rest of the family and a great subject of mirth to all the younger members.

Mrs. Hampton had been given a full report of the reception and, though she professed to be thoroughly shocked by some of the details which Caroline reported, was secretly sorry that she had not accompanied them. She also had some suspicions about the bouquet which she did not confide to her daughter. She thought she would have a little private talk with her granddaughter. She vividly remembered her own youthful days of bouquets, beaux and romance and, though she was sure the flirtation was quite innocent on Buckie's part, it was well to be careful. Paris was not Columbia where everyone knew everyone else or, at least, who they were. She thought that she had seen the girl surreptitiously remove a card from the center of the bouquet. Who could possibly have sent her the flowers? She was sure it was not Ransom, who looked upon her as a child, though she believed that view might be changing. They had not yet seen any of their friends who might have eligible relatives anxious to meet the girls. She would suspect one of the Preston or Manning boys, who were quite capable of playing such a joke, but this bouquet was far too expensive to be a prank of theirs.

Mrs. Hampton was correct in her suspicions. A card had been tucked inconspicuously in the center of the rosebuds. It said, "Demain à deux heures à la Colonne Vendôme. J.-P. B." Buckie hardly knew what to think or do. Flirting with Mrs. Gibbes' nephew or her brothers' friends was quite different from a rendez-vous with one of the Emperor's Guards. She longed to ask someone's advice, but she knew exactly what her mother or grandmother would say, given their opinion of military men. She could not bear the idea of being forbidden to go. She just had to see him again! She thought of consulting Cousin Ransom, who was a man of the world, but how could she see him before tomorrow? Finally she decided that she would persuade Mamie to come for a walk, which would seem innocent enough, as the Place Vendôme was just around the corner from the hotel. A meeting there might seem entirely accidental.

❦

The next day at lunch Buckie, knowing that her parents were going to pay a call on the Ravenels that afternoon, said to Mamie, "After lunch, let's walk over to the rue de la Paix and look at the shops. My kid gloves are a disgrace, and I would love to see those new parasols."

"Yes, may we, Mama? It is just around the corner from the hotel."

"I suppose that would be all right. What do you think, John?"

"Certainly. Be sure to walk into the Place Vendôme and look at the column. You know it is a Trajan column surmounted by a statue of Napoléon Ier with spiral decorations depicting military scenes. It was cast from the bronze of twelve hundred cannons taken from the Russians and Austrians at the battle of Austerlitz. The statue of Napoléon was removed, but I understand that Louis-Philippe put him back on his column."

Buckie could hardly believe her luck. Her father was telling her to go to her place of rendez-vous, and she certainly intended to obey him! Fate evidently meant her to see Jean-Paul again. What could be a better sign?

As the girls left the hotel, they were joined by Willie, who did not want to accompany his grandmother and the other children on a visit to the Louvre. As they walked down the rue de Rivoli and turned into the rue de Castiglione, they noticed an elegant confiserie with a window full of sugared almonds in beautiful little boxes tied with ribbons. Willie remarked, "Pity your admirer did not send you some of those instead of flowers," and cast a pointed look at Buckie. Maybe, she thought, Willie's decision to accompany them had not been as casual as it had seemed. She began to be a bit uneasy.

As she gazed anxiously around, she was startled to hear a voice at her elbow say, "Mademoiselle Preston! Quelle chance!" Capitaine Bellanger looked somewhat different out of uniform, though equally elegant and striking. He seemed a bit surprised to see Buck accompanied by her sister and brother. He had judged her to be one of those adventurous American girls (of whom he had met a good many) who came to Paris ready and hoping for an amorous adventure. He had found them to be much more unconventional than proper young French girls of good family. They seemed to be less encumbered by chaperones and more receptive to the advances of a handsome young officer. And, too, there was the thrill of a chase which was lacking with the demi-mondaines.

When he had seen Buckie looking at him from the steps of the Hôtel Meurice, he was startled by her beauty. She reminded him of his favorite Titian portrait in the Louvre, except that her figure was not quite so buxom, a good thing! When she appeared at the Tuileries reception, he blessed his good fortune. What a pity he had not seized that occasion to make the acquaintance of her parents in the proper way. He had been somewhat hesitant to do so since they were accompanied by Ransom Calhoun, with whom he was acquainted. He was not sure what report Ransom might give of him. He also suspected that Ransom was more than a little interested in Miss Preston himself. However, Jean-Paul was seldom at a loss in matters of gallantry, and he quickly revised his strategy.

Greeting Willie most cordially, as though he were the person he most wished to see, he asked to be presented to Mamie and expressed a wish to meet their parents. He told them the history of the Place Vendôme and the Colonne and, after a stroll around the beautiful square, suggested that they all go to a café in the Champs-Elysées and watch the elegant riders on their magnificent horses and the fashionable ladies being driven about in their carriages.

"Oh, yes," breathed the girls. Mamie murmured to Buck, "Remember the first night we were in Paris when Papa took us for a walk down there and it all looked so glamorous!"

Willie, remembering some of his father's remarks on that evening which the girls had not heard, had some misgivings about the propriety of such an expedition. However, he was soon caught up in his sisters' enthusiasm and eagerly agreed. They all loved horses and were excellent riders and eager to see the dashing cavaliers and amazones of whom they had heard so much. As they strolled along, Jean-Paul pointed out the guignols for children where marionettes and puppets entertained with Punch and Judy shows and the panoramas which were so much in vogue, especially the famous Bal Mabille.

After they had been seated at an outdoor café with a good view, Mamie sighed, "Wouldn't it be wonderful if we had our horses here and could ride down the Champs-Elysées to the Arc de Triomphe? Papa did say he would take us riding, but now he and Mama are going to spend a week in Tours, it will probably be a long time before he can make the arrangements. And by that time we will probably be locked away in the convent school."

Buckie sighed too. "I miss Blaze more than anyone in Columbia," she said, thinking longingly of her beautiful bay mare.

"Permit me to arrange for us all to go riding on Saturday in the Bois de Boulogne," said Jean-Paul.

"How could you do that?" asked Willie. In his delight at the prospect, he quite forgot that the young officer was completely unknown to his parents, and that they would be very unlikely to agree to such an outing. Then, when he saw the problem, he realized that they could wait until his parents were in Tours, and that their grandmother would be easier to convince.

"We are permitted the use of the Emperor's cavalry horses when they are not needed, and on Saturday there will be no ceremonies as the Emperor and Empress are making preparations to go to St. Cloud. The horses are very well-trained and would be easy for the ladies to manage."

"You don't need to worry about that. Buck can ride any horse in the world, and Mamie is not too bad either."

"Well, thank you so much. Spoken like a true gentleman."

"And a brother! Do not listen to him, Capitaine Bellanger. It is very kind of you, and I cannot think of anything that would give us more pleasure."

"Entendu," said Jean-Paul. "Shall we say samedi à dix heures? I will make the necessary arrangements and will call for you at your hotel on that morning. The Meurice, I believe?" he said, looking meaningfully at Buck.

As Buck and Jean-Paul, Mamie and Willie strolled back to the hotel, Mamie said to Willie, "What in the world are we going to tell Grandmother?"

"Don't worry," he said. "We will think of something. She is not like Mama and Papa, wanting to know every little detail. Besides, she has the others to worry about, and Wade and Lila keep her busy."

Willie was quite correct in his assumption. Mrs. Hampton, somewhat confused by their explanation, which jumbled together the captain, the Emperor, and various other people, thought that the expedition had been arranged and approved by the Prestons before they left for their visit with friends in a chateau near Tours. She raised no objections, so on Saturday at ten o'clock the girls and Willie in their riding habits waited in the lobby of the hotel, attracting quite a bit of attention from the other people waiting there. Jean-Paul arrived promptly in a cab and they all set off happily toward the Bois de Boulogne.

The captain told them that it had been modeled after Hyde Park in London. Napoléon III had much admired the English park while he had been in exile in England. Baron Haussmann had been given two million francs to spend to create a similar park in Paris. Winding walks and bridle paths circled the lakes and the Longchamp racetrack attracted many visitors. As they drove down the avenue de l'Impératrice from the Arc de Triomphe, the Prestons could hardly contain their admiration.

When they reached the stables where the cuirassiers' horses were stabled, the ladies were quickly mounted on two of the smaller horses and Willie had a lively roan. Buckie and Mamie did not like the tone of the remarks that the grooms were making to Capitaine Bellanger, but they did not understand exactly what was being said. They were quite sure, however, that it concerned them.

The Bois was in part real forest, and it had secret paths as well as wide roads for carriages and well-maintained bridle paths. There were several folies, or little dwellings, like the Bagatelle which had been built by the Comte d'Artois in seventy-four days after a wager with his sister-in-law Marie Antoinette, and the Folie Saint-James where Lucien Bonaparte had lived for a time.

As they started out, Buckie raced her horse on ahead and Jean-Paul followed. They galloped together down a winding path overshadowed by huge chestnut trees and soon outdistanced the others. The joy of being on horseback again made Buckie oblivious to her surroundings, and she was soon in the densest part of the Bois, closely followed by Capitaine Bellanger.

At length, Buck reined in her horse and Jean-Paul stopped beside her. "I think my horse has a stone in her shoe," she said and started to dismount. Jean-Paul leapt from his horse and seized her in his arms. Before she realized what was happening, he was kissing her passionately.

"Ah, ma belle, ma chérie, comme vous êtes magnifique!" he gasped.

At first, Buckie was too startled to resist. She had never been kissed by anyone except her family and several elderly gentlemen who had overindulged in the Christmas eggnog. This was thrillingly different, but she knew that she should not allow it to continue. She was both electrified and frightened by the intensity of his kisses. Pulling away from his ardent embrace, she said, "Captain Bellanger, you must not kiss me like that! I hardly know you!"

Realizing immediately his mistake, Jean-Paul bowed profoundly and murmured apologies. He had been carried away, he said, by her beauty and the magnificent way she rode her horse.

Buckie understood too late how thoughtless she had been. Her mother's advice and caution made much more sense to her now. She had always assumed that the outcome of flirtations and men's admiration was compliments, bouquets, boxes of chocolates, and proposals of marriage. She now dimly began to comprehend some of the allusions she had heard and began to appreciate what might easily have happened here in the Bois had the captain not proved to be a gentleman.

He, on his part, quickly saw what unpleasant consequences might have resulted from his impetuous behavior. He truly admired and was intrigued by Buckie, but he had no desire for a serious affair that might result in marriage. Marriage to an American, even a wealthy one, would ruin his promising career, and even a serious courtship might lessen his chances with the many desirable French girls of good family. He was relieved that Buckie so readily accepted his apology and quickly agreed with her that they should look for Mamie and Willie.

Just as Mamie and Willie had started cantering down a path at the beginning of their ride, they were hailed in English and, turning in surprise, they saw Ransom Calhoun and another American gentleman riding toward them. After cordial greetings and introductions, Mamie suggested to Willie that they had better ride on after Buckie and Capitaine Bellanger. Ransom was very surprised to hear that Buckie was with them, and even more surprised to hear the name of Jean-Paul Bellanger. He did not wish to alarm Mamie but suggested that they should all hasten on after the others. He murmured to Willie, "I am not well acquainted with the Captain, but I do know that he has quite a reputation as a ladies' man. I do not like the idea of his being alone with your sister. How did you happen to come riding with him?"

Willie did not like to explain all the circumstances so he muttered something and they all rode on.

As Buckie and Jean-Paul returned to the main path, they saw Ransom and the others riding toward them. Buckie's heightened color aroused Ransom's suspicions, but her casual manner and surprise at seeing him gave him no opportunity of finding out what had happened. Her explanation that she had galloped on ahead and become lost and that Capitaine Bellanger had found her and accompanied her back seemed perfectly logical to the others.

Ransom did not believe for one moment this explanation. A flood of jealousy swept over him and he felt an irrational desire to horsewhip the handsome captain. He realized at once what a fool he was, but it took all his self-control to restrain himself. As they circled the Lac Inférieur, on their way back to the stables, everyone except Mamie and Ransom's friend seemed lost in thought.

After they had returned the horses, Ransom suggested that he accompany the Prestons back to the hotel as he had to go back to the Embassy and it was quite close by. Jean-Paul did not object.

After many thanks and adieux, the girls, Willie and Ransom got into a cab. On the way back, Buckie said, "Perhaps it would be just as well if Cousin Ransom accompanied us to our rooms and spoke to Grandmama. She would be happy to see him and to know we were so well chaperoned on our outing."

In the fall, the girls entered a Paris convent school. Willie Preston and Dickie Manning were taken by John to a school in Switzerland. Alfred and Jack went off on the traditional Grand Tour, and Caroline, John and Mrs. Hampton traveled extensively, acquiring along the way many art treasures which they sent to their home in Columbia. On January 10, 1859, Alfred died of a fever in Rome. John Preston sadly accompanied his son's body home, while Jack remained in Europe to comfort and take care of his mother and grandmother.

Ransom Calhoun, true to his promise, looked after the girls while their parents were away, taking them on outings and being a model older cousin. While doing so, he fell deeply in love with Buck. Impetuous as he usually was, he realized that he should wait before speaking to John and Caroline and proposing himself as a suitor. She was too young and naive for any serious commitment so he kept his feelings to himself for the time being.

When the Prestons fetched their daughters from school and returned to Columbia, he knew that he had missed his chance and must now wait until his appointment at the Embassy in Paris was up and he could return to the United States. He could only hope that Buck would not find someone else before he declared his love. He had been strangely timid about expressing his feelings and had told her little of his previous life. Therefore, she never heard about his time at West Point and his classmate, John Bell Hood, who was to play such a major role in her future.

III
Columbia, 1860

At home these were tumultuous times. The question of slavery in the western territories became more and more an issue. Congress sought a compromise, but firebrands on both sides tried to inflame their supporters. In October 1859, John Brown's raid on the federal arsenal at Harper's Ferry divided the nation. The Hamptons and many others counseled moderation.

When the Prestons and Mrs. Hampton returned to Columbia in 1860, it was a different town from the one they had left. Secession was in the air. The legislature had drawn many people to the capital and the four major hotels and the rooming houses were full. The shops lining Richardson Street were doing a thriving business. However, Columbia was not such a hotbed as Charleston, and many voices urged moderation. Most people found it difficult to resist the idea of secession, and those who were pro-Union often found it best to conceal their feelings. The enthusiasm and excitement encouraged a festive atmosphere, and the Prestons arrived to be swept up in it.

Caroline decided that the best way to introduce the girls into society would be to give a large party, and her mother agreed. John Preston was so busy with politics, having been elected chairman of the South Carolina delegation to the Democratic National Convention meeting in Charleston, that he raised no objections, asking only that he have no other duty than that of receiving the guests. Invitations were accordingly issued and eagerly accepted.

The evening of the party, Mamie, Buckie, and Tudie were wild with excitement. The maid who was helping them to get dressed was almost as excited as the girls. As she laced Mamie's stays and helped her with the many crinolines, Janie said, "I declare, Miss Mamie, I ain't never seed such a beautiful sight as you in that dress! All the gentlemen going to be dying of love for you and asking your papa for your hand."

"Do stop talking so silly, Janie, and help me with this sash. I can hear Mama in the hall giving instructions to Maria, and she told us most particularly to be ready by seven-thirty."

At that moment, Caroline Preston entered the room, regally elegant in her dark green moiré dress with point de Venise lace and diamonds. She inspected the girls critically and said, "Girls, aren't you ready yet? What on earth has been keeping you? Tudie, why are you wearing Buck's earrings that she bought in Paris? They are most unsuitable for a young girl like you! People will think you are as fast as Marie Boozer. Take them off at once."

"But, Mama, Buck said I might wear them tonight."

"When did Sarah Buchanan become the authority on what is proper in this house? I want people to think you girls improved by your education in Paris, not the contrary. Now hurry and finish dressing and come down to greet the guests with your father. He is already at the door and is waiting for you."

The steps and gardens of the mansion were lighted by candles in hurricane shades, and little Negro boys hurried to hold horses so that ladies might descend from their carriages and young men dismount. Mr. Preston stood on the steps greeting the arriving guests, and William hovered in the background supervising the entire scene. He frowned disapprovingly at one of the little boys who did not seem to be taking his duties seriously enough. "You, Moses, be back on the plantation tomorrow if you don't do no better."

In the drawing room, Mrs. Hampton was seated on a long sofa ready to receive her guests and to greet old friends whom she had missed during her years abroad. All around the room were displayed many objets d'art which the family had acquired during their travels: bronzes, Etruscan vases, Swiss carvings, a set of red Bohemian glasses, not to mention the inlaid tables and carved German furniture. The French candelabra looked especially fine on Mr. Powers' beautifully sculpted mantel. It was her favorite of all the many works he had done for them, including the baptismal font at Trinity Church which she had commissioned.

In the dining room, three liveried, white-gloved servants stood over the wine coolers filled with champagne, a large silver bowl filled with punch, and many assorted wine bottles. Silver platters piled high with all sorts of sumptuous delicacies, ham biscuits, many varieties of cakes, fruits, and jellies awaited the guests. As Caroline took one last look, she could not help thinking that her refreshments were not inferior to the buffet she had seen at the Tuileries reception.

Thinking of that evening, Caroline remembered Ransom Calhoun's attentions to Buckie. She wondered if that might be a good match. She was quite ignorant of her daughter's feelings but he was, after all, a connection of theirs and also of John C. Calhoun's, and he was certainly an attractive and personable young man, if, perhaps too hot tempered. Well, she knew quite a bit about hot-tempered men: her father had been noted for his temper. Ransom had gone to West Point, not a point in his favor to Caroline, but in the present political situation it might be an advantage. She would have to ask John his opinion if she could get him to set aside politics for a moment.

The girls were soon surrounded by a swarm of young men, including their cousins Wade IV and Preston Hampton. At that moment, several young men who had just arrived and were being greeted by Mr. Preston, caught sight of the girls and, as quickly as was polite, moved toward them.

Mamie, Buck and Tudie happily greeted friends whom they had not seen for two years. Among the group was Edward Gibbes.

"Ladies, may I hope that you remember me? I am Edward Gibbes, and I made your acquaintance one afternoon before you went abroad. My aunt and uncle, Dr. and Mrs. Gibbes brought me to call."

"Indeed, Mr. Gibbes, we remember you perfectly," said Buck. "You are most welcome. Why did we not see more of you before we left for Paris?"

"I had intended to enter the South Carolina College and had come to Columbia to stand the entrance examinations, but, alas, it was not to be, and I returned to Charleston."

"Why was it not to be?" asked Tudie. Buck and Mamie tried to hush her but she repeated the question.

Edward laughed and said, "Well, Miss Tudie, to tell you the truth of the matter, I did not pass the examinations and was not accepted as a student, much to my chagrin and the sorrow of my family. I fear my previous studies had been somewhat deficient."

Tudie blushed and gazed appealingly at him. "I am so sorry," she said.

"And so am I," he answered, "as it has prevented me from becoming better acquainted with the Preston family. I hope to remedy that now, as I shall be in Columbia for a while assisting my uncle in classifying his scientific collections. Ladies, I do beg your pardon. I have been most remiss in not presenting to you my friend from Charleston, Rawlins Lowndes."

In front of the girls stood one of the most handsome men they had ever seen. Twenty-two years old, tall and slim, a perfect aristocrat in looks and bearing, no one could have better fitted a young girl's ideal. He had light brown hair, gray eyes which sometimes appeared green, long lashes, a sensitive mouth, and a fresh complexion. He was elegantly, but not foppishly, dressed.

As he bowed to the girls, he said in a decided Charleston accent, "Ladies, I am most happy to make your acquaintance. Edward has spoken so often of you."

While Rawlins Lowndes was speaking, his eyes remained fixed on Buck. He had heard much of her beauty from Edward and from various Columbia friends, but nothing had prepared him for the reality. She was, without a doubt, the most superb woman he had ever seen.

Buckie, aware of his gaze, was somewhat embarrassed and murmured, "How do you do, Mr. Lowndes."

Just then, a new group of guests arrived, consisting of several elderly couples.

"Mr. Preston, how good to have you home again! Where is dear Mrs. Hampton? And Mrs. Preston and the girls?"

Buck and Mamie and Tudie were summoned by William. "Miss Buck and Miss Mamie and you, too, Miss Tudie, your pa wants you standing beside him right now. You best move, and quick!"

Hastily telling the gentlemen that they would see them later, the girls hurried to their father's side. The hall was now full of girls in wide crinolines of all colors, low decolletages showing perfect shoulders and glimpses of bosom. Some had flowers in their hair or sewn to their gowns. They were accompanied by their beaux and closely watched by the older ladies, some of whom had taken up positions on the settees in the hall.

At the rear of the hall, near the door to the dining room the Negro musicians were tuning up. Several couples had already gone out onto the marble-tiled piazza or down the steps into the gardens, lit at intervals by torches.

When most of the guests had arrived, the girls received permission from their father to withdraw, and they gratefully moved toward the dining room.

"Look, Buckie," said Mamie, "you have lost Edward Gibbes to Tudie." Buck followed her gaze and saw her younger sister being escorted to the dining room by a most attentive Mr. Gibbes.

In the gentlemen's parlor, the talk was all of politics. Many of the gentlemen had been to the National Democratic Convention when it met in Charleston in April and had lent their voices to the growing dissension.

"The Platform Committee was a perfect disgrace from start to finish," said one elderly gentleman. "They did not take a strong stand. If Mr. Calhoun had been there, matters would have been arranged quite differently."

"What did you expect from the Northern delegates? You knew they would never enact a platform favoring laws to permit slavery in the territories," said Dr. Gibbes. "We all knew that they would reject our demands."

"The question is, what do we do now?"

"That question has been at least partially answered by our withdrawal from the Convention."

"We knew the Northern delegates meant to nominate Stephen A. Douglas from the very beginning. That is why they adjourned to Baltimore."

"I wish we knew more about what happened when the Southern states met in Richmond. Why did they choose a Kentuckian?"

"What do you know that is not favorable to Breckenridge?"

"Oh, I know nothing about Breckenridge. I just feel that it would have been preferable to nominate a Virginian or a South Carolinian."

"Well, John Preston was there, and I dare say, he can tell us all about it. However, I would not say anything detrimental about Breckenridge as he is, after all, a relative of Mr. Preston's."

"I am afraid this split insures the election of that terrible man!"

"What terrible man?" asked an innocent young guest.

A chorus answered him, "Abraham Lincoln of Illinois, the Republican candidate!"

The ladies gathered around Mrs. Hampton in the drawing room. They had other subjects to discuss. "Dear Mrs. Hampton, we are all so happy that you and the Prestons have returned to stay. Never remain away from Columbia again for so long a time. You have been sorely missed," said Mrs. Stewart.

All the ladies agreed. "And you must tell us all about the latest fashions. We have heard that they are rather scandalous. The Empress Eugénie must be quite a sight to see."

"I am afraid Columbia must seem very dull to you and the girls. Your return, however, has made it a much more lively city for us."

Mrs. Hampton laughed. "Judging from what I observed in the hall, the girls are going to find Columbia equally as agreeable as Paris. After all, in Paris they were in a convent school and the subject matter was not young men! Mrs. Gibbes, is not that your nephew, Edward, speaking to Tudie?"

"Yes, indeed. We are pleased to have him back with us. He is supposed to help Dr. Gibbes with his collection. He had brought along his friend Rawlins Lowndes with the special intention of introducing him to Buckie and Miss Mamie. He is totally captivated by your girls."

Mary Boykin Chesnut, about five-feet tall, handsome, with dark, deep-set eyes, a ready smile, intelligent, warm, and attractive, spoke up. She was the wife of James Chesnut, Jr., United States Senator from South Carolina, and a dear friend of Caroline Preston's. "It seems that all the young gentlemen are captivated by your granddaughters. I know my nephew certainly is! No wonder! Three such accomplished girls. Look at Mr. Lowndes out there in the hall, staring at Buck as if he had seen an angel. You know his mother was a Huger, and her family has many Northern connections."

"Speaking of Northern connections," said another lady, "did not Sally Baxter, Frank's wife, meet that dreadful Mrs. Stowe while she was in the South?"

"Not the woman who wrote *Uncle Tom's Cabin?*"

"The very one!"

Mrs. Hampton entered the conversation. "No, my dear, you are mistaken. It was not Mrs. Stowe whom Sally met, but Mrs. Howe, who has written many travel articles for the *Atlantic Monthly*. Sally and Frank met her in Cuba when they went there for Sally's health. Sally said she was a charming woman and a great help to her."

Mrs. Gibbes said, "Mrs. Chesnut, I know how fond you are of reading. Have you read *Adam Bede*? I enjoyed the book so much, but I cannot believe that George Eliot is a woman! And a woman of bad character. Well, I presume anything is possible these days!"

Just then Caroline Preston, having made sure that the refreshment preparations were complete, entered the room. "Is this a literary discussion? Do you all know that our own Sally Baxter Hampton is the model for Ethel Newcome in Mr. Thackeray's book? Her family are very dear friends of the author, and he has often visited them in New York.

Indeed, they say that he admired Sally most exceedingly. Frank told me that when Sally's father, Mr. Baxter, was at Woodlands this spring, he talked of going to England for a visit with the Thackerays. I wonder if they will go now. The political situation is so uncertain it is difficult to make plans."

"Caroline," said Mary Chesnut, "do you think the girls could arrange some private theatricals to entertain us this summer?"

"I am sure they would be delighted. There is nothing they love more than to act and declaim, especially tragedies. You should see Buckie dying at the stake when she plays Joan of Arc! But I rather think we will go to The Valley for a few weeks to escape the heat. Kate and the girls have invited us," said Caroline.

Mrs. Hampton sighed. "Wade and Kit have done a lot up there, but it is still a bit too rustic for my taste. I do not care for all the talk of hunting and fishing. How I wish we might go to the Colonnades at White Sulphur instead."

"Mama, you know John said that was impossible this year. The political situation is so difficult, he does not know where he will be from one day to the next."

Later that evening, as the two older girls were preparing for bed, Buck said to Mamie, "Did you ever see anyone as handsome as Mr. Lowndes? He is my idea of everything a gentleman should be."

Mamie replied, "More than Captain Bellanger?"

"Maybe not," admitted Buck, "but he is here and Captain Bellanger is in France. And we did not ever get to really know him. I will never forget that ride in the Bois! What a mercy that Mama and Papa never found out. Cousin Ransom was really a dear."

As Buckie tossed in her bed that night, still too excited to go to sleep, she kept thinking of Jean-Paul Bellanger. What was it that Mamie had said that made her recall him so vividly? The first few weeks following that ride in the Bois, she thought of him constantly, but as time went on she had been so busy in school she had thought less about him. Now she relived her first glimpse of him in uniform following the Emperor down the rue de Rivoli. And the night of the Tuileries reception when he had cleverly manoeuvered her away from Willie, and the bouquet with the concealed note, and the meeting in the Place Vendôme, and the ride in the Bois. He had awakened feelings in her that she had never known existed, troubling and yet thrilling. Why had his kisses been such a surprise to her? What might have happened if they had not so quickly joined the others?

She looked over at Mamie sleeping peacefully and wondered if her sister had ever been troubled with such passionate feelings. She couldn't even explain to herself exactly what she felt. The strange thing was that she had experienced the exact same feeling this evening when she had been introduced to that very dashing young man from Charleston, Rawlins Lowndes.

Bouquets, compliments, and teasing about her many beaux were a part of her life. She looked upon flirtations as amusing games. She had wondered at her mother's warnings about trifling with young men's affections, and could not imagine anyone being actually hurt in such a pleasant pastime. Remembering Jean-Paul, she wondered again about his abrupt leave-taking. Why had he made no attempt to see her again? It had bothered her at the time, perhaps more than she had acknowledged to herself. Suddenly she wondered if Cousin Ransom had anything to do with the matter. He had been there and had seemed quite upset when she and Jean-Paul appeared. He had rather abruptly taken them back to the hotel and had given Mrs. Hampton a very convincing, if rather confusing, account of where they had been. He certainly knew Captain Bellanger. The more she thought about the matter, the more confused she became. Anyway, the whole episode was in the past. Why had she thought of it just now? Rawlins Lowndes had awakened these same troubling emotions. Perhaps there was more to love and romance than she had previously suspected.

As she puzzled about it all, her thoughts turned to her brother Willie. Truly, he was her ideal. Fun-loving, handsome, and always protective of her, he would be a perfect husband for some lucky girl. If only she could find someone exactly like him for herself. Every man she had ever liked had possessed some of his qualities, but none had his joie de vivre and certainly none understood her so well. She sighed and turned over.

※

Fall was a pleasant time in Columbia. The heat had lifted, and while the older people were greatly worried about the presidential election, the young folk had many agreeable activities to occupy them.

The South Carolina College boys were back in school and ready to participate in all social events. Willie Preston was a popular young man at the college, not only for his cheerful and gregarious manner, but also for his three pretty sisters. He frequently brought groups of his fellow students to his parents' home where they could enjoy a game of cards or impromptu theatricals or dances.

All the Preston girls were happy to entertain Willie's friends, under Caroline Preston or Mrs. Hampton's watchful eyes. They knew most of the boys who came to call, and their families, but they also knew that college students sometimes became a bit too lively away from home, and needed some motherly or grandmotherly supervision.

One of the students who came to the Prestons with Willie most frequently was William Hayne Taylor. A shy young man, he seldom spoke, but sat quietly watching and listening to Buck.

Willie teased him. "Now, William, surely you would rather come take a hand in our card game than sit in that corner. Buck can't be all that fascinating."

"Oh, I'm perfectly happy where I am. Don't bother about me, Willie."

"Whatever you say, William. I'll come get you when the rest of us are ready to go back to the college."

William continued to gaze at Buck. In all his eighteen years he had never seen any girl nearly as beautiful. He thought he could be content forever just to be near her looking at that lovely face and hearing her speak in that voice which made everything sound like music. He resolved to write a poem for her that very evening; he had never written poetry before, but he felt inspired.

After the boys left, Mamie said to Buck, "Did you notice William Taylor? He never took his eyes off you. I tried to make conversation with him, and he acted as if he didn't even hear me."

Buck laughed. "And he never said a word to me. I can't understand why he comes."

"Oh, I understand that," said Mamie. He's another of your conquests."

"Don't be silly, Mamie. The students just like to come here to get away from school for a while."

"Perhaps, but I think William would come even if he weren't in school."

Buck said, "I'm glad Willie comes home, even if he does bring people with him. I miss having him here all the time, don't you?"

Mamie agreed. "Willie is special. I love Jack, but Willie is my favorite brother."

"Mine, too," said Buck.

A day or so later, a little Negro boy walked up on the front porch of the Hampton home with an envelope in his hand. He knocked timidly at the double doors, and when William opened the door and looked down at him with a frown, the boy said, "This for Miss Sallie Preston. One of them college boys give it to me to bring over here. He give me a nickel."

William took the envelope and shut the door, thinking to himself, "Uh huh, I bet I know which one, too."

He went up the stairs to the sitting room where all three girls were occupied in looking at drawings of the latest fashions in Godey's Lady Book.

"A letter for you, Miss Buck," said William. "A boy just brought it."

"Thank you, William."

Buck opened the envelope and discovered that her letter was, in fact, a poem. She turned the page to see who had written it and found William Hayne Taylor's name.

"Oh, my goodness! William Taylor has written a poem about me!"

"Read it to us, Buck," said Tudie.

"Let me read it myself first," said Buck. "Then I may read it to you all. Gracious, he calls me 'Sallie'; no one ever calls me that."

She began to read:

> Fair as a poet's fancied dream,
> Bright as glistening snowdrops gleam,
> Soft as warm summer's moonlight beams,
> And sweet as bygone memories seem
>   Is the gentle Sallie Preston.
>
> Her eye would shame the eagle's glance,
> Her step might lead the fairy's dance,
> Her grace would match the timid fawn,
> Her smile would vie with summer's morn,
>   The bright-eyed Sallie Preston.

Buck giggled. "So far he's compared me to snowdrops, moonlight, an eagle and a fawn. And there are eleven verses."

"Let me see," said Mamie, looking over Buck's shoulder. "Oh, Buck, he has some freshmen thinking about your feet. Your feet! And all those men in love with you. Who are they? Johnnie, and Albert, and John H., and another John. And many more, he says."

"I have no idea," said Buck. "It must be poetic license."

"Are you going to show that poem to Mama?" asked Tudie.

"I don't think I will. It might embarrass William next time he comes here with Willie if he knew Mama had read it. He is a nice boy, but not a very good poet."

"At least it scans," said Mamie, "and most of the verses rhyme. I think it's sweet."

Tudie sighed, "I wish someone would write a poem about me. It would be so romantic."

"Perhaps someday someone will. In the meantime, you can read this one if you want to," said Buck, handing the poem to Tudie, who took it eagerly.

"I like the part about 'No far-famed poet of the Greek, Can match the charm of Sallie's cheek, While thoughts of mathematics fly, Before the glance of Sallie's eye'," said Tudie.

"I wonder why he calls you Sallie instead of Buck or Buckie?" Mamie remarked.

"Perhaps he likes it better. I don't know why. Let's not worry about it. Tell me which of these dresses you like better. I think the white one with lace is the very prettiest."

And Mamie and Buck resumed their study of fashion plates, while Tudie read William's poem, substituting Tudie for Sallie in every verse.

❀

The Preston household was the social center of the town. John was deeply involved in politics, and his ambition led him to dream of great goals. Caroline and Mrs. Hampton entertained their many friends, and there were almost always visitors in the house. Everyone was alarmed when a Secession Convention was called to meet in Columbia on December 17th.

Caroline, deeply worried, asked her husband, "John, do you think that this is an end to all attempts at compromise?"

"Yes, my dear, much as I regret this move. I feel that the radicals have succeeded. Indeed, those extremists in Charleston and the abolitionists in the North have contrived to push this unhappy country into a civil war."

"Do you really believe that South Carolina will secede?"

"Yes, I do, even though I will oppose it to my last breath. I am afraid that even our own Richland County delegation will vote for it. I tremble when I think of our boys, and all our fine young men. God willing, the combat will not be long."

The Convention assembled at the new First Baptist Church on Plain Street at noon on the 17th. The church was filled to overflowing, and many fiery speeches were made. During the afternoon, word came that several cases of smallpox had been reported in the city. It was hastily decided that the Convention should recess and meet again in Charleston. As the delegates left the church in a cold sleet and started for the depot and the long trip to Charleston, no one doubted that secession was inevitable.

When John returned home to hurriedly order his things to be packed for the trip, he told his wife, "Caroline, you and your mother had better make arrangements immediately to go to Millwood. The children can go to Sally and Frank at Woodlands. I do not want you exposed to this epidemic. I also believe you should all be vaccinated. Dr. Gibbes has been advising it for some time. I'm sorry we did not follow his advice earlier!"

The next day Caroline did as John had advised and moved her family to the country. Before leaving town, she summoned Dr. Gibbes and asked him to vaccinate her and the girls. Caroline's fear of the epidemic had momentarily made her forget the terrible feeling she had about the dissolution of her country.

Everyone who possibly could was leaving town. There were thought to be about seventy cases of smallpox, and people believed it was carried by Negroes going from one place to another.

Fortunately, none of the girls had any ill effects from the vaccine, and quickly proceeded with their packing. Sending them and her mother on ahead, she closed the house, leaving a few slaves who had had the disease to keep watch over the property.

When the girls arrived at Woodlands, they found Sally suffering from her vaccination, but valiantly trying to make preparations for Christmas. On the plantation, Christmas was the Negroes' special holiday. It was then that they took their own crops to market. This year, with the smallpox quarantine that was impossible, so Frank bought their corn and cotton and provided a festival at home with a barrel of whiskey, a hogshead of molasses, and an ox for the barbecue. Sally gave out coffee, sugar, and other special treats. The cash Frank paid them for their crops gave them a little ready money, so an air of cheerfulness prevailed.

The children were also happy, and everyone's spirits lifted at the arrival of Mamie, Buck and Tudie, who rushed to greet Frank and Sally.

"Oh, poor Sally!" said Mamie. "Just look at your arm! Why, mine hardly shows. Do tell us what we can do and we will tend to everything."

"It is a good thing that Mama and Grandmama have gone to Millwood, since they are both ailing. Kate and Caroline can nurse them better than we could," said Tudie.

Buck chimed in, "Poor Mama! Now Papa has gone to Charleston with the Convention, and the smallpox is in Columbia, she is beside herself. And Christmas too! No wonder she is sick."

"And she is so worried about Jack and Willie. You know they will be in the thick of any fighting. Papa too, probably."

"Well, they aren't fighting yet," said Sally, "and we must pray it will not come to that."

"Oh, Sally, I know how you must feel with your family in New York," said sympathetic Mamie.

"I heard from Mama's Maria that she had seen people putting out flags in Columbia to celebrate secession in spite of the smallpox," said Buck.

"Well, I know that Papa is thoroughly opposed to the whole idea, he and Uncle Wade. He sent word to Mama that all anyone in Charleston can talk about is the forts and what will be done if they try to reinforce them," said Mamie.

Tudie asked, "If who tried to reinforce them?"

"Mr. Lincoln, of course. Tudie, do you never listen to the talk or look at the newspaper? I don't see how anyone can be as ignorant as you," Buck declared.

"Now, girls," said Frank, "Don't be too hard on your sister. Some people are trying their best to think of other things. And we are upsetting Sally with all this talk of war. You said you wanted to help. Why don't you take the children and go down to the quarters and distribute the coffee and sugar? The children will like to see the preparations for the barbecue. That will give Sally a chance for a little rest."

The girls collected the children and started out of the house. "Do you think Papa and Uncle Wade will be back for Christmas?" asked Buck.

"No," said Mamie. "I don't believe they will leave Charleston with all the excitement there and the smallpox here. Christmas this year will certainly not be the way it usually is."

"And our first Christmas at home since 1857! It seems a shame. I was so looking forward to all the parties!"

"Well, perhaps next year will be different. If we do go to war it could be quite different," said Mamie.

"Oh, yes. Think of all the boys in their uniforms. They will be so handsome!"

"Trust Tudie to see the bright side!"

"Come on, children. You'll have to walk. We can't possibly carry you all the way to the quarters. You are much too heavy. Don't you want to see the barbecue?"

Christmas was celebrated as happily as possible under the circumstances, and shortly thereafter the Prestons returned to Columbia.

John Preston also returned from Charleston with the news that on the night of December 16th Major Robert Anderson and the garrison had abandoned Fort Moultrie and moved to Fort Sumter, an island in Charleston Harbor. Many Charlestonians felt this to be an act of aggression.

In January, six other states seceded and the Confederacy was formed. Newspaper headlines proclaimed, "THE UNION IS DISSOLVED!" and Columbia responded with bonfires, ringing of bells, and militia company parades.

In Paris, Ransom Calhoun, who had already made preparations to return home and resigned his position at the Embassy, left as soon as he learned that the South had, indeed, seceded from the Union. He had no doubt that his duty was to his native state. With his West Point background, he knew he would be needed when war came. Before he left Paris, he wrote a letter to John Preston, saying that he hoped he would soon be back in Charleston and would then call on him in Columbia on a matter of some importance. In all the political turmoil and the smallpox scare, John quite forgot about Ransom's letter. He never thought of connecting it with his daughter Buck, supposing it to be about a military appointment.

By mid-Jamuary, Jack had already joined the Charleston Dragoons. Willie decided to join the artillery company attached to the Charleston batteries. He had discovered that his senior officer would be Ransom Calhoun, very recently arrived from Paris. This pleased him very much, and his parents were relieved to think that Willie had someone to look after him. (Willie, of course, felt sure that he was well able to look after himself.)

On the last day at home before leaving for Charleston, Willie went to his room to pack his valise with things he thought he would need as a soldier. He expected to have his uniform provided for him, but he planned to take socks, underwear, shirts, his shaving gear, and a change of clothes, not knowing when his uniform might be ready. As he took his valise out of the closet and laid it on his bed, he heard a soft knock at the door.

"Who is it?" he asked.

"It's Buck. May I come in?"

"Of course. Come on in. You can help me pack—maybe that way I won't forget anything."

"Oh, Willie, I am so proud of you for enlisting, but I truly will miss you," said Buck, as she moved toward the shuttered windows and sat in a low chair facing Willie. "I can't believe we are really going to have a war against the North."

"Well, they haven't given us much choice. We can't let them dictate to us. Anyway, I'll be in Charleston for the time being, and I'm certain to have a leave sometime so I can come home."

"That can't be too soon for me, Willie. You know how much I depend on you, both for amusement and for good advice," said Buck.

Willie turned from the tall walnut bureau, a pair of socks in each hand. He dropped them on top of the clothing in his valise and said, "Buck, let me give you some advice now. We may be involved in a war which could go on for a long time. Don't listen to those people who say we Southerners could whip the Yankees with cornstalks; they aren't going to be fighting with cornstalks. The North has more men and factories than we do, and it's going to be a tough fight if war comes, and I fear it will. There will be many of my friends who will become soldiers, and I'm sure they will look very smart in their uniforms. They may appeal to your sympathies and ask you to give them some commitment. Don't do it. Don't be carried away by the thought that they may be going into battle and promise them something you don't really mean. I know you, Buck. You are a sensible, level-headed girl, but you have a soft heart. Promise me you won't do anything foolish."

Buck stared at her brother, her violet eyes wide with surprise. "Why, Willie, you sound so serious. I have no intention of doing anything foolish. I can't help it if young men make a fuss over me. When William Taylor used to come to visit with you I hardly said a word to him, and he wrote that ridiculous poem to me anyway."

"Buck, I'm serious. I'm going to be down in Charleston, training with the artillery company, and I can't keep an eye on you from there. Just don't be swept up in the excitement and do something you'll regret."

"Oh, Willie! You know Mama would never let me do something if she didn't approve of it."

"Mama might not, but you know as well as I do that you can persuade Papa to let you do anything you want. Remember the time you wanted that pony everyone said was too lively for you? You teased Papa till he gave it to you."

"And I rode it, and it wasn't a bit too lively," retorted Buck.

"Honey, what I'm talking about is something more serious than a pony. I haven't forgotten that time in the Bois in Paris when you went riding with Captain Bellanger. You know you were attracted to him, and there will be lots of men just like him, soldiers who claim your attention because they may be risking their lives in a war."

"That was a long time ago, Willie. I'm older now and I think I know how to behave."

Willie sighed. "I hope you do, Buck. I hope you do. But you don't realize how you affect men. You sit there smiling, murmuring soft replies in that mourning dove voice of yours, looking at them with those big violet eyes and nodding your pretty red head, and they all melt."

"I don't do it on purpose, Willie. I can't help the way I look, or talk."

"I know that, Buck. I just want you to be careful."

"Careful, Willie?"

"Yes, careful. Don't give your heart away too soon. Listen to Mama. And don't use your wiles on Papa to get something you shouldn't have."

"I'll try to be careful," said Buck. "But suppose I meet someone I love as much as I do you? What then?"

Willie looked at his sister and smiled fondly. "Buck, if you find someone like that, marry him. And if I find a girl I love as much as I do you, I'll marry her."

Buck laughed. "That seems fair."

"You know, there may be an exception to my advice to not become too involved now. Cousin Ransom Calhoun is a senior officer with the company I'll be in. I have always liked and admired him, and I know how highly he thinks of you."

"Now, Willie, Cousin Ransom just looked after us in Paris to please Mama and Papa. I don't believe he has any special feelings for me."

Willie regarded Buck quizzically. "You must know better. I saw how he looked at you that day we said goodbye in Paris."

"Then you saw more than I did. I think you are imagining things."

"We'll see. Now hand me those shirts in the bottom drawer and let me finish my packing."

IV
Columbia, 1861

About eight o'clock on a snowy evening in February, Ransom Calhoun appeared at the Preston home. Handing the reins of his horse to a little Negro boy who appeared around the corner of the house, he instructed him to take it around to the stables, ran up the front steps of the house and rang the bell. When William opened the door, he urgently asked him if Miss Buckie were at home.

"Yes sir, Mr. Calhoun," said the surprised butler. "Mr. and Mrs. Preston have gone to call on Mrs. Chesnut who is staying at the hotel. Mrs. Hampton is feeling poorly and she has retired. The young ladies are in the parlor getting up one of their theatricals."

"Please tell Miss Buckie that I need to speak to her privately on a most urgent matter," said Ransom.

"Are you all right, Mr. Calhoun, sir?" asked William, noticing the visitor's agitation. "Should I fetch you some of Mr. Preston's brandy? It's mighty cold out there tonight."

"No, thank you, William. Just tell Miss Buckie that I am here. I will go into the gentlemen's sitting room."

Ransom paced back and forth. Was he being an utter fool? Ever since he had returned from France, he could think of nothing but Buck. Perhaps it was the war. Perhaps it was talking with Willie. All he knew was that he had to act. He could no longer hide his feelings from himself or from her. He could no longer play the role of the indulgent older cousin. The door opened and Buckie entered the room.

"Cousin Ransom, what a surprise! Why didn't you let us know you were coming? We just found out that you were back in Charleston. Mama and Papa will be disappointed that they have missed you. They have gone to visit Mrs. Chesnut, who is ill at the hotel, and Grandmama has gone to bed."

Seizing her in his arms and kissing her passionately, he said, "It is not them I came to see but you, my darling. Oh, Buckie, I can't stand this another minute! You must know how I feel about you. I am in torment. Say that you will be my wife or I don't know what will become of me."

Buckie, completely astonished by this outburst, did not know what to do or say. Trying to withdraw from his embrace, she said, "Ransom, you are my favorite cousin, and that is how I have always thought of you. You were so good to us while we were in school in Paris. I don't know what Mamie and Tudie and I would have done without you, taking us places and all, while Mama and Papa were traveling. Please do not spoil things by speaking of marriage." Buckie could not help thinking of what Willie had said to her before he left.

"Spoil things! How can you be so cruel! Think what may happen to all of us in this horrible war! I want to be with you every moment and protect you as your husband."

"Dear Ransom, I have Papa and Jack and Willie to protect me if it becomes necessary. I don't wish to cause you pain, but I do not love you as a wife should. Please, please, don't say anymore."

"I hope the first shot from Fort Sumter will go right through my heart!"

"Oh, Cousin Ransom, how can you say such a dreadful thing? I would be heartbroken if anything should happen to you."

"Well, you will be to blame."

"How can you be so cruel?"

She left the room sobbing, and Ransom, after a moment, turned and walked despondently into the hall. Seeing William, he said, "Tell Mr. and Mrs. Preston I regret that I could not stay."

He left the house abruptly, shouting for his horse.

When the Prestons returned from visiting Mrs. Chesnut, they found Mamie and Tudie in tears in the parlor. Buckie was nowhere to be seen.

"Girls, girls," said their mother, "whatever is the matter? What has happened?"

When his wife was unable to get any coherent response, John Preston went into the hall to speak to William, whose gloomy face indicated that he knew something. "William, do you know what has happened in our absence to upset the girls so? Tell me at once!"

"Yes, sir. Mr. Ransom Calhoun came running up the steps a little after you and Mrs. Preston left to go to the hotel. He looked like a wild man possessed and said that he have to see Miss Buckie right away."

"Did he say why?"

"No, sir. I even ask him if he want some of your brandy and he say no."

"Then what happened?"

"He go in the gentlemen's parlor and pace up and down till Miss Buckie come. They stay there for a few minutes. Then she come running out crying like her heart was broke and he come out and say, 'Send for my horse,' and run out the door. Miss Buckie, she go in and talk to her sisters. Then they all start to cry. Miss Buckie run upstairs and Miss Mamie and Miss Tudie just sit there crying."

By this time, Mamie had managed to stop sobbing long enough to speak. "Oh, Mama, Buckie has refused Cousin Ransom, and he says he hopes the first shot from Fort Sumter will go through him. And it most likely will since he is there at Fort Moultrie with Willie! They will both be killed!" And she started another fit of tears.

"Mamie, my dear, control yourself! It was very wrong of Cousin Ransom to behave in this impetuous way and upset you all. He should have spoken to your father first. I fear he too often acts before thinking. I do not understand what has happened to all his diplomatic training. He could not have behaved in this manner at the Embassy. Where is your sister now?"

"She said she wanted to be alone and has gone upstairs."

"I will go to her. Now you try to tell your father what you have told me. Girls, do try not to cry. You know how that upsets him."

Caroline sighed and started up the stairs. She had been afraid that something like this might happen. She had heard several tales of impetuous engagements in the last few weeks.

When Caroline arrived in Buckie's room, she found her daughter huddled on the bed. She was not crying now, but her face was red and her eyes swollen.

"Oh, Mama, I have done a terrible thing."

"What have you done, Buckie dear?"

"I have told Cousin Ransom that I don't love him. How could I have been so cruel?"

"Well, Buckie, if you don't love him, it is far better to tell him the truth now than to give him false hope. That would be very cruel."

"But Mama, he may die of a broken heart or try to get himself shot. That's what he said."

"Very few people die of broken hearts in spite of what you read in novels. He may put himself in danger, but you cannot stop him."

"If I had promised to marry him, he would have been so happy. Oh, I wish that I had!"

"If you had married him, feeling as you do, he would have been still more unhappy in the long run. And you would have been miserable."

"I am miserable now!"

"Yes, but you will get over it and so will Ransom. My dear, you did the right thing. Now get undressed and try to calm down. You will feel better tomorrow."

As Caroline left the room, she decided to go and see if her mother were still awake. She wanted to talk to someone, but not John just yet. She feared his reaction. Willie was serving under Ransom with the artillery in Charleston. She wondered what role, if any, he had played in this drama.

Mrs. Hampton's lamp was still burning and Caroline knocked lightly at the door. Her mother sat propped up in bed reading. "Come in, daughter. How did you find Mrs. Chesnut? Why, what is the matter? You look so distressed. She is not much worse, I hope."

"No, Mama. Mary Chesnut is better. It is something which happened while we were out. I am surprised that you did not hear anything."

"I may have slept a little. My neuralgia bothered me, so I decided to read some more. That's why I am awake now."

"Well, shortly after John and I went out, Ransom Calhoun arrived. You remember in Paris how we all thought he seemed to take a particular interest in Buck? This war fever seems to have inflamed his emotions. He came up here to propose to her. Just left his company and rushed up. I cannot believe that he would do such a rash thing!"

"Caroline, he always was an impetuous young man. All the Calhouns are. I am afraid someday it may cause him great harm."

"According to Mamie and Tudie, he proposed an immediate marriage and Buckie refused. The girl really does have good sense. She does not love him in that way. She is fond of him. We all are. But she is not in love. He behaved very melodramatically, and told her he would die of a broken heart or be shot. Now she is regretting that she did not accept him. She is so afraid of what may happen to him. I have tried to tell her that she did the right thing, but she is terribly upset. I could shoot him myself for what he has done to her!"

"You are working yourself up into a frenzy, my dear. Please try to be calm. You will have to deal with John later on. I am afraid, Caroline, with the secession and the war fever, we will have many more of these hasty proposals and unwise engagements to deal with. You had better prepare yourself and speak to the girls of the dangers of rushing into marriage. I will talk to Buckie myself tomorrow, if you like."

"Thank you, Mama. I wish you would."

※

John was very upset with Ransom Calhoun. He hated disruption of any kind. However, after talking with Caroline, he decided not to take any action on the matter. The imminent danger of war was changing all their lives. Emotions ran high and why should he think his own family would escape?

In March, John Preston, then fifty-two years old, went to Charleston as a volunteer on General Beauregard's staff. Willie, an artillery lieutenant, and Jack, who had volunteered as a private, were already there. Frank Hampton, with his cavalry company, was on the coast, accompanied by Sally and the children. Caroline Hampton, Frank's sister, had gone along to look after Sally, whose lung disease had made her very weak and incapable of caring for the children.

Several days later, Caroline Preston came into the sitting room with a letter in her hand. "Girls, I have just heard from your father. He has been inspecting Charleston's defenses, along with General Beauregard and Colonel Chesnut."

"Whatever in the world does Papa know about defenses?" asked Tudie.

"Nothing. But I guess he knows as much as Colonel Chesnut and Governor Pickens. Much better send Mrs. Chesnut! She knows a lot about everything!" replied Buck.

Mamie added, "We must all just hope that General Beauregard knows something or we will be in a really bad fix."

"Girls, that is very disrespectful. Both to your father and to the others!"

"Well, Mama, it's true and you know it. They are all having a good time down there in Charleston playing at being soldiers."

Buckie added, "Grandmama had a letter from Aunt Caroline. She said that they were being entertained all the time. She can't do much as she is busy nursing Sally and taking care of the children. She said Papa and the others were going to parties every night. And you should hear what she said about Mrs. Pickens and all the young men. The governor would be really jealous if he weren't so busy with the defense. All the young ladies are furious at Mrs. Pickens for trying to take their beaux and...."

"Buck! That is enough! I am surprised at Caroline Hampton writing all that to your grandmother."

"She probably has nothing else to do. She can't leave Sally, and you know how Mrs. Gibbes and Mrs. Chesnut and all those ladies sit around and gossip. Dr. Gibbes and Colonel Chesnut can't stop them. All they do is sit around in the lobby of the Mills House and talk."

Shortly afterward, Caroline Preston decided to go to Charleston and stay with her friend Mary Chesnut. She wanted to visit John and the boys. Therefore, she was in Charleston when the first shots were fired at Fort Sumter on April 13th. Despite their opposition to secession, the family was proud that it was Willie Preston's shot which broke the flagstaff on Fort Sumter.

The next day, Major Anderson surrendered the fort and President Lincoln called for 75,000 volunteers to put down the insurrection. When the news reached Columbia, Mrs. Hampton and the girls were in a frenzy of excitement. Mrs. Hampton, opposed as she was to the war, sent Willie a telegram to congratulate him. The girls could talk of nothing but their adored brother Willie.

Later Buckie stood alone in her room examining herself in the mirror. Something had made her think of the things Ransom Calhoun had said on that memorable night when he had proposed so unexpectedly. She shuddered. The memory of those passionate words and caresses troubled her more than she cared to admit, even to herself. She had told her mother only a small part of what had actually occurred after she had rejected Ransom's proposal. He had, indeed, said he hoped he would get shot, but before saying that, he had seized her, spoken to her in a way she had never imagined, and kissed her ardently. And she, not knowing what else to do, had let him, until she became really afraid. She felt terribly guilty now about the whole episode. What she really wanted to do was to confide in Willie and ask his advice. If only he were at home. But he was in Charleston with Ransom and not likely to return soon to Columbia. She had not told Mamie and Tudie the whole story either. Their knowledge of men's behavior was no greater than her own.

Ideas of confiding in Willie and asking his advice were crushed a few days later when she received a letter from him. Surprised that he had found time to write to her, she was dismayed when she read the letter.

Dear Buckie,

Why did you refuse Cousin Ransom? He loves you and always has. You may not have known it, but he told me of his feelings for you. He hoped you loved him too. He's sorry he didn't ask Papa's permission first. He is very depressed, and I'm worried about him.

      Your brother,
      Willie

P.S. My friend Rawlins Lowndes is coming up to join Cousin Wade's legion. He will probably come to call.

Buckie ran to show the letter to her sisters.

"Oh, how mean!" said Tudie. "Willie would take Cousin Ransom's part. It sounds to me as if it were all Willie's idea in the first place. Rushing up here like that instead of first speaking to Papa."

"Who is Rawlins Lowndes?" asked Mamie.

"Why, you remember, Mamie, that divinely handsome man who came to the party Mama gave when we first came back from France. He came with Edward Gibbes. You remember, don't you, Tudie?"

"Yes. The one with the Charleston accent. I could hardly understand a word he said."

"You were too busy gawking at Edward Gibbes!"

"Girls, what are you fussing about now?" asked Mrs. Hampton as she came into the room. "I have just heard from your mother that she is returning on Friday. Charleston is too crowded and she can rarely see your father and the boys. Mrs. Chesnut is going to Camden before going on to Montgomery, so they can travel up here together."

"Don't say anything about Willie's letter," Buck whispered to her sisters, but too late.

"Grandmama, Buckie had a letter from Willie this morning fussing at her for refusing Ransom. He didn't say anything about Mama's coming home."

"Mamie, I don't see that *Cousin* Ransom and Buckie are any concern of Willie's. He should have enough to occupy his thoughts without worrying his sister. My dear, you did the right thing. Willie should keep his opinions to himself."

"Thank you, Grandmama. Do you remember a man named Rawlins Lowndes from Charleston? Willie says he is coming up to join Cousin Wade's legion and will probably call on us."

"Isn't he the Lowndes boy whose mother was a Huger? I believe his father is a banker in Charleston."

"And he is the most handsome man Buckie has ever seen!" exclaimed Tudie.

"I never said that! You are making that up!"

"You did too. Just before Grandmama came into the room. You asked Mamie if she remembered him and said he was divinely handsome."

"Stop, girls. If Mr. Lowndes calls, we will be glad to receive him. Your mother also mentions that John Darby from Orangeburg may be joining the Legion as a surgeon. She says not only did he graduate from the medical college in Charleston, but he also attended medical school in Philadelphia. It will be very pleasant for you girls to have all these young men in Columbia while they train with Wade. It is truly a noble thing for Wade to do. Imagine financing a legion of one thousand men with his own money. I'm sure President Davis was very pleased. He commissioned him a colonel."

"Well, he certainly ought to," said Mamie. There aren't many people like Cousin Wade around."

Several days later, two young gentlemen went up the steps of the Hampton home. When William opened the door, they asked him to tell Mrs. Hampton that Dr. Darby and Mr. Lowndes had come to call.

John Darby was not quite as tall as Rawlins, with chestnut hair and moustache and deep-set brown eyes. Though not handsome, his charm, intelligence, and wit made him popular wherever he went. "John, do you think it was proper for us to invite ourselves like this?" Rawlins asked his friend.

"Certainly. Mrs. Preston told me to send a note and call as soon as I arrived in Columbia. She was a little worried about her mother and the girls being alone. Though I don't call thirty or so servants and a lot of friends and relatives all over the place being alone."

"I guess she meant without herself and Mr. Preston and the boys. Willie also told me to come."

Just then William reappeared and asked them to follow him into the parlor where Mrs. Hampton was seated by herself. Trying not to look too disappointed, the two young men introduced themselves and told her the latest news of the Legion.

"It's really wonderful, Mrs. Hampton, the way it is all coming together. In Charleston, twice as many men answered Colonel Hampton's ad in the *Courier* as he could accept. We are to train at his old racetrack at Woodlands. It will be called Camp Hampton."

Rawlins joined in. "Each volunteer is to bring his own horse and body servant. The uniforms are to be gray with gold buttons and braid."

"We will need body servants just to keep our uniforms in order," laughed Dr. Darby.

There was a rustle in the hall, the door opened, and three girls entered the room. "Why Grandmama," exclaimed Buckie with an air of surprise, "we did not know that you had visitors."

Mrs. Hampton suppressed a smile for she knew the girls had been at the upstairs window for at least half an hour. "Girls," she said, "I believe you have met Mr. Lowndes. This is Dr. John Darby, a friend of your parents. Dr. Darby, may I present my granddaughters, Mary Cantey, Sarah Buchanan, and Susan Frances?"

The young men bowed to the girls and glanced at each other. Rarely had they seen three more elegant, vivacious, and attractive girls. John Darby could not take his eyes off Mamie.

"We have been discussing Hampton's Legion," said Mrs. Hampton. "I am glad to hear some of the details from people who know what they are talking about. We hear so many rumors and stories. It is hard to know what to believe these days."

"Grandmama, they say Cousin Wade is finally going to allow Preston to join as a private," said Mamie.

"Imagine having to salute your own father and call him Colonel Hampton!" laughed Buck.

"I'm afraid if you did not you wouldn't last long in the Legion," said Rawlins. "You could hardly address the commanding officer as 'Papa'."

As he looked into her laughing eyes, he felt the same thrill he had the night of the party almost a year ago when he had first met her. Back in Charleston, he had managed to convince himself that it had been a momentary sensation but now, seeing her again, he knew it was far, far more than that.

And Buck, still laughing, felt all the charm of the dashing young man. He was mocking himself, as well as her. He knew that right now they were all playing soldier like little boys. The glamorous uniforms and talk of body servants and camps on race tracks helped keep everyone from thinking of the inevitable bloodshed ahead. For now, it was better to concentrate on frivolities.

"Well, Miss Preston, will you not give a farewell party for all us brave men who are going off to defend you?" he asked.

"Oh, yes, Mr. Lowndes. We will give lots of parties and barbecues and dances. We will all fall in love with you and promise to wait forever!"

Ever practical Tudie joined in. "Won't you have to ask Mama?"

"Yes, dear," replied Buck. "Actual plans for a party will have to await Mama's return. But that should be soon. In the meantime, we have Grandmama's approval, don't we?"

"I do approve of parties and entertainments for our brave men," replied Mrs. Hampton. "I am not so sure however, about falling in love and promising to wait forever!"

"But that is the best part, ma'am," laughed Dr. Darby, with a longing glance at Mamie. "Don't you think so, Rawly?"

Rawlins, looking at the blushing Mamie, said, "Oh, I wouldn't want to wait forever. Why not hurry things up!"

※

"Hurry things up" expressed the exact mood of the two young men when they left the house later that afternoon. Mrs. Hampton had supplied them with tea, and the conversation had centered on the formation of the Legion. In spite of hints from all sides, Mrs. Hampton had never left the room. As she had told Caroline, engagements and hasty marriages were all too likely in wartime, and she was not going to help things along. She had noticed the admiring glances that John Darby had been giving Mamie. Mr. Lowndes and Buck also seemed very attracted to each other. This after the tears and trauma of Ransom Calhoun's proposal! It was going to be quite a summer. She would be thankful when Caroline and John returned to deal with some of it. She realized, though, that John's immediate return was unlikely now that he had been put on General Beauregard's staff. Well, she had every confidence in her daughter's ability to deal with almost anything. Caroline was an extremely competent woman, as she had proved more than once!

As Rawlins and John Darby were walking down the street, John said, "What a beauty Miss Mamie is! And so agreeable! How soon do you think it would be proper for us to call again?"

"Why, John, I have never seen you so smitten before! Usually you let the young ladies do the courting." Rawlins laughed good-naturedly at his friend.

"I don't know what you are talking about. Anyway, when did you have time to notice what I was doing? You spent the whole time flirting with her sister! What about all those heartbroken girls in Charleston who have just kissed you goodbye? One dark-haired beauty in particular!"

"Oh, don't mention her. I may have problems there. Right now I don't want to think about her. I no longer fancy dark-haired beauties anyway. Let's fall in love while we can and 'Hurry things up!'"

When Caroline returned, she agreed that a party for the Legion was a good idea, and plans were started right away. Needless to say, John Darby and Rawlins Lowndes were deeply involved in the planning and many hours were happily spent on this task. Caroline and Mrs. Hampton began to wonder if these two soldiers had any duties at all at the camp. John assured them that so far no one had need of his medical attentions, and that Rawlins was the one in charge of all duties in town.

The laughter and joking in the parlors and gardens seemed to be a daily thing. It was not always laughing and joking, however, and sometimes the conversation became more serious. The Legion had heard that they were to be ordered to Virginia in late June or early July, so all their time was precious.

In the Preston kitchen, preparations for the party were moving ahead despite frequent interruptions from Mamie and Buck. Harrison, the Prestons' gifted cook, was able to ignore the girls' efforts to supervise the elegant foods he was devising for the party. As the head cook he commanded respect from all, and it was beyond the girls' powers to make suggestions regarding cookery to Harrison. This was not the case with his helpers, and Buck and Mamie made many trips down the basement stairs to make sure everything was done just so for their evening's entertainment.

"Pearlie, are you sure you're making enough beaten biscuits? You know how much everyone likes those, especially with ham," said Buck.

"Now, Miss Buckie, how many years I been making these biscuits for your mama's parties? More than you been alive. I know how many we needs."

Mamie was watching Eloise stir the batter for pound cake. "Did you sift that flour? I don't want these cakes to have sad streaks. Maybe you need to beat that batter some more too."

"Have mercy!" said Pearlie. "We been cooking all these years and now you all gon' tell us how to do it? I tell you, Miss Buckie, Miss

Mamie, if you all don't quit coming down here and meddling, we never gon' be ready for tonight."

"Oh, Pearlie," said Buck, "this is an important party for us. We want everything to be just perfect."

"It will be, Miss Buckie, if you and Miss Mamie stay upstairs and leave us be."

Mamie stuck her finger in the pound cake batter, licked it thoughtfully and said, "Eloise, you do make the best pound cake. But do you think you used enough vanilla?"

"Shoo, shoo! Get out of my kitchen," said Harrison. "Can't you young ladies find something to do upstairs in the parlor? How you expect us to fix all this food when you come down here and pester us? Next time, I tell y'all's mama what you doing."

Buck and Mamie retreated up the stairs. They knew everything was being done well in the kitchen, but they were too excited to stay away.

"Maybe we could cut some flowers and put them in vases in the parlors," said Mamie.

"I think Mama has already done that. Let's look at our dresses for tonight and be sure everything is ready. I want to look my best for Rawlins."

"So do I," replied Mamie. "Not because of Rawlins though."

"Oh, I can hardly wait till tonight! It's going to be a wonderful party. There's even a full moon and the garden is looking its best. Anything can happen!"

Downstairs in the basement, Pearlie laughed. "Do, Lord! Miss Mamie and Miss Buckie got their beaux coming tonight. You reckon we have a wedding in the family soon?"

Eloise put her hand in the oven to check the temperature and then slid the cake pans in. "I doubt Miss Caroline thinks these girls is old enough to be getting married. But Miss Mamie and Miss Buckie is hard-headed. They may say yes, no matter if Miss Caroline say no."

"I put my money on Miss Caroline!" said Pearlie.

That night at the party, Rawlins led Buck down the steps, into the garden. They could hear the music and laughter in the house, but, as they walked farther down the boxwood bordered path, the noises grew softer and the loudest sound was the splashing fountain at the end of the path. Her arm linked through his and her white dress glowing in the dark, Buck felt a thrill of excitement. Rawlins looked down tenderly at her, and she felt sure that this was to be the time he would speak to her. She could hardly wait! Drawing her down on a bench somewhat hidden in the shrubbery, he put his arms around her. She lowered her head to prolong the magic moment. He touched her chin with his fingertips, and slowly raised it so he could look into her eyes. As he kissed her, at first gently, then with passion, she felt a thrill like nothing she had known before. Every other time a man had kissed her, it had been a surprise, and not a pleasant one. She did not like to feel that she was not in control of events. But this time, she had eagerly anticipated the moment and done everything in her power to bring it about.

"My darling, how can I bear to leave you?" he whispered softly. "Now that we have just found each other."

"Don't talk about leaving," she said, "not now. This moment must last forever." As they clung to each other, it seemed to her that nothing could spoil anything so perfect.

"You know we leave soon for Virginia?"

"Dearest, please, please don't say any more about leaving. I can't bear it."

"I don't say it to hurt you, my darling. I want you to be brave. But I don't want you to spend years waiting for me and always hoping and being afraid. I want to think of you having fun with your sisters and being just as you are now."

"How can I not think of you? I didn't plan to fall in love with you. When the war is over. . . ."

"That will be a long time, Buckie. Who knows what may happen. Let's not spoil the time we have now. Kiss me again, my love!"

※

Hampton's Legion was ordered to Virginia in early July 1861. The Confederate capital had been moved from Montgomery to Richmond in May. An invasion by Federal troops was expected imminently.

The day the Legion left Columbia, Mrs. Hampton, Caroline and the girls went down to the station to see them off. Bands were playing *The Bonnie Blue Flag* and other patriotic tunes, and flags were waving in the breeze. It was an exciting, if sorrowful, moment. Few thought of what lay ahead.

One who did was Mrs. Hampton, sitting in her carriage with Caroline. The girls had gotten out of the carriage, much against their mother's wishes. They were determined to find Dr. Darby and Captain Lowndes and say another tearful good-bye. Mrs. Hampton said to her daughter,

"I am very worried, Caroline. I do not think this will be a short and bloodless war. In fact, I am sorry Fort Sumter fell the way it did, though it was a glorious moment for Willie. I am afraid another such easy victory will be our downfall."

"Why, Mother, do you think there will be a battle soon?"

"I don't know, but I'm afraid all the parties and festivities are taking our minds off what may happen. I hate to see the girls fall in love so quickly. This is not just another flirtation for either of them. I must confess that I was very surprised to see Buckie so in love with young Mr. Lowndes after all her tears over Ransom Calhoun."

"I don't believe Buckie had any idea what love could be until she met Mr. Lowndes. It was all just sentimental play-acting. But Rawlins Lowndes is certainly a most charming and well-bred young man. I could almost fall in love with him myself!"

"My dear, beautiful as Buckie is, she would not stand a chance against you!"

"Thank you, Mama. What a nice compliment. But I think I had better devote myself to John. He must be in Richmond already. I understand the Legion is to be attached to General Joseph E. Johnston's army, with General Beauregard in overall command."

"Do you think you will go to Richmond?"

"I am going to wait and see what the situation is when John arrives there. If we can be together, I will certainly go. But if it will be as it was in Charleston where I just sat around the hotel all day and hardly got to see him, I will stay here in Columbia. I will do whatever John wishes."

"Well, I do not think the Yankees are anything to be scornful of. They will not give up easily, and I am afraid for our boys, brave as they are."

Caroline decided to go to Richmond, and joined her friend Mary Chesnut at the Spottswood Hotel where many officials and their wives were staying. The ladies exerted themselves to visit with the boys from home. This was not hard to do as the Legion was camped just east of the city.

On July 16, Union soldiers marched from Washington to Manassas, and Beauregard moved to stop them. General Johnston's forces, including the Legion, were moved to the front. On July 22, news reached Columbia that a great battle had been fought. Colonel Hampton had been wounded, as well as many others. Quite a number had been killed. With thankful hearts, the girls and Mrs. Hampton learned that their loved ones had survived.

In August, John Preston was assigned to command the prisoner-of-war camp in Columbia. He and Caroline returned home to everyone's great joy.

"Oh, Mama," exclaimed Tudie, "you can't imagine how lonely we have been without you! *Nobody* is in Columbia. All we do all day long is knit and sew for the soldiers and talk about how we miss them. And I don't have anybody in particular to miss! Mamie has Dr. Darby and Buckie has Captain Lowndes and I don't have anybody!"

Trying not to laugh, Caroline said,"What about young Mr. Gibbes?"

"Oh, he is nobody. And besides he belongs to Agnes Smythe now. He never did belong to me."

"Well, my dear, I would not say that Dr. Darby belonged to Mamie, or Mr. Lowndes to Buck! People do not belong to each other until they are married, or at least officially engaged. And your sisters do not know either of these young gentlemen well enough for that."

"They act like they do. Always sighing and moaning and writing letters."

"Well, they had much better get on with their work!"

"Mama, were there a lot of funerals for the soldiers in Richmond?"

"Why do you ask, Tudie?" said Caroline.

"Mary Jones had a letter from her cousin in Richmond, and she said there was a funeral every day and that it was so sad. Everyone was dressed in black with veils, and crying. She said they led a horse with an empty saddle and the band played the 'Dead March' from Saul. What is Saul, Mama?"

"An opera. You have been to funerals, Tudie. Why are you so interested now?"

"I've never been to one like that. Just ordinary ones at Trinity. Never with horses and bands."

"Mama," said Mamie, "did Mrs. Chesnut ever tell you about the slave who killed Mrs. Witherspoon? Her son was going to punish him for taking some of Mrs. Witherspoon's things while she was away on a visit. She had spoiled her slaves terribly and her son was mad at her about it and said there would be trouble. But I don't imagine he thought his mother would be murdered in her bed. Anyway, that night she was murdered. And another man in Camden had his throat cut by his slaves. And they hanged the woman who did it!"

"Who told you these stories, Mamie? I'm sure it was not Mrs. Chesnut! She is much too sensible to go about frightening people. You do not need to repeat such tales and scare others. Our people would never harm us. Now let us talk of something more pleasant than murders and funerals. When your father returns from the camp, he would like to hear something agreeable. Why don't you sing us a song?"

Mamie went over to the piano and struck the opening chords of *Lorena*. As she began to sing, Buck exclaimed, "Not that! Mamie, you know that always makes me cry."

"Who are you crying for?" asked Tudie. "Cousin Ransom or Mr. Lowndes?"

"Mama, make her stop! She is so mean!"

"Girls, girls, do stop fussing. Your father hates to hear you fuss."

"Do you think Papa beats the prisoners?" asked Buck.

"Of course not! What an idea. They are prisoners of war, not criminals. Would you like to think of our boys being beaten if they were captured? They are to be treated humanely until they can be exchanged. Do you never listen to Dr. Shand's sermons about doing unto others as you would have them do to you? Why do you think we go to church and pray to be forgiven? The very idea that your father could be cruel to anyone!"

"Not Papa. He is far too soft-hearted. But I'll bet the guards are mean. Why, Pearlie says she knows a man who. . . ."

"Enough! Sarah Buchanan, I forbid you to say another word about prison camps. Here comes your father."

John Preston was not a very successful prison camp superintendent. In fact, he only held this position for a few months. Far from beating the prisoners, he was much too lenient with them. They were allowed out in the town and seemed to have friends, including the notorious Amelia Boozer Feaster, reputed to be a Union spy. There was a lot of criticism which hurt John very much. In January 1862, he was relieved of this job and put in charge of the Columbia Conscription Camp where new recruits were trained.

V
Columbia 1862

Early in 1862, Mary Chesnut arrived in Columbia for a visit. She enjoyed visiting the Prestons, and she was such good company that Caroline, Mrs. Hampton, and the girls begged her to stay. They were sick and tired of the gloom that had settled over the city since the fall of Port Royal and the departure of the Legion.

Sitting in the parlor one morning in January, Caroline said to her friend, "I do hope your neuralgia is better this morning. Did you sleep any?"

"Yes, some, but I believe I am going to have to consult Dr. Gibbes. The doctor in Camden did not help me at all. I really wish I could see that wonderful Dr. Adams in Richmond."

"Are you not going to accompany Buck and Mamie to the Gibbes' party this evening?"

"Oh, I had quite forgotten! Yes, indeed. He will probably not believe I am ill if he sees me at his party. But I must go. I promised the girls."

"It seems rather strange to me that being so 'in love' as they are with absent beaux, they are eager to go to parties and meet more young men."

"Well, they are young. And I like to meet new young men, too!"

"Mary! What would Mr. Chesnut say?"

"Oh, he knows me very well. He is not worried. He doesn't mind if I flirt a little. It is good for my nerves, he says. Besides, I understand Dr. Darby may be back in town quite soon, so Mamie had better get her flirting with others done before he arrives."

"Why would he be coming to Columbia? I thought he was attached to Wade's Legion?"

"It has something to do with establishing a hospital."

"You mean the Young Ladies Hospital Association that the girls are all involved with?"

"Either that or that project of Mrs. McCord's."

"Well, I know all the young people are very concerned about the wounded soldiers arriving at the depot and having to wait long hours with no arrangements for their comfort. However, Mama and I are worried about the girls. Who knows what they may come upon at the depot. Not only the wounded soldiers but the people who hang around down there."

"If Dr. Darby and Wade come back to set it up, you may be sure it will be done well."

Just then Mamie came into the room. "Are you talking about the hospital? We are all so excited. I am so tired of knitting and sewing all day. I am even tired of entertaining all these men on furlough."

"Well, dear, if what I have heard is true," said Mrs. Chesnut, "you girls will have plenty to do if the hospital becomes a reality. Only don't call on me to be a nurse. You would end up having to nurse me. You remember how frightened you were, Mamie, that day you thought I was going to die?"

"Oh, Mrs. Chesnut, please, I beg you, don't bring that up! Mama never lets me forget how I ran for her and left you to die alone because I was so frightened of the way you looked."

"I am sure you will make a splendid nurse, Mamie. Particularly if you are assisting Dr. Darby."

"Dr. Darby has absolutely nothing to do with it," said Mamie, blushing bright red. Her mother and Mrs. Chesnut burst into laughter.

Wade and John Darby, on leave from the army, arrived in Columbia in March to set up the hospital. Naturally, John's first moment of freedom found him at the Prestons. He was warmly welcomed by William and ushered into the parlor, where he found a crowd of young officers talking to Mamie, Buck, and Tudie.

As he entered the room, Mamie jumped to her feet and almost fell over two men in her haste to greet him. Oblivious to the stares, she flung her arms around him and said, "Oh, Doctor Darby, how happy I am to see you!"

Drawing her into the hall, he tried to control himself and murmured softly to her, "Come out into the hall away from all those people. Who are they anyway and what are they doing here?"

"We always seem to have a crowd. It is driving Mama and Grandmama to distraction. They can scarcely wait for you and Cousin Wade to set up the hospital so we will all be busy and unable to receive callers."

"I don't want *you* to receive 'callers.' Leave that to Buck and Tudie. While I'm in Columbia, I want you to receive only *me*."

As Dr. Darby was speaking, John Preston entered the hall from the library. "Well, John, I thought I heard your voice. How did you leave things in Virginia? I hope the McCord company has been a help to the Legion. Conscription is going very slowly these days."

Mrs. Preston came from the back of the house. "Doctor Darby, we are all so delighted to see you. William told me you were here. How is Wade? Do come in the back parlor and have some tea and tell us the news."

As John Darby and Mamie followed her down the hall, they heard the sounds of the piano in the parlor and a rousing chorus of *Bonnie Blue Flag* followed by *Dixie*. Colonel Preston said, "Caroline, do you think you can get rid of those boys before I come home? I would like to conscript them and send every one to Virginia! I would do just that if they weren't already in the army and some wounded. Then I might have some peace at home."

"I will try, dear. It is not only the girls. Mary Chesnut also encourages them to come. It is very trying for Mama, too. I'm becoming really worried about her. She spends so much time in bed lately. Usually she enjoys company, especially when Mary is here. I think she feels worse than she lets on."

Just then Buckie came flying out of the parlor. "Papa, have you heard about Cousin Ransom? One of the officers from Charleston says he is under arrest for writing an insulting letter about General Ripley."

"I had not heard of it, but nothing Ransom does would surprise me too much now. Not after the way he behaved with you. I only hope Willie was not involved."

Caroline said, "You remember that time last year in Virginia when they all got into a fight with a Maryland company over a camping ground. Something about picketing their horses."

"One would think they could exercise more self control. We have plenty of enemies to fight. There is no need to be quarreling with each other and insulting superior officers. I pity General Beauregard! Someday Ransom will go too far. I am very thankful Buck didn't marry him. She has saved herself a lot of grief. I must go to my office. John, please stay and visit with the ladies. I hope you will come to dinner soon."

"Thank you, sir. I would like that."

Caroline said, "I hope your father will not get too upset over this affair of Cousin Ransom's. We are all so fond of him and he was wonderful to all of us when we were in Paris. Besides, your father has had much to worry him lately. All that unnecessary business of the prison camp."

Buck said, "And it was so unjust! Even Dr. Gibbes criticized him. As though Papa could have done anything about that Feaster woman. Her daughter, Marie, is very nice. Poor thing. To have a Yankee spy for a mother."

Mamie added, "Those prisoners have certainly caused a lot of trouble. Why in the world did they send them to Columbia?"

John Darby said, "I imagine because it is quite removed from the fighting in Virginia and on the coast. How did they cause so much trouble?"

Caroline explained. "They wanted to visit friends in town. And John is so kind-hearted, he allowed them to do so. But it turned out some of them were passing information to a woman named Amelia Feaster who was sending it to the Yankees. Of course, Colonel Preston was blamed and it was very hard for him."

※

The young ladies' idea of a hospital at the depot was eagerly embraced by the ladies of Columbia. The Preston girls and their friends canvassed the town for funds. Caroline and Mrs. Hampton, along with Mary Chesnut and many others, gave generously. As the project grew, it was decided that older women should be in charge. Although this annoyed the girls, their mothers were relieved. They did not want their daughters exposed to the suffering and perhaps dying soldiers without capable women who knew something about nursing to direct and guide them. Most of the older women had, of necessity, nursing experience, having cared for their families and slaves through all sorts of illnesses and accidents. Mrs. John Fisher was named to head the project, and it was universally agreed that she was the best possible choice.

Mamie, Buck, and Tudie immediately volunteered to help. Mamie and Tudie proved to be very capable nurses, helping to bathe the soldiers, dress their wounds, read to them, and write letters. Buckie soon found that she was so affected by the suffering that she was of little help. Most of her work became collecting supplies, making bandages, and helping with the preparation and serving of food. This was a humiliating experience for her, but Mrs. Fisher was very kind and kept assuring her that the work she was doing was vital.

The Preston girls were a little worried at first about their relations with Dr. Gibbes after his public criticism of their father. However, as he seemed to have forgotten the whole matter, they wisely decided that they had better forget it also.

The developing romance between Mamie and Dr. Darby was a subject of endless conversation among the girls, the ladies, and even the soldiers being cared for. Mamie seemed quite oblivious to this gossip, but it annoyed Buckie and Tudie very much.

"I declare," said Buck to her sister, "Mama would have a fit if she knew how everyone is talking about Mamie and Dr. Darby. And Mamie has really done nothing."

"Oh, Buckie, how can you say that? Think how she blushes when anyone mentions his name and how she watches his every move. She's always trying to help him with the soldiers."

"He is just as bad. Always telling her not to work too hard and wanting her to assist him. 'Get Miss Preston to help me.' No wonder people talk."

"Well, it will soon be over. I heard Papa say that Dr. Darby and Cousin Wade have to return to Virginia next week. Please don't tell Mama about the gossip. It will just upset her. She has enough to worry about with Willie and Jack in the siege in Charleston and Grandmama being sick."

Later that day, after the girls had returned from the hospital, Mary Chesnut suggested that they go pay a visit at the convent. Buckie and Tudie did not want to go, but Mamie wanted to see her friend Ellen Spann, who had just become a nun. Mrs. Chesnut liked to go to the convent from time to time and visit with the Mother Superior whose brother, Bishop Lynch, she had known in Charleston. She and Mamie went off in the Preston landau.

Upon returning home, Mary Chesnut sought out Caroline. After telling her of their visit, she said, "I wonder if Mother Superior Baptista Lynch is not thinking of Mamie's joining them. Aren't you worried, Caroline? Mamie called her 'Mother' and was very affectionate."

"No. It is so peaceful in the convent. I think it does the girls good to go there after all the pressure at the hospital. Besides, Mamie would never become a nun. She loves the world and Dr. Darby too much. If I thought she had such an idea, I would ask Dr. Shand to speak to her. I am sure she will remain a devoted Episcopalian and plan to have a wedding at Trinity Church and wear a wedding veil, not a nun's veil!"

"Speaking of Episcopalians, well, not really, but of Presbyterians, did it not annoy you and Colonel Preston to have the seminary right across the street? I always had the feeling that they disapproved of our parties and lively behavior."

"Oh, Mary, I don't let things like that bother me. I'm sorry if they disapproved, but we cannot run our lives to suit them. Right now I am so worried about the boys and Mama that I need a little distraction. John says the situation in the West is very bad. General Grant has captured several forts and New Orleans may fall. When I think of Houmas in Yankee hands! And Mr. Burnside still owes us money from the sale."

On April 27th came news that New Orleans had fallen and all up and down the river cotton was being burned to prevent it falling into Yankee hands. Only a short stretch of the Mississippi between Vicksburg and Port Hudson remained in Confederate hands.

In the East, by mid-May, McClellan was within a few miles of Richmond. The army needed reinforcements from Charleston, but these could not be spared as the city was under bombardment and besieged. There was some good news however. Stonewall Jackson's victories in the Shenandoah Valley and consequent threat to the city of Washington offered some relief to Richmond. In June, the Seven Days Battles forced the Union Army to retreat down the peninsula and the city was spared. In the course of these battles, Wade Hampton was given the rank of general. He was also wounded in the foot and returned to Columbia to recuperate.

While Wade was in Columbia, word came that Hampton's Legion was to be broken up. When General Robert E. Lee took command of the Army of Northern Virginia, he reorganized it. Special units such as the Legion were impractical, and Wade III and his cavalry were placed under the command of General J.E.B. Stuart. Though much younger than Wade, General Stuart was a West Pointer and outranked him. Rawlins Lowndes remained with Wade as his aide. John Darby went with the units assigned to General John B. Hood. It was hard on all of them to be separated, but they recognized the wisdom of General Lee's decisions.

General Lee's encouraging effect on the army was evidenced in a victory at the Battle of Second Manassas, which sent the city of Washington into a panic, and by the successful cavalry raids into Pennsylvania which were led by Stuart and men from the former Legion.

September brought news of a great battle in Maryland at Antietam and also of President Lincoln's proclamation declaring that all slaves in states or parts of states still fighting against the United States on January 1, 1863 would be emancipated when liberated by the Union armies.

John Preston was very aware of the implications of this proclamation concerning the slaves. He told Caroline, "This is the end of any hope of aid from England or France. They will not help us now. Whatever the politicians may wish to do, their constituents would oppose it. As long as the war was about a state's right to leave the Union, there was a chance they would come in on our side. Now there is none."

"That is exactly what Mary Chesnut has maintained all along. She never did think they would help us. And everyone said she was just a prophet of doom."

"Well, she was right, which may be some consolation to her, if not to the rest of us."

"Yes. Mary does like to be right. Do you think we have a chance of winning without European help?"

"No, my dear, I don't. We do not have the resources. Much as I hope I am wrong, I do not see how we can prevail."

But in the Preston household these national events were overshadowed by what was happening at home. Sally was dying at Millwood. Frank was with her, having delayed his departure for Virginia. He had been appointed a lieutenant colonel after the reorganization of the army and was to join the South Carolina Cavalry in August. This was the unit commanded by J.E.B. Stuart where Wade was serving.

The morning of September 6th, while the girls were preparing to leave for the Wayside Hospital, Mamie came running up the stairs and into the bedroom. Tudie and Buck knew at once that something terrible had happened.

"Have you heard the news?"

"No, what? Not Willie!"

"No, Cousin Ransom. He has been killed in a duel."

"Killed! By whom? Why?"

"I don't know why, but Alfred Rhett has killed him."

Buck turned pale and collapsed on a sofa. Just then Caroline entered the room. "I see you have heard the news. Willie has just telegraphed us. He is distraught. I always felt something might happen to Ransom but never dreamt of this."

Buck was inconsolable. She refused to leave her room for several days and would wear nothing but black. She grew so pale and thin that her mother became worried. Caroline made up her mind that she would have to try to shock her out of this excessive grief. At first she had thought there might be a certain amount of dramatization involved, but now she was really concerned. "Buckie, dear, you are doing no good to yourself or anyone by taking on this way. Your father and grandmother and all of us are worried about you. And heaven knows we all have more than enough to worry about besides you. Do try to get up and put on some other clothes and come downstairs. Mamie and Tudie are just leaving for the hospital and you can sit with Grandmama for a while and relieve me."

"Oh, Mama, I can't! Poor Cousin Ransom. I can never forget how sweet he was to me in Paris. And how sad he was when he proposed to me and I refused him. He said then that he would be shot, and now he has been, just as he predicted."

"Well, not *just* as he predicted. As I remember, he said that he would be shot at Fort Sumter. This duel had nothing to do with that."

"And that horrible Rhett man has been put in charge of the Second Artillery! After he killed Cousin Ransom. Oh, I hate the army. You and Grandmama were right about military men!"

"Well, we don't know all the details. We shall have to wait until we hear more from Willie. In the meantime, so many of our friends are being killed or dying, we must make an attempt to be cheerful for the sake of others. It is very selfish to give way to our own feelings, as though no one else had any. I fear also we may soon hear sad news from Millwood."

"Is Sally worse?"

"Yes. I have had a note from Kate this morning. Frank is beside himself. He cannot remain away from his regiment much longer and he cannot leave Sally. Wade has done all he can to have the leave extended this long. I don't know what will become of those poor children. I suppose they will stay with Ann and Kate and the others at Millwood."

"You are right, Mama. I'm a selfish pig. I'll go sit with Grandmama a while and tomorrow I'll go back to the hospital with Mamie and Tudie."

Sally died at Millwood on September 10th and the family went into mourning. She was buried with the Hamptons in Trinity churchyard and Frank left shortly for Virginia.

VI
Richmond and Columbia, 1862-63

All fall the girls continued their work at the Wayside Hospital, while Caroline nursed her mother and John was occupied with the conscription camp. Mamie's thoughts were with John Darby. Buckie still mourned for Ransom Calhoun, but her thoughts now more often dwelt on Rawlins Lowndes. Why, after such an ardent leave-taking when the Legion went to Virginia and several sentimental letters, had she not heard from him in the past few months? He had not come to Columbia with Wade on his several visits, so she had had no opportunity to see him and judge for herself what might be the matter. When she asked her cousin about his aide, he always replied that Rawlins was a brave and loyal soldier and an excellent aide, but that was not what Buck wanted to hear. Wade had mentioned in passing that Rawlins did not write often enough to his mother and that she worried about him, but that was not quite the same thing. Buckie could not forget him, and Darby's constant attentions to Mamie made Rawlins' inexplicable conduct even harder to bear. She did not say anything about her worries to anyone, knowing how greatly her parents would disapprove of any young lady expressing an interest in a man who did not seem to favor her.

When, in December, President Davis sent James Chesnut a commission as colonel and summoned him to Richmond as a personal aide and Mrs. Chesnut invited Mamie and Buck to come immediately for a visit, it seemed a heaven-sent opportunity to see Rawlins and find out the truth. As soon as the Chesnuts were settled in Richmond, Caroline agreed to let the girls go. She thought it would do them good, and she knew how eager her friend was to have them come.

Almost as soon as they arrived, word spread to their many friends and the Chesnut home was besieged with callers—among them Cousin Wade, now a general, and his aide Captain Rawlins Lowndes.

Buck was quite astonished when she saw him enter the room. Still handsome and charming in appearance, there was something very changed. He had lost much of his lively manner and looked rather somber and downcast. She attempted to conceal her concern and spoke first to Wade and some of the other officers. Finally, when he approached her, she attempted a few light remarks, but the look in his eyes made her pause. He drew her over to a corner of the room somewhat away from the others and said, "I know what you must think. Come with me for a carriage ride tomorrow afternoon and I will try to explain."

As two young officers approached, she quickly answered, "I don't know what I will say to Mrs. Chesnut, but I will try."

"Don't worry. We can tell her that I am taking you to see the camp. If she objects, we can take her or Mamie with us and let them visit with General Hampton while we talk."

Fortunately, Mary Chesnut had other plans for the next afternoon and wanted Mamie to accompany her. She was not pleased at the prospect of Buck's going out unaccompanied but decided allowances had to be made in wartime and, since she knew both Rawlins and his parents to be models of propriety, Buck would be safe with him. She tried not to think of what Caroline might say.

As they drove out of Richmond toward the camp, Rawlins said, "You cannot imagine how many times I have pictured this moment—sitting beside you. You must think me very strange not to have written or have come to Columbia!"

"Indeed, I have wondered. I could not believe that you would forget me so easily after what you said in the garden that last night in Columbia."

"As though anyone could forget you! No, it is the war. I have seen things I could never have imagined. Every day is so uncertain that sometimes I feel I can scarcely go on. Every time I would start to write to you, I could not force my pen to put down the words. I have longed to see you and dreaded it too. Every time General Hampton went to Columbia, I almost begged him to allow me to accompany him, and then became afraid of what I might say or do. I never asked. I am afraid of the future—for all of us."

"But Rawlins, we are all afraid. Mamie and Tudie seem so confident in their work at the hospital, but I dread going there and seeing those poor wounded men. I cried so much they made me help in the kitchen and not be a nurse."

"My dearest, I cannot think past today until the war is over. Can you accept that? I know it is not what you want to hear, but it is all I can say now."

Tears were falling on Buck's beautiful face, but Rawlins made no attempt to wipe them away or to comfort her. At last she dried her eyes and said in a low voice, "You had better take me back to the Chesnuts." As she got out of the carriage, she said, "Good-bye," with a heartbroken sob.

Going directly to her room, she thanked heaven that Mamie and Mrs. Chesnut had not yet returned and that the servants were all in the kitchen so she was unobserved. She managed to compose herself sufficiently before dinner and vowed silently that no one would ever know what had taken place that afternoon.

In late February, after the girls had returned to Columbia from Richmond, Buckie was sitting with her grandmother in her room. Mrs. Hampton was almost a complete invalid now, rarely leaving her bed. On her good days, she enjoyed visits from her granddaughters, and was especially pleased to see Buckie this afternoon. She had missed her greatly. She was struck by Buckie's downcast face, a contrast to the smiling, happy Mamie who had visited her yesterday, full of tales of good times in Richmond and blushing references to Dr. Darby.

"Buckie, something is the matter," said Mrs. Hampton. "There is no use saying there isn't, for I can see it in your face. Don't you want to tell me about it? I may not be able to help, but it is always better to talk to someone than to brood alone."

"Oh, Grandmama, you are right. I just have to tell someone. Mama and Papa wouldn't understand, and all Mamie can think of is John Darby. I would tell Willie but this horrible war has kept him away so long."

"Well, tell me. I am old and I have lived through a lot and very little upsets me."

"You remember before the Legion went to Virginia and how we were all so happy and had such fun? Well, Rawlins Lowndes almost proposed to me that night in the garden. He didn't because he thought it would be wrong when he was leaving so soon and didn't know what might happen. He said he loved me and I told him I loved him. He wrote me a few letters from Virginia and then they stopped. I knew nothing had happened to him because Cousin Wade said so. When we arrived in Richmond, he came to the Chesnuts. He looked so different, rather woebegone, not dashing and elegant as he used to be. He came over and asked me if I would go for a buggy ride with him the next day so he could explain something. While we were going out to the camp, because we had told Mrs. Chesnut we were going there to visit friends, he said he couldn't think of anything but the war and all the terrible things he had experienced and seen. He said he was sorry to hurt me and hoped I could forgive him."

"What did you say?"

"Grandmama, I couldn't say anything. I just started to cry and told him to take me back to Mrs. Chesnut's. I suppose I should have said something, but I couldn't. Nobody knows. You are the first person I have told."

"My dear, I know how devastated you must be. When your grandfather came back from the War of 1812, he was a changed man from the one who had left. I knew he loved me and the children, but sometimes it seemed as if we weren't there. He never was able to speak of his experiences, but as time wore on, it seemed to affect him less. I know he never forgot, but he slowly seemed to come back to us. The same thing may happen with Mr. Lowndes, but certainly not until this dreadful war is over. It is affecting so many lives in such terrible ways."

"And Grandmama, I don't see how I can live through Jack's wedding in April. I know it will be a quiet wedding because of the war, but to see him and Celestine walk down the aisle in Trinity will be more than I can endure. I know I shall weep."

"Now, Buckie, it would be most unkind of you to spoil your brother's happiness. You must think of him and act happy whether you feel that way or not. As you say, you haven't told anyone but me about Mr. Lowndes; people will think you are unhappy about Jack's marriage. April is a good while away so don't worry now."

"You're right, Grandmama. I won't disappoint you. And thank you. You make me feel much better."

Buckie was very relieved to have confided in her grandmother, even though her words did not offer much hope. She made up her mind to try to forget Rawlins and to devote herself to her work at the hospital.

"Come with me to the Chesnuts', Sam." Dr. John Darby looked into the room where his friend and commanding officer, General John Bell Hood, sat at his desk. (Hood had acquired the nickname "Old Sam" as a cadet at West Point for no more reason than J.E.B. Stuart had been called "Beauty" at the Academy.)

"I'm writing a letter, John. Go on without me."

"Now, Sam, that letter can wait. I want you to meet Mamie's sister,

Buck. If you think Louly Wigfall is handsome, wait till you see Buck! She is stunning. Every eligible bachelor in Richmond has been calling on the Chesnuts."

"Maybe that's a good reason I shouldn't go. She can't be wanting for callers."

"Oh, Sam! Come just to oblige me. I promised Mamie I'd bring you. And you must let me present you to Mrs. Chesnut; she is a great friend of President and Mrs. Davis, and she could introduce you to people you might find helpful to know."

Pushing his letter aside, Hood leaned back in his chair and groaned, "John, you are a nuisance. Very well, I'll go with you, but promise me we won't stay too long."

Darby laughed. "Once you see Buck, you won't want to leave."

As they set out for the Chesnuts' residence on Clay Street, they made an eye-catching pair. John Bell Hood was tall, over six feet, with golden-brown hair and beard, blue eyes that usually had a look of secret sadness (not necessarily reflecting his feelings), a broad chest, though slenderly built, and, for his size, surprisingly small, well-shaped hands. His gray Confederate officer's uniform was well-cut, and his broad-brimmed hat shaded a face that was considered handsome, even when compared to Preston Hampton's, generally regarded by the ladies as the best-looking man in the entire Confederate Army.

Darby and Hood arrived at the Chesnuts and discovered that, as usual, there were crowds of visitors who had preceded them. Mrs. Chesnut was one of the most popular hostesses in Richmond, and always welcomed young and old alike. Her home was only one floor of a not-too-large house, but she somehow found room for the Preston girls and their maids, in addition to her own servants Molly and Laurence. Buck and Mamie had been given what had been the dining room for their apartment, and the parlor had become a room for all social occasions. Colonel Chesnut, to his dismay, found himself the host for a never-ending series of tea parties, card parties and dances.

John Darby was an old friend of the Chesnuts and was greeted warmly by Mary.

"May I present my friend, Sam Hood? Officially, he is General John Bell Hood, but we have called him Sam so long we almost forget his real name."

"It is a pleasure to meet you, General Hood. I'm glad John could persuade you to call on us; I know how busy you must be."

"Thank you, Mrs. Chesnut. John has told me so much about you and Colonel Chesnut. He says there are no people like South Carolinians for hospitality, and I believe, for once, he speaks the truth."

"I understand you are a Kentuckian, General."

"Yes, ma'am, I was born in Kentucky, but I was in Texas so long and was so taken with that state, that I feel more Texan than Kentuckian now."

"Well, whichever you are, we are delighted to have you with us."

John Darby broke in, "Mrs. Chesnut, I promised to introduce him to Buck. I've looked but I don't see her anywhere."

"Oh, John. You know Buck. She is in her room. She said she didn't feel like company today, so we left her to herself."

"Then perhaps tomorrow you and the girls could come out to Drewry's Bluff for a picnic. We can dine with my Texans at camp. I can promise you a military band for music, and turkey, chicken, and buffalo tongue for a repast," said Hood.

Mamie had come up to speak to Darby and Hood just in time to hear the end of Hood's invitation.

"Buffalo tongue! My stars, where in the world could you find such a thing?" shrieked Mamie, who frequently spoke more loudly than she intended.

"Oh, we Texans can manage to come up with almost anything if we put our minds to it," laughed Hood. "Say you all will come. The weather should be just right for a picnic."

"Thank you, we accept," said Mamie, more quietly, "and I'll make sure Buck comes too."

"Then we will see you tomorrow," said Dr. Darby, giving Mamie an ardent look as he took her hand and pressed it gently.

Mamie blushed and pulled her hand free. "Yes, tomorrow. Will you come for us, or shall we meet you at Drewry's Bluff?"

"I will be happy to escort you," said Darby eagerly.

"No, that won't be necessary," said Mary Chesnut. "We can easily rent a hack and meet you there."

She had watched the exchange between Mamie and Darby with some amusement. John was becoming a very persistent suitor. "Then you won't have to trouble yourself to see us home after the picnic."

With a downcast look, Darby said, "If you insist. Till tomorrow then."

And with that, Hood and Darby took their leave, bowing to the ladies with great panache.

As they went down the stairs, Darby turned to Hood, "I'm sorry you didn't get to meet Buck, but I'm sure Mamie will see to it that she comes to the picnic. You know, Buck may have heard rumors about you and Louly Wigfall, even that you are engaged. Some people claim that Miss Wigfall is more beautiful than Buck, but Buck has something special about her. I dearly love Mamie, but I can understand why so many men have lost their hearts to Buck."

Sam Hood smiled rather wryly. "I don't think I'm the sort of man who loses his heart to anyone. I'm past thirty and so far I haven't seen the girl who could make me want to trade my bachelor's life for marriage."

"Just wait. Better men than you have sworn to resist Buck and have failed miserably."

"We'll see. In the meantime, I've got letters to write. I'll make the arrangements for our picnic when I ride back to camp."

A beautiful May morning greeted the girls when they looked out their window the next day to see if it was indeed picnic weather. The sun shone brightly, and the young green leaves on the locust trees blew gently in the warm airs that caressed Buck and Mamie's charming faces.

"Oh good," said Mamie. "We can wear our best hats and dresses, and not worry about showers spoiling them. Buck, wear that hat with the pheasant feathers you bought in Paris—it is one of the most becoming you've ever had. Just think—three years ago we were shopping in Paris for our clothes, and now we feel fortunate if we can find even a new pair of gloves or a linen handkerchief here in Richmond."

"Do you remember those ballgowns Mama bought us from Worth's?" Buck asked wistfully. "They were lovely, and we had slippers and stockings and everything to match. I wonder if we'll ever see Paris again?"

"Let's just be glad we're in Richmond with Mrs. Chesnut. We never went to so many parties or met so many entertaining people when we were in Paris. Those years we spent in school learning French and German and elocution weren't as jolly as all that anyway. I'm glad to be here, even if it is wartime. And we have a picnic to look forward to today. General Hood is a fascinating man, a hero, and so different from the boys we know from South Carolina. Of course, he can't compare to Dr. Darby, who is perfect! I don't understand why you were determined not to meet the general yesterday."

"If he really wants to know me, he'll have his chance today. I'm not sure someone from Texas will be a gentleman like John Darby or Rawlins Lowndes."

"Hood isn't from Texas. He's really a Kentuckian, and his mother was a French, one of the best families in Kentucky, and his grandfather was from Virginia. John told me so."

"All right, Mamie. I'm willing to go to this picnic and meet General Hood, and then that will be that. Now let's get dressed and have breakfast. I'm starving."

"Me, too. But let's save some room for those buffalo tongues the general promised us. I wonder what in the world they taste like?"

The two sisters opened the door to their room, and Mamie called up the attic stairs to their maids. "Lena! Patsy! Come help us get ready. We don't want to be late for the picnic."

After breakfast with Mrs. Chesnut, who had sent Laurence out earlier to engage a hack, the ladies found their hats, parasols, and shawls, just in case the day turned cool later. Buck wore her hat with a pheasant feather tucked in the ribbons which encircled the crown, and Mamie wore a tiny hat tipped forward over her eyes, with flirtation ribbons of dark green to match her dress.

Just as Laurence was helping the ladies into the rather shabby hack, which was all he had been able to find for them, and apologizing to them for its appearance, "I'm sorry, Miz Chesnut, but this was all they had," a horseman approached, riding very fast and waving his hat as he shouted, "Wait, wait!"

As he drew nearer, they recognized Dr. Darby, who dashed up on a roan gelding with foam-flecked sides. He dismounted hastily, throwing the reins to Laurence, and said, "Stop! It's all off. I'm sorry to tell you this, but our picnic must be postponed. The Army has orders to move out at once, and they are already marching toward the Rappahannock."

Mary Chesnut, Buck. and Mamie sat, stunned, in the hired hack. What could have happened to make this sudden movement of the troops necessary? They looked at each other apprehensively. Being in Richmond seemed all at once much more dangerous than it had even yesterday. Quietly, the ladies collected their belongings, alighted from the hack, and dismissed the driver. Dr. Darby, as he stood beside them, helping hold their shawls and parasols, said "Suppose you walk over and see them pass the turnpike?"

The ladies were delighted with his suggestion, and set off immediately, with Dr. Darby leading his horse. They had only gone a few steps when they were joined by Captain Johnny Chesnut, Mrs. Chesnut's dashing nephew, and his friend Samuel Shannon, ironically called "The Infant Samuel" because of his large size. Both were in civilian clothes.

John Darby, in his surgeon's uniform, walked with Mamie, Buck, and Captain Chesnut, while Mrs. Chesnut and the "Infant" followed more slowly. The group arrived at the turnpike and found a position on the sidewalk with hundreds of other onlookers, citizens of Richmond who had also heard of the army's imminent departure.

As they stood there, thousands of men marched by, their uniforms ragged and torn, pots and pans hanging from their waists, tied on with rope or bits of string. Their bayonets were tipped with loaves of bread or slabs of bacon. As they passed, the troops shouted and cheered. Some sang as they marched. "The Southern Wagon" (Wait for the wagon, the dissolution wagon, The South is the wagon and we'll all take a ride) was a favorite, as was "Goober Peas" (Goodness, how delicious, eating goober peas!), but as the men moved past the spot where Mrs. Chesnut and the others stood, they were singing "The Yellow Rose of Texas".

> She's the sweetest rose of color
> A fellow ever knew,
> Her eyes are bright as diamonds,
> They sparkle like the dew.
> You may talk about your dearest May,
> And sing of Rosalie,
> But the Yellow Rose of Texas
> Beats the belles of Tennessee.

Some of the men caught sight of Johnny Chesnut and Shannon, who appeared to be civilians. This brought on jeers and catcalls. "Come on, ladies, send those puny conscripts on to their regiments! Maybe you didn't know there was fighting going on!"

Captain Chesnut muttered under his breath, "This is my first furlough. I haven't missed a battle, not one!"

John Darby said, "Don't answer. Those are the Texans, and they'll make you sorry you did."

As Darby spoke, General Hood and his staff galloped up. Hood dismounted and stood holding his horse's reins as he greeted the ladies. Mamie had brought a bouquet of spring flowers with her, and offered them to Hood, with a sidelong glance at Dr. Darby. Hood accepted the flowers with thanks, and removed a single blossom from the bouquet, which he carefully placed between the pages of a small book which he took from his breast pocket. "This is the Bible my mother gave me," he said.

Mamie, seeing the pages of the Bible were as pristine as if it had never been opened, commented, "I don't think you have read it since it was given to you."

Mamie seldom troubled to lower her voice, and some of the Texans passing by at that moment heard her, and began to make jokes about their general and his Bible reading. He was not known for reading anything, since in his four years at West Point he had taken out two books from the Academy's library, *The Scottish Chiefs* and *Rob Roy*.

When Hood stopped to speak to Mrs. Chesnut and Mamie, Buck remained aloof, ignoring Hood and the comments made by his Texas soldiers. John Darby was determined that today Buck and Hood would meet, even if Buck seemed unwilling. He called to her, "Buck, please come here. I want you to meet my friend, Sam Hood."

Buck walked toward him, saying, "Oh, very well."

Hood went to join Darby, who said, "Miss Preston, may I introduce General Hood?"

"How do you do?" said Buck coldly, and turned away.

Mounting his horse, Hood looked down at her and then said something quietly to Dr. Darby. Darby laughed, and returned to say goodbye to the girls and Mrs. Chesnut. Buck's curiosity got the best of her. "What did General Hood say to you about me?" she asked.

"Only a horse compliment. He is a Kentuckian, and he said you stand on your feet like a thoroughbred."

"Oh!" said Buck thoughtfully.

John Darby mounted his horse and prepared to join his commanding officer. "Good-bye, ladies. I hope to see you all again soon."

"Please write and tell us how you are. You will all be in our prayers," said Mary Chesnut.

Mamie looked at her gratefully. She had wanted to ask for a letter, but not in the hearing of the rest of the group. It seemed more suitable coming from Mrs. Chestnut, as she was an older lady and a long-time friend of John Darby.

As they watched him disappearing in the distance, they wondered if they would ever see him again, or any of the other men who had marched so jauntily down the turnpike on their way north, and though they could not know it then, to Gettysburg.

A day after Mary Chesnut and the Prestons had watched the army leaving Richmond, a letter came from Caroline Preston:

> My dear Mary,
>
> I regret that I must ask you to send Mamie and Buckie home. Mama's condition is worsening, and she is anxious to see the girls again. You know that they have grown up with her, and she has always been so devoted to them. It is hard for me to realize that she is eighty-three, her spirit seems so young. I pray that she may be spared, but I am fearful that she may not survive much longer. But God's will be done.
>
> If you could arrange for the girls and their maids to take the train to Columbia, we would be so grateful. Please send us a telegram if you can. If we do not hear from you, we will send someone to meet the train every day.
>
> Thank you for sharing your home with Buck and Mamie. I know they have enjoyed being there in Richmond with you.
>
> Affectionately, your friend,
> Caroline Preston

As soon as she finished reading her friend's letter, Mary Chesnut hurried to find Buck and Mamie, who were in the parlor, idly thumbing through the books stacked on the center table.

"Girls, I have just received a letter from your mother. She wants you at home; your grandmother is failing and she wants to see you."

"Oh, poor Grandmama! She hasn't been really well for ages, but I can't bear the thought of losing her," said Mamie. "How soon can we leave?"

Buck's violet eyes brimmed with tears. "Grandmama is the dearest person. She has always been someone we could depend on. How can we do without her?"

Mary Chesnut agreed. "Mrs. Hampton is one of my favorites, too. I will see about tickets for you all and Patsy and Lena. Perhaps we can find a place for you on the train leaving tomorrow. I know your mother would not write unless she felt it was important for you to come home."

Buck and Mamie left the parlor to find their maids and tell them to start collecting their belongings and to pack their trunks for the trip back to Columbia.

"Patsy, Lena," said Mamie, "Grandmama is very ill and we are all going home to be with her. Find our trunks and pack our things. We may be able to leave tomorrow if Mrs. Chesnut can get train tickets for us."

"Yes'm, Miss Mamie," said Patsy. "We sorry to hear Miz Hampton be sick. She looked right peaked last time I seen her."

Lena added, "But she always be smiling. Miz Hampton never complain."

"That is true," Buck said, "she never does. I want to see her so badly. I hope we leave for Columbia first thing tomorrow."

Patsy and Lena went to look for the girls' trunks and to begin the task of fitting everything the Prestons had brought with them back into the trunks so that their clothes would be as little wrinkled as possible, as Mrs. Preston had taught them. They too were glad to be going home. In Richmond they had been sharing a tiny attic room and, with the coming of summer, it was becoming hot and stuffy. They had missed the company of the other servants at the Hampton house as well. Molly and Laurence had been kind to them, but they were older. It would be good to get back to Columbia and be with the other maids who were nearer their own ages. And they would enjoy telling their friends who had never been farther from Columbia than Millwood or Woodlands about life in Richmond.

Mrs. Chesnut was able to get tickets for them all, and they boarded the train leaving Richmond the next day. It was crowded, but they found seats in one of the coaches and, after a long, uncomfortable journey they reached Columbia.

"This isn't the way we expected our visit to Mrs. Chesnut to end," said Mamie.

"No, but I am glad that Mama wrote and asked to have us come home. Darling Grandmama is more important than all those people we saw in Richmond," said Buck.

Mamie sighed. "If Dr. Darby were here maybe he could help Grandmama."

"Oh, Mamie! You think Dr. Darby can do anything, no matter what. Look, there is Henry waiting for us, just like he did that time we came back from Houmas so long ago. It is good to be home."

❧

Caroline Preston, wearing a dress of somber black batiste, with long full sleeves and a small ruffled collar fastened with a dark cameo brooch, was seated at a fragile fruitwood desk in the upstairs sitting room. The black-edged writing paper she had ordered after the death of her mother had arrived that day, and she had begun replying to the many letters of condolence she had received. Mrs. Hampton had died on the nineteenth of June at the age of eighty-three, after a long illness.

Caroline lifted her head and looked across the room at her three daughters. How glad she was that Mamie and Buck had come home from Richmond in time to be with their grandmother before her death. Mrs. Hampton had loved her granddaughters dearly, and had always enjoyed hearing about their parties and outings. She had listened eagerly to their accounts of life in Richmond. She knew Mary Chesnut well, and could imagine the entertainments she had provided. Caroline smiled rather sadly as she thought of her mother's last days, spent lying quietly in her enormous tester bed, propped up on a multitude of pillows covered in the finest linen, looking out the window at her beloved garden and listening to Buck and Mamie regale her with tales of supper parties, dances, and carriage rides through the shady streets of Richmond.

Buck and Mamie were sometimes more forthcoming to their grandmother than to their mother and, as Caroline moved quietly between her mother's room and other parts of the house, she occasionally heard snatches of conversation that made her wonder if Buck had met some new young man who had replaced Rawlins Lowndes in her affections. She did not like to ask Buck or her mother directly, but she hoped her daughter would eventually confide in her.

Having all the girls at home had made Mrs. Hampton's gradual decline more bearable for Caroline. They had been helpful in sitting with their grandmother and in speaking to the many friends who had called to ask about her condition. They were dear girls. How fortunate she and John had been in all their children.

Caroline sighed, and turned back to her desk, but Buck, seeing that her mother had paused in her writing, said, "Do let's go out into the garden for a while, Mama. It is so hot in the house. There's no breeze coming in at all today, even with every window open."

Mrs. Preston agreed. "Yes, let's go out and see if it's cooler under the shade trees by the fountain. At least the sound of the water splashing will make us think we are cooler."

As the ladies started toward the door, Tudie, looking out the window, said, "There is Papa coming up the walk. I wonder why he is home so early."

As John Preston crossed the black and white marble-paved porch and reached for the door's brass knob, the door was opened by the Prestons' butler, William Walker, who prided himself on having the door open before his master could open it himself.

"Thank you, William. Is Mrs. Preston in?"

"Yes, sir. She and the young ladies are in the upstairs sitting room."

Colonel Preston handed his hat to William, glancing briefly in the ornate gilt-framed pier mirror which stood in the hall near the staircase. Despite the July heat, he looked comfortable in his gray Confederate uniform which fit his tall, muscular form perfectly.

As he ascended the stairs, reaching the spot where he could see the upstairs hall, he saw the women of his family walking out of the sitting room.

"I am glad to find you all together. I have news—we are to go to Richmond as soon as possible. I have been given the post of superintendent of the Confederate Bureau of Conscription. President Davis asks that I take up my duties at the earliest possible moment."

"Oh, John, I am so proud that your accomplishments with the local conscript camp have been recognized. I know you will be just as successful when you are in charge of conscription for our whole country."

Buck, Mamie, and Tudie joined their mother, like her, happy to hear of Colonel Preston's promotion.

"Papa, do you mean we will live in Richmond, and not just visit as we did before?" asked Mamie. "I hope we can have a house near the Chesnuts. Mrs. Chesnut was so kind to Buckie and me when we stayed with her in May."

Tudie, who had not been to Richmond with her sisters, asked, "Will I go too? I am so tired of hearing about all the things Buckie and Mamie did there."

"Of course you will go with us, Tudie," said her mother. "You certainly could not stay here alone."

Buck said teasingly to Mamie, "You just want to be able to see John Darby again."

"Girls, girls!" said their mother in reproving tones. "Your father will tell us everything we need to know, if you all will give him a chance to do so. Now please sit down and be quiet."

"Yes, Mama."

"But Papa, please tell us quickly," said Tudie.

"Well, as Richmond is the capital, there will be a great many people, many important officials, living there. I understand that it may be very difficult to find a suitable residence for us, but I want us all to be together. I am sorry that it is necessary to leave Columbia so soon after Mrs. Hampton's death. I know it will be particularly difficult for you, Caroline, but with Jack and Willie away, I think it will be better to have all the females of the family with me in Richmond. I would not like to have you stay in this house without someone besides the servants to protect you, although I have every confidence in the loyalty of everyone who works for me."

He added, "Richmond is suffering from overcrowding and scarcities, and life is not easy there now, but I'm sure I can rely on all of you to make the best of things, and be a comfort to me and others who live there. Mrs. Davis, I know, looks forward to seeing you again. She is a charming woman and her niece, Maggie Howell, will be good company for the girls."

Caroline Preston leaned forward. "How many servants should we take with us, and which ones should we leave here to take care of the house and garden?"

"I leave that to you, my dear. You always have such good judgment in matters like that."

Colonel Preston walked toward the door, saying as he left the room, "I will be at my desk for some time. I have a number of letters to write and arrangements to make for our transportation. When you pack, do remember that our living quarters will not be as spacious as those we are accustomed to here."

As soon as he had gone, the three girls advanced on their mother. Tudie said, "Mama, I want to go to Richmond with you, but I think I ought to stay here. All my friends are here. And I want to help at the Wayside Hospital. They depend on me."

"I am sorry, Tudie, but if your father feels that he needs us in Richmond, it is our duty to go there. I'm sure you will find many ways to be useful to our soldiers in Richmond, as you have here. Mrs. Fisher can manage without you for a while."

"Yes, Mama. But..."

"That is enough, Tudie. You and your sisters had better go to your rooms and make lists of the things you will need in Richmond. We must be ready to go as soon as your father makes the arrangements for our departure." And with that, Caroline Preston left the sitting room, in search of Maria, her reliable maid. They had many things to see to, and Caroline wanted to make a start immediately.

She found Maria in the Prestons' large, comfortable bedroom, mending the lace on a fine cambric petticoat.

"Maria, we are to go to Richmond. Colonel Preston has been given an important post in the government. I want you to go with us. We can only take a few servants, since our accommodations will be much smaller than we have here in Columbia, but we will need you, and William and John, and Harrison to cook for us, and, of course, two or three of the younger girls to help with the cleaning and washing."

"Yes, ma'am," said Maria. "I'd like to go."

"Do you think Janie and Lizzie would be able to help Harrison in the kitchen, and keep up with the housecleaning and laundry?"

"Yes, ma'am, I do. Those two girls are well-trained, and they know how to do housework and kitchen work too. I can help you and Miss Mamie and Miss Buck and Miss Tudie with your clothes and all."

"Thank you, Maria. I know I can depend on you." She smiled at Maria, remembering how she had found her and her brothers, William and John Walker, offered for sale in Columbia after their master, who had owned their mother and had fathered her three children, died. He had married a white woman, who, not wanting the illegitimate children of her late husband to remain where she would see them daily, had sent them to be sold. Caroline Preston had bought them and never regretted it. They had become her most valued servants, especially Maria.

William had become an impeccably-mannered butler; John was somewhat less reliable. Mrs. Preston recalled one occasion when she had had to deal with John at a very inopportune moment.

She and her mother had given a party at their home in Columbia while John Preston was in Louisiana, at Houmas. Her brother-in-law, Governor John Manning, had been there, as well as Mrs. Chesnut and many other friends. She remembered her dress, a white silk velvet gown, with point lace, and she had worn her diamond earrings and necklace with it.

While she was chatting with her guests, William had come and, in a low voice, told her that John, his brother, was in the cellar, drunk, and threatening the other servants with a carving knife. Excusing herself with a murmured, "Something seems to need my attention," she followed William down the steps to the basement, where she found the servants dashing about like frightened sheep. John was shouting and cursing everyone in his vicinity, waving the knife and promising to kill anyone who interfered with him. She had gone up to him and said, "Give me the knife," looking at him sternly, but with inward tremors. To her great relief, he handed it over to her without a word. After putting the knife on a nearby table, she had grasped him by the collar, saying, "Come with me," and led him to the empty smoke-house, where she had locked him in. She had pocketed the key to the smoke-house, taken several deep breaths, and returned to her guests, hoping that they could see no trace in her demeanor of what had taken place. Apparently they could not.

Later that evening she had told John Manning what had happened. He was lavish in his praises of her courage, but she had only been able to think, "What if he hadn't given me the knife?"

But that was in the past, and Caroline Preston brought her mind back to the present, to make the decisions necessary to ensure that her family would be comfortably established in Richmond, and that her home in Columbia would be well taken care of in her absence.

She thought of the lovely garden that she and her mother had planned so carefully, with the advice of a landscape gardener from England. Mrs. Hampton had taken such pride in having exotic as well as native plants in her garden, and now in July many of the flowers were in full bloom. It would be hard to leave the garden, which had meant so much to her mother. Last month, at Mrs. Hampton's funeral in Trinity, the altar flowers had come from her own rose garden, roses of all colors, pink, white, yellow, deepest crimson, filling the church with their fragrance. Caroline sighed. It was such a short time since her mother's death; somehow she still expected to see her walking down the path between the tall box hedges, making sure that the path was properly raked and the hedges pruned just so.

She resolved to have a long talk with the head gardener, to leave a list of things to be done, and to remind him that the townspeople of Columbia were to be allowed to enjoy the garden as they had always done.

Maria had been waiting patiently as her mistress stood lost in thought.

"What would you like me to do first, Mrs. Preston?" asked Maria.

"Oh, Maria, I think we had better make sure all the girls' clothes are clean and mended. I don't know how long we will be in Richmond, perhaps for months, so we will have to take our warm clothing as well as our summer things. Let's go look in the attic and see what we have in storage. We may have to make some alterations."

"It's so hot in that attic, Mrs. Preston. Shall I bring the boxes down to one of the bedrooms?"

"What a good idea, Maria. Thank you. I have so many things on my mind, I'm afraid I hadn't considered how uncomfortable the attic will be now. Ask Isaac to help you carry the boxes—they will be heavy. I am going down to speak to the staff, and then out into the garden. You might ask Miss Mamie to show you which dresses she wants, and then Miss Buck and Miss Tudie.

"Yes, ma'am. I'll get started right away."

Caroline Preston made her way down the elegant staircase to the main floor of the house, and then down the rather dark, narrow stairs to the raised basement, where she found Harrison, their very accomplished cook, and several other servants discussing the news of Colonel Preston's appointment and the coming move of the family to Richmond. William, taking advantage of his position as butler, had heard most of what John Preston had said to the ladies, and had reported the news to as many of the staff as were in the house.

Caroline, realizing that she had been forestalled in telling the servants of the changes in store for the Prestons, smiled at the black faces turned toward her.

"I see William has told you our news. We will be going to Richmond as soon as Colonel Preston can arrange it. Some of you will be going with us. Harrison, I shall depend on you to cook for us, and Janie and Lizzie will help you in the kitchen when you need them, and help with the washing and housework. Maria will go as my maid, and William and John will have their usual jobs. I shall rely upon the rest of you to keep things in order here. The Misses Hampton will be at Millwood, and they will be able to advise you if something happens you cannot manage. All of you have worked here long enough to know how the house and grounds are maintained, and I have every confidence you will do your jobs as well as if I were here. Colonel Preston and I will, of course, be returning from time to time to Columbia."

"Miz Preston, when will we all go to Richmond?" asked Harrison.

"I'm not sure yet, Harrison, but I will tell you in time for you to pack all your special pots and pans."

"Thank you, ma'am. I just can't cook with some strange pots, and my skillets are seasoned just right. I don't want nobody else messing with them."

Mrs. Preston turned to go back upstairs, leaving the servants to discuss all the possibilities they saw opening before them.

"Mind now," said Lucy, one of the older women, "this don't mean some of us won't be called to go too. And Miss Kate Hampton is sure to keep a sharp eye on us here. We better mind what Miss Caroline says."

"That's so."

"You right, Lucy."

"But things gon' be different without the family here."

※

July was a bitter month for the Confederacy. The long siege of Vicksburg ended on July 4th with the surrender of the city, and Union troops at the Battle of Gettysburg inflicted a stinging defeat on the armies of Robert E. Lee on the same day.

At Gettysburg, John Bell Hood was shot from his horse, badly wounded in his left arm. He was treated hastily on the battlefield and then put into an army ambulance, part of the retreat from Pennsylvania back to Virginia.

The journey south was long and painful. Hood felt not only physical pain, but a burning resentment. To lose a battle the Confederate Army could have, should have won! If only Longstreet had heeded his advice and let his Texas brigade attack the enemy from the flank and rear of Round Top, and not insisted on his attacking up the Emmittsburg Road, directly into a heavily-armed Federal position! In his mind, he re-fought the battle over and over again.

One of the other wounded men in the ambulance with him was General Wade Hampton, who had received two sabre cuts on his head and a shrapnel wound in his thigh, charging with Stuart's cavalry against George Custer's troops.

They had many days to discuss the battle, reviewing each movement of the armies and regretting lost opportunities. During the seemingly endless retreat to Virginia, they also had time to become better acquainted. Hood knew that Wade Hampton was closely related to the Prestons, and he was interested in learning something about the family.

He had been impressed with the two Preston daughters he had met in Richmond. Buck's reluctance to meet him had intrigued him. Most other girls in Richmond had been flattered to receive his attentions. Louly Wigfall, a dark-haired beauty and one of the reigning belles of the city, had welcomed his visits. Her father, Louis Wigfall, a Texan in the senate of the Confederate legislature, had encouraged Hood in his army career, and had entertained him many times while his brigade was stationed near Richmond.

Hood was well aware that Wigfall opposed Jefferson Davis, and that John Preston was one of the president's supporters. It could do Hood's career no harm to meet someone as close to President Davis as John Preston, and if he wanted to know Buck Preston better, it would be important to have her family think well of him.

"Tell me something about the Prestons, Hampton. I have met their daughters, and I know they are relatives of yours."

Wade Hampton, shifting uneasily on the hard floor of the army ambulance, his wounds making it impossible for him to sit up comfortably, was glad to talk about something besides the loss at Gettysburg.

"Well, John Preston was the brother of my first wife, Margaret. He is a Virginian by birth, but I'm sure after all these years he thinks of himself as a South Carolinian. He married my grandfather's daughter, Caroline, one of the children by his third wife, Mary Cantey, who was considerably younger than he. So Caroline Preston is both my aunt and my sister-in-law, a rather complicated relationship! John and Caroline moved to Columbia after my grandfather died, and lived with Mrs. Hampton there when they were not in Louisiana. John managed the sugar-cane plantation there for the family. He and Caroline traveled to Europe many times. In fact, the children were educated there. The Prestons have had a great deal of sadness in their lives. They lost several children and their son Alfred died when he was in Rome on the Grand Tour. But they have two sons, Jack and Willie, and the three daughters. They are a very close family. The boys volunteered as soon as the war began, and the girls are as pretty and intelligent as any you'll ever meet."

"John Darby and I had hoped to entertain Miss Mamie and Miss Buck and Mrs. Chesnut, with whom they were staying, at a picnic when we were in Richmond, but we were ordered to leave for the Rappahannock, and you know what that led to," said Hood. "But I would like to know Miss Buck better. She seems to be a most unusual young lady."

"She is," said Wade Hampton. "She has an air about her that all the young men seem to find irresistible. It isn't just her appearance—it's that soft voice, just like a mourning dove you hear, late on a summer afternoon, and that manner which seems so distant. She is a challenge to any man. You'd better watch out, Hood. You may find yourself in the same boat."

"Oh, no, not me," said John Hood. "I'm too old to be caught by a beautiful face and a gentle voice. I've managed to live thirty years without a woman in my life. But Buck Preston does interest me."

"Well, when we get back to Richmond, you'll have to call on the Prestons. I hear that the whole family is living there now that John Preston is the superintendent of the Conscription Bureau. I'm sure John Darby will be happy to take you there with him. He really seems to be serious about Mamie Preston. I miss having him with me. You know he began with Hampton's Legion when I first organized it."

"Yes, I know," said Hood. "He has spoken of it often to me. I am fortunate to have him as my surgeon now. He is a gifted doctor. I am always amazed how well he does his job despite all the shortages of drugs and even bandages we have had."

"I wish we had him with us right now. I'm sure we'd be a lot less miserable," said Hampton, as he tried, vainly, to find a more comfortable position in the wagon, which seemed to find every rut and bump in the road. "I hope this journey won't go on much longer."

Hood concurred. "I do agree. With this arm, I haven't been able to lie down since we left Gettysburg."

And with that, they both fell silent, remembering their friends and comrades left lying on the battlefield, while they at least had been able to return to Virginia, however unpleasant the trip.

After they crossed the Potomac, their train of wagons was met all along the way by women of Virginia, standing by the roadside to greet Lee's army, and to offer food and care. There were so many men in need of both, and Virginians gave what they could, hoping that someone, somewhere, would do the same for their sons or husbands or brothers.

In Richmond, the Prestons were settling into their temporary home, finding it very different from their spacious house and grounds in Columbia. Mamie, Buck and Tudie were obliged to share a room, but they found it less difficult than they had anticipated. In fact, it was rather pleasant to be able to chat about the events of the day as they sat on the sides of their beds in their frilly pastel silk dressing gowns, brushing their hair and counting slowly to one hundred, the number of strokes, as everyone knew, necessary to have really shiny hair.

"I wish I had red hair like yours, Buck," said Tudie wistfully. "Mine is such an ordinary brown."

"My hair isn't red—it's auburn. That tacky Wilson girl has red hair, that awful carrot color, and freckles as well," said Buck.

"Buck, just because your hair is dark red doesn't mean you should call somebody else's carrot-colored and tacky," cried Mamie.

"I didn't say her hair was tacky, I said she was tacky," retorted Buck.

"I must admit, the way she was flirting with Charles Bryan, hanging on his every word and fluttering her eyelashes at him was very improper. Maybe she is tacky." Mamie paused in her hair-brushing. "Sixty-two. Don't let me lose count. But you better not let Mama hear you say that. She would think you were being unladylike, criticicizing May Wilson. Poor thing, she can't help it if she has freckles and no waistline. Hers must be at least twenty-seven inches around."

"Who's being critical and unladylike now? Watch out. I may tell Mama," laughed Buck.

"Tell Mama what?" asked Caroline Preston as she stood in the doorway of the girls' bedroom surveying her daughters as they sat brushing their long hair. Three pretty faces looked at her innocently.

"Oh, nothing much, Mama. We were just talking about what a good time we had at the Davis' the other day," said Mamie.

"Yes," added Buck. "I like Maggie Howell. She's such an entertaining girl, and Mrs Davis is always so gracious."

"President Davis told me that he wants us to come to breakfast one day. I imagine he needs some distraction from all the things that are happening now. It has been such a blow to lose Vicksburg and to be defeated at Gettysburg. I hope Wade and all the men we know from home will be back in Richmond soon," said Caroline.

"Especially John Darby," said Tudie mischievously, looking at Mamie. "We all know who Mamie is thinking about, and it's not Cousin Wade."

"Tudie, you talk too much," said Mamie, blushing bright pink.

"Never mind, girls. It's time to put out your lamp and go to bed. Tomorrow you must help me decide what we need to send for from home. I did not realize how scantily furnished this house would be, even though Mrs. Chesnut warned me that we would probably have to make do with much less than we were accustomed to at home."

"How long do you think we'll be in Richmond, Mama?" asked Buck.

"I really don't know, dear. It depends on what your father has to do. We'll just have to wait and see," said her mother. "Now say your prayers and go to sleep. Pleasant dreams."

She closed the door, and the girls turned to each other and giggled.

"Thank goodness she didn't open the door a minute sooner. We would all have been in trouble," said Tudie.

"But she didn't," said Mamie.

VII
Richmond, 1863

General John Bell Hood paused at the front door of the Chesnuts' home on Cary Street. He had not seen Mrs. Chesnut since his return to Richmond. After coming back to Virginia, his left arm shattered by a bullet, he had spent several weeks in Staunton at the Wigfalls' summer home. Now that his arm was better, he was ready to enjoy life among his friends in the Confederate capital until he was called back to active duty.

This was the first time he had called on Mrs. Chesnut unaccompanied by Dr. John Darby, and he hoped he would find a welcome. Raising his right hand, he knocked softly and then loudly, on the paneled door. When no one answered, he tried the door handle, and when it turned, he opened the door and entered the hallway.

Mary Chesnut, from her rooms on the second floor, heard the knocking and came to the top of the stairs. Looking down to see who was there, she recognized Hood immediately. His height and tawny blond beard made him unmistakable.

She called out, "General Hood, hello. I have not seen you for a long time."

Hood removed his broad-brimmed hat, decorated with a silver and diamond star, and said, "I have been in Staunton lately."

"We had heard that you were seriously injured, but you are looking very well," said Mary Chesnut. "Do come up and tell me about yourself."

"Thank you, ma'am. I hope I haven't called at an inconvenient time."

"Not at all. I am happy to see you. For once, I am by myself, so we can have a nice quiet chat."

Hood walked up the short flight of stairs and joined Mrs. Chesnut.

"Let's sit in the parlor, General. Would you care for some lemonade? It's such a hot day, and we are fortunate enough to have lemons and sugar and even ice," she said.

"That would be a real treat," said Hood, seating himself in one of the chairs nearest the windows.

"I'll ask Molly to bring us a pitcher of lemonade and some glasses. Excuse me for a moment."

As she left the room to find Molly, her maid, Hood looked around the rather small room. There were several books lying on side tables, but few other personal items. He had heard that Mrs. Chesnut was a great reader. These volumes must be hers.

When she returned, she said, "Molly will be here soon. Tell me, how long have you been in Richmond? Wade Hampton told us a little of your journey back to Virginia together. It must have been a very painful trip."

"Yes, ma'am, it was, but we were fortunate to be alive. I've only been in Richmond a few days."

"I understand you spent some time in Staunton with the Wigfalls. I have heard that Louly Wigfall is an excellent nurse. Your convalescence couldn't have been too unpleasant with such a pretty girl in attendance. I do admire brunettes."

"The Wigfalls were very kind to me, and Miss Wigfall is a fine nurse. Like you, I admire brunettes, but somehow I prefer auburn hair to dark," replied Hood with a rather conscious look at Mrs. Chesnut.

"Here is Molly with our lemonade. Thank you, Molly. Just put the tray down there on the table. I will pour."

"Yes, ma'am," said Molly, cutting her eyes at John Hood. She had seldom seen a gentleman so large and so handsome. Captain Johnny Chesnut was a good-looking man, but not nearly so tall. And certainly without so many whiskers!

Molly left the room, and Mrs. Chesnut poured two glasses of lemonade, thinking regretfully of her own fine crystal glasses far away in Camden.

She handed a glass to Hood, and he sipped it, enjoying the cool tartness of fresh lemonade, something he had not had in a long time. After a moment he said, "John Darby is certainly happy to be here in town. I think he has called on Miss Mamie Preston every day. He has let me accompany him on some of his visits, and I have met Colonel and Mrs. Preston and Miss Tudie."

"The Prestons are very old friends of mine. I miss having Buck and Mamie here with me. They are delightful girls."

"Perhaps one day you would go out for a carriage ride with me, Mrs. Chesnut? And I would like to invite Miss Buck Preston too."

"Thank you, that would be most agreeable," said Mrs. Chesnut, smiling inwardly. She knew that she was not Hood's most wanted guest but she would be welcome as a chaperone.

"If you would be able to go tomorrow afternoon, and if that suits Miss Preston, I will engage a carriage for us," said Hood.

"Oh, I am sorry, General Hood, but tomorrow evening we are invited to a reception at the White House, and I don't believe I could go out in the afternoon and then again later."

"Mrs. Chesnut, Mrs. Davis very kindly sent me an invitation to that reception also. I will look forward to meeting you and Colonel Chesnut there, and perhaps we can set another day to go out in a carriage."

"I'm sure we can."

Hood stood up to go. "I appreciate your hospitality, Mrs. Chesnut. The lemonade was very refreshing."

"Come and see us again soon. John Darby is teaching us all to play casino, and we have had some lively games."

"I would like that. And I would like it if you could call me 'Sam' as John Darby does. All my friends have called me that since my West Point days, and I hope that you consider me a friend, too," said Hood.

"Why, thank you—Sam. I would be happy to do that," said Mary Chesnut. "Good-bye."

As Hood went down the stairs and out the door, she thought, "That man thinks I may be useful to him with Buck. I wonder what Buck thinks of him. She seemed very interested in Rawlins Lowndes, but it has been so long since he's been in Columbia or Richmond. Is it 'out of sight, out of mind'? Goodness knows, there have been a great many young men who have come and gone in her life, but I thought Rawlins might be someone she could truly love. He surely is a handsome thing, and such manners. And that Charleston accent, and a good family. Well, we shall see. . . ."

Strolling down Cary Street, Hood's thoughts centered on one thing, Buck Preston. He had dreamed of her so often since they met. No other girl had ever made such an impression on him. He had admired Louly Wigfall. She was a lovely girl, a slender, brown-eyed brunette, who had eyes only for him, but she had never made his heart beat faster, as Buck Preston had, the first time he saw her. Her face haunted him and he, who never noticed what ladies wore, could still recall her jaunty hat decorated with pheasant feathers. What was it about her that was so captivating? Her smile? Her voice? Whatever it was, he knew that every time he left her he could hardly wait to see her again. He thought that her parents would surely be at the reception given by President and Mrs. Davis, and he hoped that Buck would be with them.

The sultry August evening darkened. Lights began to shine out of Richmond's windows, and mothers called their children in to supper, ignoring pleas to stay out longer to catch the fireflies rising out of the dusty grass, their small lights glimmering in the early twilight.

At the White House of the Confederacy, the house formerly owned by the Brockenborough family, all was in readiness for the President's levee. The Greek Revival mansion, designed by Robert Mills and completed in 1818, had been leased to the Confederate government for the Davises. Standing on a hill above the James River, at the corner of Twelfth and Clay streets, it was a three-storied brick building covered in gray stucco. The front of the house, on Clay Street, had a small portico with marble steps leading directly to the street. A larger portico in the back had eight plain columns arranged in pairs, a marble floor, cast iron railings, and cast iron steps. It overlooked the terraced garden, planted with fruit trees and flower beds, which also contained a sentry box, built to house a guard for the President and his family.

Among the first arrivals at the levee were the Prestons. They entered the oval entrance hall, where they were greeted by the Davis' butler. The hall was fashionably papered in a pale gold marbleized wall-covering. A niche on either side of the door opening into the parlor held a statue of a woman in classical draperies, made of plaster painted to look like bronze, each carrying a lighted globe. The painted canvas floorcloth was terra cotta with a black and white checkerboard border.

As they walked into the parlor to speak to President and Mrs. Davis, Mamie whispered to Buck, "Isn't this the most elegant house we've seen in Richmond? Just look at the wallpaper! And those beautiful statues!"

Caroline looked back at Mamie and shook her head slightly, which Mamie knew meant "hush".

The Davises greeted the Preston family warmly. Jefferson Davis, a tall, erect figure with deep-set eyes and a gaunt, lined face, was happy with his choice of John Preston to head the Conscription Bureau, and pleased that he had come to Richmond so promptly. His wife, Varina Howell Davis, a lovely brunette, her dark hair parted in the center and drawn smoothly back from her oval face, and her deep brown eyes sparkling in the lamplight, said, "I am delighted to see you again, Mrs.

Preston. Do come and see me one afternoon when we can have a real visit, and bring the girls."

"Thank you, we would enjoy that," Caroline answered with a smile.

Other guests pressed into the parlor, anxious to speak to the Davises, and the Prestons moved away.

Looking around them, the Preston girls admired the dark red flocked wallpaper and the rich red and gold figured curtains, edged in red and gold braid, with matching silk cord tiebacks. The rosewood chairs were covered in red damask. The white marble mantel had large carved figures representing Cupid and Psyche, and there were pictures and mirrors hung from the cornices with tasseled cords. The chandeliers were intricately designed brass with large white globes lit by gas.

Each room had something to catch the eye. In the smaller parlor, similarly decorated, they found Mrs. Davis' collection of Parian ware statuettes, including two they recognized as Perseus and Andromeda. Chess sets and backgammon boards and pieces lay on small tables around the room.

"I could spend hours looking at all the interesting things in this house," declared Tudie.

"So could I," said Buck. "I heard Mrs. Davis invite Mama to come for a visit and bring us, so perhaps we'll be able to do that."

John Bell Hood arrived shortly after the Prestons, and went immediately to speak to President and Mrs. Davis.

"How good to see you looking so well, General. I trust you have completely recovered from your wound," said Varina Davis.

"Yes, thank you, ma'am. I have not regained full use of my arm, but I am ready to return to action as soon as possible," said Hood.

Jefferson Davis nodded approvingly. "Just what I like to hear, General. I wish all our soldiers felt as you do. I know you are eager to speak to your friends who are here tonight. Come and see me another day when we can talk," said Davis, who had noticed Hood's eyes straying toward the corner of the room where Buck Preston stood, surrounded, as usual, by most of the young men at the levee.

"Thank you, sir, I will. Perhaps we could go riding one morning if you are free."

"I would like that, General. Now go and join the others. I see several people waiting for an opportunity to speak to you."

Hood bowed and moved away, as other guests came into the parlor where the Davises stood. As he started toward Buck, Louly Wigfall, standing a few feet away, attempted to catch his eye, but Hood could see no one but Buck. Louly recognized Hood's intense expression, for only a few weeks ago he had looked at her like that. Now all his attention was for Buck Preston. Louly turned her head, not wanting to see Hood's eagerness to reach Buck's side. Before she could move away, into another room, she heard whispers, and then someone laughed, "It never fails. Buck Preston attracts men like a magnet. The rest of us might as well not be here."

Louly walked away, a dull ache in her heart. She had believed that John Hood was falling in love with her. Now she feared she had been mistaken.

Buck had been listening to a very young lieutenant describe life in camp and had not noticed Hood's approach until some of the other officers said, "Good evening, sir." She lifted her head and smiled at Hood, saying softly, "I did not expect to see you here tonight, General."

"I certainly could not fail to be here, knowing you would be a guest, Miss Buck. May I escort you to the dining room? I believe they are serving lemon punch there," said Hood, offering his arm.

"Why, thank you, General. That would be delightful." Buck took Hood's arm and strolled with him toward the dining room, leaving the junior officers muttering quietly among themselves. "Damn, rank does have its privileges," whispered a disgruntled lieutenant.

Hood brought two cups of punch over to Buck, and as he offered one to her, he said, "Miss Buck, I have invited Mrs. Chesnut to go out with me one afternoon for a carriage ride. I would be honored if you could join us."

"Why, I would like that very much. Mrs. Chesnut is one of my favorite ladies," said Buck. "I believe I'm free almost any afternoon next week."

"That would give me great pleasure," said John Hood. "May I call on you tomorrow and you and Mrs. Chesnut may choose a day?"

"I shall be happy to see you, General Hood. Now I must find my parents. They are probably looking for me. Till tomorrow then." Buck walked away, her full lavender skirts rustling softly, as Hood stood gazing after her, gently smiling, with an expression that would have greatly astonished his Texas soldiers, unaccustomed to seeing such a look on their commanding officer's face.

Later that night, as Caroline Preston brushed and braided her hair in front of her dressing table mirror, she said, "John, I saw General Hood speaking to you at the President's reception. And he seemed very attentive to Buck."

"He does seem very interested in furthering his acquaintance with her. I did say that he might call. We can hardly refuse to see him when he is John Darby's commanding officer. Mamie seems to think well of him."

"Mamie thinks whatever John Darby thinks, I'm afraid. I do believe he is serious about Mamie. I just hope they will wait to marry until things are more settled."

"That may be a very long time. John Darby is a fine young man, well-bred and well-educated. And Mamie is almost twenty-three now, old enough to be married. We can hardly justify asking them to postpone marriage if they really want to be married while the war is going on."

"Well, Dr. Darby hasn't asked your consent, and until he does we need not worry about it. But I do think of all the girls we know who married soldiers and are now widows."

"Very true, very true. But it is hard to be young now. All the uncertainty and turmoil we are going through makes life very difficult for young people."

"And old people like us too," replied Caroline.

"To me you are as young as the day we met," said John Preston gallantly.

Caroline blushed. After all these years, she still felt like a girl with her handsome husband. "Put out the lights, dear. It's very late. We can discuss all this tomorrow."

In the following weeks, John Bell Hood was a frequent caller at the Prestons. He had no formal duties, so he was able to take Buck out in a hired carriage, with Mary Chesnut as chaperone, as often as she would consent to go. Some days he and Buck were to be seen riding horseback together along Richmond's shady thoroughfares. Hood was an excellent rider, able to control his horse despite having little use of his left arm, and Buck was a notable horsewoman. They made a most attractive picture as they walked or trotted along the streets bordering the Capitol or near the river, a favorite locale.

Sometimes in the evening Hood and John Darby met Mamie and Buck at the Chesnuts, where games of casino were all the rage. Darby was a skilled player, the others less so, although Buck was one of the most frequent winners. They usually played partnership casino, in which the two players who were partners were able to help each other secure desirable cards and therefore increase their chances of winning.

After a game that Buck won, Mamie complained, "Buck always wins. People give her cards. No one ever gives me anything!"

John Darby placed two fingers on his heart and looked at Mamie, who was contemplating her score and not paying attention to him.

Hood asked, "Now, Darby, what is the meaning of that signal?"

"You caught me!", said Darby. "I put two fingers on my heart to hint to Mamie that she should play the deuce of hearts."

Mamie looked up. "What in the world are you two talking about? I haven't seen any signal."

"I know," said John Darby mournfully. "I know."

Buck found the attention she was receiving from General Hood very flattering. He was an older man, at least ten years older than she, impressive in appearance, and a war hero as well. She knew that there were girls in the capital who envied her, especially Louly Wigfall. Buck was well aware that Hood had spent a great deal of time with the Wigfalls in Staunton, and Louly had made no secret of her feelings for him.

And yet Hood seemed to be interested only in Buck. The last time they had been riding together, he had paid her extravagant compliments: "There is no one as beautiful as you, Miss Buck. I have seen girls in Kentucky and Texas who were well-enough looking, but they were plain as posts compared to you."

"Surely you don't mean that, General Hood."

"Oh, but I do. And please don't call me 'General Hood'. Call me Sam. I'm more accustomed to answering to that."

"Perhaps I could do that—when I know you better."

"Miss Buck, I want to know you very well. I've never met a girl I wanted to know as much as you. You are the kind of girl I'd like to spend the rest of my life getting to know."

Buck felt this was moving a bit too fast. "You don't really know me at all—Sam. And I hardly know a thing about you. Tell me what you were like as a little boy."

"You don't want to hear all that, do you? I'm from Kentucky, I went to West Point, I served in the United States Army in Texas, and now I'm in the Confederate States Army, and right this minute I'm with the prettiest young lady in Richmond."

Buck pouted . "That doesn't tell me very much. What do you enjoy doing? What do you like to read?"

Hood thought for a moment. "Well, I like commanding my Texans, the finest troops in the army. And I like to read a newspaper occasionally."

This was not what Buck expected to hear. Most young men of her acquaintance had been students at South Carolina College, and while they had not been scholars, still they read some of the current books, and could discuss poetry or the latest novel. She thought of Rawlins Lowndes, who could quote Shakespeare or Wordsworth, and who paid her much more subtle compliments. It seemed ages since the last time she had seen him. Sometimes she wondered if he had forgotten her. She knew that no matter how many other men she danced or rode or flirted with, she would never forget that night so long ago now when he told her of his love and kissed her for the first time.

Buck felt differently with Hood. She could not tease him as she did Rawlins or Johnny Chesnut. Hood took everything she said seriously. He was not at all like the boys she had grown up with, who came from the same background and had the same friends. The South Carolina boys knew exactly what to do when she flirted with them. They flirted back, knowing just how far to go. She wasn't sure Hood knew the rules of the game of flirtation. She realized this could be a problem.

But she intended to enjoy their rides together. Her mother, she was aware, was not altogether happy to have her spend so much time with the general, but Buck was confident they could be friends. And what girl would not be pleased to have a tall, distinguished escort, wounded in action, commended by Stonewall Jackson himself, and a friend of President Davis?

All too soon, as far as Hood was concerned, in September the orders came to rejoin his troops. Part of Longstreet's corps was to move west, to Tennessee, to reinforce Braxton Bragg's army, just south of Chattanooga, near a creek named Chickamauga. Hood was again in command of his old brigade, and his men rejoiced to have their leader back.

His orders were to go to Petersburg, to take the train there and head west, through Wilmington, Charlotte, Augusta, and then Atlanta, where the troops would assemble to move on to Chattanooga. His brigade left Richmond by rail, but Hood rode to Petersburg in a carriage with Buck and Mary Chesnut.

At the train station, Hood managed to snatch a moment alone with Buck when Mrs. Chesnut paused to speak to someone she knew.

"Buck, I must speak before I go. I love you more than anyone else in the world. Say that you will marry me when I come back," begged Hood, as he took Buck's right hand and held it between his own hands.

Buck attempted to release her hand but could not pull it from Hood's firm grasp. She was completely taken by surprise, and took a deep breath before she answered him. "No, I cannot say that. I like you very much, but I don't love you, and I could never marry you if I didn't love you."

"I know I can make you love me in time. I will consider myself engaged to you. I believe sincerely that you will come to love me too."

"You may believe what you like, but I am not engaged to you," said Buck firmly.

Hood smiled at her wistfully. "I will miss you. Think of me while I'm gone."

"I will—as a friend, Sam. Good-bye." Mary Chesnut joined them just in time to see Hood gently lift Buck's hand, turn it, and kiss her palm, looking down at her as if he wanted to imprint her face in his memory. "Good bye, Buck. Remember me."

He bowed to Mrs. Chesnut. "Good-bye. And thank you."

She replied, "Good-bye, Sam. You will be in our prayers."

Hood boarded the train, and as it began to move away from the station he stood on the steps and waved his hat as long as he could see Buck's lacy white handkerchief fluttering in the hazy September air.

The Battle of Chickamauga, fought on September 20, 1863, was one of the South's last decisive victories. Hood commanded eight brigades, which charged through a gap in the Federal lines, the rebel yell sounding as they drove the Northern troops in retreat. As Hood led his men, on horseback, he was shot from his saddle, gravely wounded.

In Richmond, three days after the battle, the *Enquirer* reported "Major General Hood is dead." Hood's friends were shocked and saddened by this distressing news, but later reports contradicted this, saying instead that he had been shot through the right thigh, shattering the bone. It was impossible to save his leg, which was amputated a few inches below his hip. Dr. Darby had not left Richmond with Hood and his troops, and so the surgery was done by the chief medical officer of the Army of Tennessee, Dr. T. G. Richardson.

Hood was carried to the nearby home of one of his officers, where he spent a month convalescing under the care of John Darby, belatedly arriving from Richmond.

Hood's Texas brigade contributed nearly five thousand dollars to pay for the best possible artificial limb, a "cork leg," named not for its material but for a Dr. Cork, who invented it.

By October, Hood was able to travel to Atlanta, and in late November he returned to Richmond, having been promoted to lieutenant general.

Buck Preston had been horrified to read of Sam Hood's supposed death. Too many of her suitors had lost their lives on the battlefield, so many indeed that Johnny Chesnut had remarked wryly that anyone rash enough to fall in love with Buck Preston could expect to have his name appear on the next casualty list. She knew she had been right to refuse Hood's proposal of marriage, but she had come to respect and admire him. The news that he had been wounded and had had his right leg amputated was shocking, but she was thankful that he had survived.

She knew that he was in Richmond, staying with friends. Every day she expected to receive some message from him, but none came. Perhaps he had fallen out of love with her as fast as he had fallen in. She wondered if he had renewed his courtship of Louly Wigfall, as was rumored by the local gossip.

Buck was ready for distractions, and an unexpected event provided a welcome diversion.

On the first of December, Mary Chesnut arrived at the Prestons quite early in the morning, asking for Buck and Mamie. "Girls, girls," she said, "the most exciting news. Mr. Chesnut has just told me that a French frigate has arrived and is lying at anchor down the river. The officers will disembark soon, and we must go down to the dock right away and meet them and invite them to my party tonight. It will be a wonderful opportunity for you to use your French again."

Mamie smiled, knowing Mrs. Chesnut's fondness for all things French and her constant search for some new attraction for her parties. Glancing at Buck, she said, "What a good idea. Buck and I had a wonderful time while we were in Paris, even if we were locked up in a convent school most of the time. Willie can go with us. You know he just arrived home on leave."

In a short while Mrs. Chesnut's carriage was at the door, and the two girls and Willie, who had been persuaded to accompany them, climbed in. As they were driving along, Mary Chesnut explained that her husband had told her that the frigate Grenade had been sent to bring the French consul to Washington for negotiations over some tobacco which the French had bought but had been unable to ship through the Federal blockade.

"They may be in Richmond several days, and it will be such a treat to have new visitors and talk about something else besides the war."

Laurence, Mrs. Chesnut's servant, who was driving the carriage, spoke up. "Ladies don't need to be going to no riverfront to see no sailors. Mr. Chesnut be cross if he knew and mad at me for taking you."

"Be quiet, Laurence. We are going for the purpose of improving our French."

Willie laughed. "Mrs. Chesnut, you just can't resist anything new and different."

"Especially when they might be handsome young Frenchmen! So nice for the girls, and for me too. Mr. Chesnut says I must stop giving parties. The times are too serious, he says, for me to be so frivolous. But he never cared much for parties anyway!"

When they arrived at the dock, they found quite a crowd of Richmond ladies already there, and the officers just getting out of a small boat. Willie, being taller than the ladies, could see them and said, "Buck, you will never believe who is here!"

Behind the naval officers, escorting the consul was a tall aide in a military uniform she well remembered. "It can't be," she exclaimed. "Look, Mamie, it is Captain Bellanger!"

Just at that moment, Jean-Paul saw Willie, who, in his gray uniform, stood out among the ladies, and hastened forward to greet him.

"Monsieur Preston, quelle bonne surprise! I have never expected to see you in Virginia." Then seeing Buck and Mamie standing behind Willie, he greeted them enthusiastically, thinking that they were prettier than ever.

"But it is too wonderful to find the Preston ladies here also. Do you remember our ride in the Bois? I have never forgotten. And you are looking more charming than ever," he said, with a soulful glance at Buck.

Blushing furiously at the memory of his kiss, she could think of nothing to say. Mamie hastened to introduce him to Mrs. Chesnut.

"Enchanté, madame," he said, bending over her hand. By this time, all eyes were fixed on them, and the other officers had come up to be presented. Mrs. Chesnut invited them all to her party that evening, but unfortunately their escort was waiting to take them on to Washington.

As they were being hurried off, Captain Bellanger said to the Prestons,

"I have found you to lose you again. What a sad world. Perhaps when we have concluded our business in Washington we may pass through Richmond again and be able to renew our acquaintance."

Mary Chesnut was most distressed. "What a charming man, and to think you knew him in Paris. What a shame they have to leave so soon. Now, Mamie, start at the beginning and tell me all about how you all met him."

Mamie said, "Well, Buck could tell you a lot more than I. It was when we first arrived in Paris, and we saw him riding down the rue de Rivoli with the Emperor. Buck waved to him and. . . ."

"I did not," Buck said indignantly. "We met him at a reception at the Tuileries. He was a friend of Ransom Calhoun's."

Mamie added, "Tell her too about how you were lost in the Bois and we were all so worried."

"I am surprised your mother has never mentioned the captain to me."

"She didn't really know him very well," said Buck. "Oh, look, Mrs. Chesnut! There is Mrs. Davis calling to you and beckoning."

Later, Buck told Willie and Mamie, "If you ever tell Mrs. Chesnut or Mama about Jean-Paul, I will never forgive you."

"Why Buck, what really did happen when you were in the Bois?"

"Not as much as you may think. But you remember we covered it up pretty well, thanks to Cousin Ransom."

The visit to the French frigate left Buck feeling pensive. The episode with Captain Bellanger seemed to have occurred in another lifetime. So much had happened since that day in Paris. Ransom dead, Rawlins remote and indifferent, and now Sam Hood seemed to have lost interest in her. She was glad that Mamie and John Darby were officially engaged now, but she felt alone and left out, as she had felt when her brother Jack married Celestine Huger.

It had been particularly difficult to say good-bye to Willie at the end of his brief leave. Every time she saw him she feared it might be the last. So many men she knew had died of disease in camp or wounds received in battle. It sometimes seemed that the war had taken all their lives and turned them upside down. No one could feel secure and comfortable in the way they once had.

Willie had tried to reassure Buck before he left Richmond. "Now, Buck, you know I won't take unnecessary risks. My artillery company is well-trained and experienced, and we usually aren't on the front line.

It's important that we preserve our guns. We don't have any to spare, or gunners either. Why, the artillery is probably the safest unit in the whole army."

Buck looked at him, smiling reluctantly. "You are just saying that to make me feel better. I know no one is really safe."

"I hope you are, here in Richmond. And if the Union Army gets too close, you know Papa will see that you all can return to Columbia. Anyway, from what I've seen everyone seems to be having a pretty good time despite the war."

"It's true. We have all sorts of parties and theatricals. Some people say we shouldn't have parties with the war going on, but the soldiers we entertain say they need something to take their minds off what may happen to them, and they want to dance and enjoy themselves while they can."

"I agree with that. Keep up their spirits, and yours too. Just remember what I told you a long time ago — don't let your heart run away with your head. Speaking of which, I hear that General Hood has been calling on you, and quite frequently, too. Are you encouraging him?"

Buck blushed. "No, I'm not. But he doesn't seem to need encouragement. Don't tell Mama, but he proposed to me before he left Richmond in September."

"And what did you say?"

"I told him I wouldn't marry him because I didn't love him in that way, but I would be his friend."

"Oh, Buck, that sounds like he still has a chance."

"Well, what else could I say? And he hasn't tried to see me since he's been back."

"Perhaps he's concerned that a man with only one leg would not be an acceptable suitor. What do Mama and Papa say about him?"

"Mama doesn't approve of him. She thinks he's too unrefined. Papa says he's an excellent leader, and must have good qualities to be so highly regarded by President Davis."

"And what do you think of him?"

"I'm not sure. I do admire his courage, and he is handsome, but he's so different from most men I know. He frightens me a little sometimes. He is too intense and serious. I don't feel comfortable with him. But I can't help feeling attracted to him too."

Willie looked at his sister and sighed. "You are looking for trouble, honey. Don't do anything impulsively. Listen to Mama. Promise me?"

"I promise, Willie. But sometimes it's hard to know what I want or what to do."

"I know that. Just remember you have a family that loves you and wants what's best for you."

"I wish you didn't have to go back to camp. I will miss you so much."

"I'll miss you too, but you know I have to go. How can they run the war without me? None of the generals ever make campaign plans without asking 'What do you think of this, Major Preston?'"

"They should do that. Lately some of their plans haven't worked too well."

"Now hush. Everything will be fine. You stay here—I'm going to tell Mama good-bye. I'll see you again as soon as I can. Good-bye, Buck."

Buck put her hand lightly on Willie's face and kissed his cheek. "Goodbye. Take care of yourself," she said, and turned away so that he would not see the tears brimming in her eyes.

Mary Chesnut, perceptive as always, realized how much Buck and Mamie missed their brother, and tried to keep them entertained and amused. She decided that a luncheon for several of their friends would be a good way to achieve this. Invitations were issued, and accepted, for the ninth of December. To Buck's great disgust, she became ill with a fever and cough. It was not possible to re-schedule the party, so Buck resigned herself to staying home in bed while Mamie went to the luncheon.

Mamie, the punctual member of the family, was the first to arrive. Mary Chesnut greeted her warmly, and then went into the dining room to give orders to Laurence about the table settings. Mamie stood in the parlor, looking out the window. As she watched the activity on the street, she suddenly called out, "Mrs. Chesnut, do come and look! Here is Sam Hood at the door!"

Mrs. Chesnut hurried from the dining room and stood beside Mamie. "Oh, my! Everyone has seen Sam except your family and mine, and now here he is on my doorstep, just when I'm about to have a ladies' luncheon."

Mrs. Grundy, the Chesnuts' landlady, who lived on the ground floor, met Hood at the door and invited him into her drawing room.

"Please come in , General. The sofa should be a comfortable seat for you. I'll call Mrs. Chesnut. I know she'll be delighted to see you."

Mrs. Grundy bustled out the door, but before she could reach the stairs, Mamie and Mrs. Chesnut came rushing down.

"Oh, Mrs. Chesnut! And Miss Preston! General Hood is here," said Mrs. Grundy breathlessly.

"Yes, we saw him arrive and came right down," Mary Chesnut replied, as she went over to greet Hood.

"How good to see you again, Sam," she said. "It seems ages since we left you at the train station in Petersburg."

"Yes, welcome back," said Mamie. "John told me you were in Richmond."

"I am very glad to be back," said Hood. "Please forgive me for not standing to speak to you ladies."

"Oh, goodness, Sam, pray do not attempt it. I hope your wound is not too painful still," said Mrs. Chesnut.

"Only an occasional twinge," Hood assured her. I'm becoming used to moving around on crutches, and I hope to be able to ride my horse again when I have my artificial limb fitted."

"John has told me that he will be going abroad to purchase supplies for the Confederacy, and a suitable limb for you, as soon as he can make the necessary arrangements," said Mamie.

"Yes, my Texas brigade has given enough money to buy more than one limb for me. They are the most generous men in the world. I don't deserve such devotion."

"I'm sure you must; otherwise they would not have contributed their money for you," said Mrs. Chesnut.

"Well, I hope I can soon rejoin them. Being in Richmond is pleasant, but I'm used to army life, and I miss it."

"Don't try to do too much too soon, Sam. The war may last for years, and you will be needed," said Mary Chesnut.

Just then, the rest of the luncheon party arrived, very surprised to find John Bell Hood there. Mamie and Mary Chesnut had tried to treat Hood as they always had, but the other ladies were determined to make a fuss over him. They could hardly look at him without tears, seeing his empty trouser leg and his drawn, pain-scarred face. They hovered over him, murmuring, "Oh, your poor leg! However will you manage? Is it very painful?" till Hood became quite ill-at-ease.

Finally he turned to Mrs. Chesnut. "How is Buck?"

"She has been ill for a few days, but she is better. I had hoped she could be here with us."

"I'm sorry to hear she's not well. I look forward to seeing her again."

Richmond, 1863 115

"I'm sure she'll be able to receive visitors soon, if you call on the Prestons."

"Yes, I will. I intend to be as active and happy as a one-legged man can be. Now I expect I'd better be going. Thank you for your hospitality, Mrs. Chesnut."

"It is always a pleasure to see you, Sam. Do come again soon."

"Thank you, ma'am. If you would call my driver I would appreciate it. I still need a little help getting around."

"Certainly," said Mary Chesnut. "I'll send Laurence out for him immediately."

In a moment, Laurence returned with the driver, who gave Hood his arm and helped him rise from the low sofa. He handed the general his crutches, and Hood walked awkwardly toward the door, watched sympathetically by the women in the room, who recalled how differently Hood had looked, tall, athletic, confident, the last time they had seen him in Richmond, before Chickamauga.

※

General John Bell Hood was the man of the hour in Richmond, He was invited to dinners, luncheons, card parties, charades, the theater: anywhere he was willing to go he was a welcome guest. Men admired his courage, and women his noble suffering for the Cause. Hood had never been so popular. As the Hero of Chickamauga he was in the spotlight wherever he went.

Often, his companion was Buck Preston. He had called on the Prestons soon after he had seen Mrs. Chesnut and Mamie. Buck had recovered from her illness, and was happy to see him. She had missed his admiring attention. To have it again was a salve to her feelings of neglect by Rawlins Lowndes.

Caroline Preston was not as glad to see General Hood as her daughter, since she still had reservations about him, but she could give no concrete reason for refusing to allow Buck to attend the many functions to which Hood invited her. John Preston, as always, wanted Buck to do whatever would please her, and felt that there could be no objection to her going to public places with someone who was a friend of President Davis and universally recognized as a great soldier.

Caroline had expressed herself rather forcefully to her husband. "John, I really do not think Buck should see so much of General Hood. She may expose herself to gossip, which I cannot like. You know how rumors spread here in Richmond, even when there is no basis for them. Surely you don't approve of Buck's becoming seriously involved with that man? We know so little about him, and now that he has lost his leg I feel he is even less eligible than before."

"I think you are making too much of this, my dear. Let Buck enjoy herself. She is young, and she deserves some happiness."

"Very well, John, as you wish. I merely feel I should give Buck a hint that she must not make herself an object of gossip."

"Oh, for goodness sakes! Let the child alone. Our daughter would never do anything improper. You have brought our girls up to be ladies and I'm sure they will always be a credit to you."

"Thank you, dear. But with so many of the girls' friends marrying in haste. . . . I just don't want our daughters to make a mistake."

"Neither do I. Nevertheless, Buck and Mamie, and even Tudie, are old enough to make their own choices, and we may have to learn to accept them."

"You may be right, but I still think it is our responsibility to make sure that the girls marry well. I certainly cannot fault Mamie's choice of John Darby. I only wish that Buck and Rawlins Lowndes had had a chance to know each other better. Buck seemed to be very interested in him when the Legion was in Columbia, and he would be a quite suitable match. His family is prominent in Charleston, and well-to-do."

John laughed. "First you don't want Buck to be involved with anyone, and now you want to marry her off to Rawlins Lowndes."

"You are the most exasperating man sometimes. You know exactly what I want. I want the girls to be as happy as I have been with you. And I don't think Buck would be happy with John Hood."

"Let's not cross that bridge till we come to it. As far as I know, he hasn't proposed. And Buck is too devoted to her family to do anything that we would not approve of."

"I hope you are right, John. At any rate, let's not encourage General Hood's attentions."

"Very well, my dear. I trust Buck's judgment, and I'm sure Hood will be leaving Richmond before long anyway. I understand John Darby will be running the blockade to go to England for medical supplies and an artificial limb for Hood sometime soon. When he returns, he and Hood may both be rejoining the army for the spring campaign."

"Yes," said Caroline, "Mamie is very worried that Dr. Darby may be captured by the Yankees, but he assures her that he will be perfectly safe.

I hope he is right. How I wish this dreadful war would end, and Jack and Willie and all the other men we know could come home."

"So do I, Caroline. So do I."

Buck was happy to attend the various social functions to which Hood escorted her. She was well aware of the envious glances of other girls, and could not help feeling fortunate to be squired by so distinguished a soldier.

One cold winter day, Sam Hood called on Mary Chesnut and invited her to go for a drive.

She looked at him in surprise. "Sam, don't you think it's rather chilly to be out riding in a carriage? It must be nearly freezing today."

"Oh, do come, Mrs. Chesnut. I have all sorts of carriage rugs, and there are foot warmers too."

"Very well. Let me find my heaviest cloak and I'll come with you."

Hood handed her into the carriage and tucked the robes around her. "There now. You'll see, we'll be perfectly comfortable."

"Where are we going?"

Hood said casually, "Oh, I thought we'd go and see if Miss Buck would like to go with us."

Mary Chesnut eyed him in amusement. "Now I know why you invited me!"

Hood looked at her sheepishly. "You don't mind, do you?"

"Not at all. I'm always happy to see Buck."

They soon reached the Prestons' home. Hood walked carefully up the front steps and knocked firmly at the door, which was opened promptly by William, the Prestons' indispensable butler.

"Hello, William. Is Miss Buck in?"

"Yes sir, she's here, but she's upstairs. I think she's feeling poorly."

"Well, would you tell her General Hood and Mrs. Chesnut are here and would like to have her join us for a carriage ride?"

"Yes, sir. I'll go tell her," said William doubtfully.

He walked slowly up the stairs and knocked softly at Buck's door. "Miss Buck, General Hood and Miz Chesnut are here. They say can you come for a carriage ride with them. It's mighty cold out, Miss Buck. I don't believe yo mama would like it if you go someplace in a buggy."

Buck had been lying on her bed, reading a rather dull novel, feeling slightly feverish and bored. She was glad to have a diversion, and called out, "William, you tell them I'll be downstairs in a few minutes."

William said crossly, "Yes'm, I will, but you don't need to be outside today."

Buck ignored his comment and went to her closet to find her black velvet cloak, hooded, and lined with ermine. The contrasting black and white set off her fair coloring and made her auburn hair glow. Her cheeks were delicately flushed, with fever and excitement. Glancing in in her gilt-framed mirror, she knew she looked her most striking.

As she came down the stairs, Hood gazed at her with an expression reflecting his admiration. Every time he saw Buck he was more impressed with her beauty, which was matched by the sweetness of her disposition.

She smiled at him and said, "How kind of you all to include me. I was getting very restless this afternoon."

"How kind of you to come, Miss Buck."

Mary Chesnut leaned out of the carriage window and said, "Buck, come in and sit next to me. I hope you'll be warm enough. The air is chilly even in the sunshine with the carriage open like this."

"Oh, I never mind the cold, and my cloak is very thick," said Buck cheerfully. "Where are we going?"

"Just driving around," said Hood as he entered the carriage and told the driver to proceed.

They drove slowly along the city streets, admiring the handsome red brick houses, many with double balconies overlooking a garden whose boxwood hedges were the only note of color on this wintry day. In downtown Richmond around Capitol Square there were mansions, business establishments, and boarding houses side by side. Franklin was the fashionable street, where bankers and wealthy merchants lived in their large, elegant homes. Richmond was a city built on hills, and the numbered streets sloped down to the James River, referred to by the citizens of Richmond as the Jeems.

As the carriage passed the Elliott house, Mrs. Chesnut remarked, "I heard the other day that Alice Elliott was engaged to that nice Captain Smith from Lynchburg."

"Yes, someone mentioned that to me," said Buck.

Hood grinned. "I heard that I was engaged too, to four different young ladies."

"Oh?" said Buck, looking straight ahead. "To whom do they say you are engaged?"

"To Miss Wigfall."

"And who else?"
"Miss Buck Preston."
"Really?"
"Yes. Are you annoyed?"
"Oh, no, not at all. You know how people in Richmond talk. They say I'm engaged to Phil Robb and Shirley Carter."
"Don't you mean or Shirley Carter?" laughed Mary Chesnut.
"Perhaps I do," said Buck, looking mischievous.
Sam Hood frowned. "I'd like to set a trap by your door and break some of these fellows' legs. Your father should send them packing."
Buck looked sideways at Hood through her long eyelashes and thought, "I do believe he's jealous."

※

"Mama, could we invite Sam Hood to dinner on Christmas Eve? I know you have asked General Buckner, who is a Kentuckian like Sam and a friend of his." Buck had found her mother in the dining room, counting damask napkins to be sure there were enough for their expected guests.
Caroline Preston paused and studied her daughter's face. "I suppose we could include him. Senator Orr and Mr. Miles will be coming, and of course the Chesnuts."
"I know he would appreciate it. May I ask him, then?"
"No, I will. He seems to be here every day. I have lost count of the times he has escorted you to some party or other."
"Not that many, Mama."
"Buck, I do wish you would see other men besides General Hood. We really know very little about him."
"I do see other men. Captain Robb took me riding just yesterday, and Johnny Chesnut calls whenever he's in Richmond. And Shirley Carter too."
"That is true, but General Hood is more conspicuous somehow."
"You know he is a friend of John Darby, and John is here to see Mamie all the time. Sam Hood comes with him."
"Yes, and Mamie and John are engaged, which is a different situation altogether."
"Are you saying I shouldn't see Sam?"
"No, I'm not," sighed Caroline. "Just less often, perhaps."
"But he can come to dinner on Christmas Eve?"

"Yes, child, yes. Now let me finish what I'm doing. I've lost count of these napkins. Go find Maria for me, please. I need her to help wash the goblets."

"Thank you, Mama." And Buck whisked out the door before her mother could change her mind.

After sending Maria to her mother, Buck went upstairs to look for Mamie. She found her sitting in their small bedroom mending a rip in the finger of one of her kid gloves.

"I asked Mama to invite Sam to dinner Christmas Eve, and she said she would," said Buck, as she picked up Mamie's other glove and smoothed it out over her hand.

"Whatever for?" asked Mamie, snipping the silk thread she was using with her small scissors.

"Why shouldn't he come to dinner? You will have John Darby, and there won't be another man under the age of fifty here."

"Oh, Buck, do you always have to have an admirer around? Goodness knows you have enough of them. There can't be an eligible man in Richmond who hasn't called on you."

"Mama says I'm seeing too much of Sam."

"She may be right. I think he's more interested in you than you are in him, and it's wrong to give him false hopes," said Mamie. "Besides, I thought Rawlins Lowndes was the man you really cared for."

"I thought so too, but it's been such a long time since I've seen him, and he hasn't written to me. I'm afraid he's forgotten all the things he said to me when we were together before the Legion left Columbia. The last time we met he wasn't at all the same."

Mamie nodded. "Men do change."

"But John hasn't, has he? He's loved you for years now. Why should Rawlins be different?"

"I don't know. Perhaps Rawlins has had things happen to him that make him less willing to plan for the future. Life in the Legion as Cousin Wade's aide can't be easy for him. They have been in so many battles now, and have lost so many men. Maybe he thinks it wouldn't be fair to ask you to marry him under the circumstances."

Buck sighed. "I wish I knew. I'm all confused."

Mamie looked at her glove. The mend hardly showed. "At least we learned something useful in the convent besides French and manners. It does help to be able to mend things neatly these days, when there is so little to buy to replace them. And as far as Sam Hood and Rawlins

Lowndes are concerned, you might as well forget both of them. You know perfectly well that Mama and Papa won't let you marry someone like Sam, even if he is a hero."

"I thought you liked Sam."

"I do. I admire him, but you must admit he's not the sort of man Mama approves of."

"That is so unfair! Sam is a fine man. And he loves me, I know he does."

"Yes, but do you love him?" asked Mamie.

Buck shook her head. "I don't know. Sometimes I think I do, and then he does something that makes me doubt it."

"If you're not sure. . . ."

"But how can I be sure?" asked Buck wistfully.

Mamie said confidently, "I was sure I loved John almost from the day we met, and I've never had any doubts about it."

"I envy you. It must be wonderful to feel that way."

"Someday you'll feel the same way, I know you will. And everything will work out for you."

"But when?"

"Oh, Buck! Let's go find Mama and see if there's something we can do to help her. With all those people coming to dinner she'll need all the extra hands she can find. And being busy will take your mind off things."

Dinner on Christmas Eve was a great success. The Prestons were able to have food and wine shipped up to them from Millwood and from their townhouse in Columbia. The quantity and quality of their dinner was almost equal to those they had before the war began. Their guests were served steaming oyster soup, followed by succulent boiled mutton, a perfectly cured ham, dark red and salty, thinly sliced, a boned turkey roasted and basted till it was browned and shiny, wild ducks stuffed with onions and apples, partridges delicately flavored with sage, candied sweet potatoes, green beans cooked with bits of the ham, and a flaming plum pudding for dessert, all served with the appropriate wine, sherry, burgundy, or sauterne.

Caroline Preston graciously accepted the compliments of their guests.

"A wonderful dinner, Mrs. Preston. I don't see how you do it." "Yes, everything is delicious. Such a treat to have a dinner like this."

Caroline responded, "We are very fortunate to have supplies sent to us from South Carolina. There are not such shortages of food in Columbia as here in Richmond. Now, if you gentlemen will excuse us?"

As she spoke, she rose from the table and the other ladies present rose also and prepared to retire to the parlor, leaving the gentlemen to pass the Madeira and port.

When the gentlemen eventually rejoined the ladies, both groups were glad to find other topics than the war to talk about. The gentlemen had criticized every aspect of battlefield tactics and government incompetence, and the ladies had told stories of the high cost of everything in the markets and the shocking behavior of certain young women, none of whom could be regarded as ladies.

Sam Hood approached Buck, who was standing near the fireplace, warming her hands. "You are looking lovely today, Miss Buck. I like that dark green dress you are wearing."

"Thank you, Sam."

"May we go and sit in the alcove? I've wanted to speak to you ever since I got here, and it will be a little more private there."

"Why, certainly. You don't need to tire yourself out standing."

They moved slowly toward the alcove, where two chairs were partially concealed by heavy dark blue damask curtains. Buck seated herself and waited for Hood to sit down and prop his crutches against the chair.

He gazed at her intently. She realized at that moment that this would not be a casual conversation.

"Buck, do you remember what I told you when I left you at the train station in Petersburg, on my way to join the western army? I told you I loved you and wanted to marry you. And I told you that I considered myself engaged to you. I still do."

Buck shifted in her chair. She hesitated for a moment and then said, "Yes, I remember. I remember I told you that I couldn't marry you because I didn't love you in that way. And I never regarded myself as engaged to you. I thought you knew that."

"All these weeks I've been seeing you, couldn't you tell how much I love you?"

"I think you do, but you know you've been seeing Louly Wigfall too. You even said people thought you and she were engaged."

Hood said impatiently, "You know I was just teasing you a little bit when I said that. I didn't mean it. You are the only girl I've ever loved. Say you'll marry me. I cannot live without you."

Buck looked at Hood in distress. "I'm sorry, Sam, but I can't say I'll marry you. My answer must be 'no.'"

"Please, Buck, don't say 'no' right away. Give me a hope that you'll change your mind."

"No, I cannot. Please don't ask me again. I don't want to hurt you, but I can't marry you."

Hood rose slowly from his chair and felt for his crutches. "I'll say good-bye now. But I'm not finished with this. I won't believe that your 'no' really means you can't ever love me. I always win, one way or the the other, and I'll win you too."

As he moved away from the alcove, Buck stared after him. She had wanted to invite him to dinner, but she had had no notion that he would choose this day to propose to her again. She felt that she was being forced into making decisions she wasn't ready to deal with. As she had told Mamie, she was confused. It was immensely flattering to have a man declare that he couldn't live without her, but she did not like to feel rushed or pressured. She could not deny that she found Hood attractive. He had a forcefulness about him that most young men she knew lacked. And yet something about him bothered her. He was sometimes awkward in company, and said things that showed his inexperience in the circles of society in which he now found himself. And yet he commanded the respect and admiration of the men in his beloved Texas brigade. Men liked him, and women regarded him as someone needing comfort and understanding when he looked at them with sad, soulful blue eyes.

Buck wondered why she could not learn to love someone who seemed truly in love with her. Could she ever love anyone as much as she had loved Rawlins that June when the war was just beginning and life was filled with both excitement and apprehension? She wondered if she was destined to go through life never knowing the feeling of being absolutely sure of doing the right thing.

"Buck, come and say good bye to our guests," said her father, interrupting her agitated thoughts.

"Yes, Papa, I'm coming."

At the door, Sam Hood was speaking to Caroline Preston. "You were very kind to have me, Mrs. Preston. Thank you."

"Not at all, General. We were delighted you could come."

As Hood turned to leave, John Darby stopped him and said, "How are you, Sam?"

Hood smiled wryly and said, "I've been better, but I'll manage."

"I'll be leaving soon for England. Is there anything else I can bring you besides the cork legs you asked for?"

"Yes," said Hood. "Bring me a diamond ring."

Darby looked at him sharply. "I didn't know you were engaged!"

"I'm not right now, but I have hopes. So bring me the prettiest ring you can find."

"Am I supposed to guess the size?"

"Oh, I think you can figure out the right one," Hood laughed, as he went out the door into the frosty evening, balancing carefully on his crutches.

On Christmas Day, Hood attended another dinner, this time at the Chesnuts. Alex Haskell, a longtime friend of the Chesnuts, was the other guest.

As they sat down at the table, Mary Chesnut said, "After yesterday's dinner at the Prestons, mine will seem quite simple. We are only having oysters, ham, turkey, partridges, and a good wine."

"I'm sure yours will be equally delicious, Mrs. Chesnut. I don't know when I've had such feasts as these."

"You know, Sam, I have always regretted that the picnic you invited us to at Drewry's Bluff couldn't take place. My curiosity has never been satisfied about the taste of buffalo tongue."

"I don't think you would have liked it too much. It's an acquired taste."

"Nevertheless, I'm sorry we missed it. All that seems so long ago now."

"Yes, it does. That was the day I first met Buck Preston." Hood sat in silence, a faraway look in his eyes.

Mary Chesnut turned to Alex Haskell, and the conversation became general. There were mutual friends to remember and past Christmases to recall with nostalgia.

After dinner, Haskell and James Chesnut sat drinking wine at the table. Hood and Mrs. Chesnut moved to sit on a low sofa, where Hood could be more comfortable.

As they settled themselves, Hood asked quietly, "May I tell you something confidentially, Mrs. Chesnut?"

"If you wish, and are sure you want me to hear it."

"I do. I have to tell someone or I'll burst."

"Then by all means, tell me at once."

"Well, yesterday when I was at the Prestons, I proposed to Buck again, and she said there was no hope for me. I asked her to marry me that time we were in Petersburg. You remember, you and she went with me when I was leaving to join the western army. And when I asked her then she almost promised me to think about it. When I left I told her I was engaged to her, and she said she wasn't engaged to me, but I still hoped that she loved me a little. Then when I came back from Chickamauga so badly wounded I thought it was no use. But as soon as I saw her again, I knew I could never give her up."

"Do you mean to tell me that you had proposed to her before you talked about being engaged to her and to Miss Wigfall? What impudence!"

"Yes, but now she says she'll never marry me. I told her I wasn't giving up, no matter what."

"Do you really believe you can win her?"

"I have to believe it. And I still think I have a good chance."

"Sam, you are amazing! No wonder you have had such success as a soldier—you never concede defeat."

Hood chuckled. "No, I don't. I think persistence will pay off in the end."

"I almost feel sorry for Buck," said Mary Chesnut.

VIII
Richmond, 1864

John Bell Hood was true to his word. He persisted in calling on Buck and inviting her to accompany him to a variety of functions. And, somewhat to her surprise, she did.

A particularly gala occasion was a party featuring charades, given by Mrs. George Wythe Randolph, one of the premier hostesses in Richmond. President and Mrs. Davis, Colonel and Mrs. Preston, Colonel and Mrs. Chesnut, General Breckinridge, General Buckner, General Stuart, members of the cabinet, members of both Houses of Congress, visiting dignitaries, and all the beautiful belles of Richmond, including Hetty and Constance Cary, who rivaled Buck Preston in quantity of admirers, were there. The guests comprised the very highest levels of society and of political and military circles.

Buck, looking radiantly lovely in blue silk, sat with Hood near the Davises. There was a program listing the charades to be given, among them "The Fair Penitent", done by Lizzie Giles, "Coming Through the Rye", by Hetty Cary, and "An Elegy Written in a Country Church Yard", by Isabella Martin. However, the charade which excited the most enthusiasm was the one performed by Mamie Preston, whose word was "knighthood". Dressed in flowing Grecian robes, she recited:

> 'Knight' is my first, my second is a name
> That's doubly linked unto enduring fame;
> The gentle poet of the Bridge of Sighs,
> The hero, cynosure of tenderest eyes,
> 'Hood', whose keen sword has never known a stain,
> Whose valor brightened Chickamauga's plain,
> Well might he stand in glory's blazing roll
> To represent to future times my whole;
> For goodlier knighthood surely never shone
> Round fair Queen Bess upon her stately throne
> Than his, whose lofty deeds we proudly call our own.

As she finished, the audience broke into tumultuous applause, The performance could not continue until Hood, blushing with embarrassment, stood and bowed repeatedly to the crowd.

He was finally able to regain his seat, and murmured to Buck, "Did you know Mamie was going to do that?"

Buck said softly, "No, I didn't. I knew she was to do one of the charades, but she wouldn't tell me what word she had chosen."

"I wish I'd known. I wouldn't have come."

"Oh, Sam, you mustn't be so modest. You deserve that applause."

"No, I don't. The soldiers I lead deserve it far more than I."

Someone behind them whispered, "Shhhh. The next charade is beginning."

Hood and Buck fell silent, and the program continued.

At another affair, one of the many festivities taking place that winter, as Hood stood in the hallway, ready to leave, so many people pressed around him that he was in danger of losing his balance. Buck, seeing what was happening, moved to his side and held her arm out in front of him to protect him from the crowd.

Caroline Preston heard about it the next day from a friend of hers who had seen the whole thing. As they sat sipping tea from Caroline's rose-patterned china cups, Mrs. Evans eagerly told her what had happened.

"Oh, Mrs. Preston, it was the bravest, dearest thing I ever saw. Buck guarded General Hood from that throng of people, standing in front of him and looking quite fierce. I declare, she is a remarkable girl, and seems so devoted to the general."

Caroline with difficulty managed to say, "Yes, Buck is very thoughtful. She would have done the same for anyone who needed help."

"Of course she would," said Mrs. Evans with a knowing look.

"More tea?" asked Caroline. "Now do tell me how your daughter and her sweet children are."

"Thank you, I will have just a little more. Celia and the girls are well, although the baby is teething and rather fretful."

The conversation moved on to the difficulties of teething, finding a really reliable nursemaid, and life in Richmond during wartime, until Mrs. Evans was incapable of returning to the more interesting subject of Buck and General Hood.

After her visitor left, Caroline went in search of her daughter. She found her sitting by the window in her bedroom, writing a letter.

"Buck, I have just had a visit from Mrs. Evans, who told me that last night at the Ives's you stood in front of General Hood, warding off the other guests. Is that true?"

"Yes, Mama, it is. They were about to knock him down, and I came to his aid."

"That is exactly the sort of thing that makes people talk about you. It makes you conspicuous. Ladies should never be conspicuous."

"I didn't intend to be. It all happened so fast."

"Nevertheless, I wish you would not seem so intimate with that man. I cannot like your being talked about, as I have told you before."

"Yes, Mama. I understand."

Caroline sighed. "I know you think I'm being unreasonable, dear, but I worry about you."

"You don't need to worry. I won't do anything conspicuous again."

"I hope not. But knowing you, I doubt it. You attract attention just by existing."

Buck rose from her chair and went over to hug her mother. "I love you, Mama, and I promise to be good."

"You are a dear daughter. I wish. . . ."

"What, Mama?"

"Never mind. Finish your letter."

"I'm writing to Willie. Shall I give him your love?"

"Do, and tell him we are all well. Sometimes I think he worries about us as much as we do about him."

"I will," said Buck. "Won't it be good to have him home again when the war is over?"

"I pray every day that will be soon," Caroline replied as she turned to leave the room.

Toward the end of January, Hood was able to be on horseback again, much to his satisfaction. This meant that he could invite Buck to go riding, an activity at which they both excelled. Buck never looked more charming than in her English style riding habit, which fit her tall, elegant figure to perfection. Having Buck all to himself gave Hood the opportunity to advance his cause, which he did as often as Buck would allow him to speak of it. She did her best to prevent his proposing to her again, changing the subject abruptly every time the word "marriage" was mentioned. It became almost a game between them, with Hood finding ingenious ways to introduce the subject, and Buck becoming equally clever at evading it.

Caroline Preston was not happy with her daughter's continuing association with Hood, but she felt that she had said all she could to Buck. When she brought up her concerns to her husband, he was quick to say, "Now, Caroline, the more you tell Buck not to do something, the more likely she is to do it. You know she is just like you, strong-willed and proud, and you wouldn't want to listen to someone who kept telling you over and over that you were making a mistake."

"No, I suppose not. Perhaps if you spoke to her?"

"What could I say you haven't already said, more than once. Let's just depend on Buck's good sense."

"Very well. But. . . ."

"Please, dear. Say no more about it. I'm sure General Hood will be gone from Richmond soon, and the problem will be solved."

On the last day of January, Sam Hood went to visit Mary Chesnut, and found her and Buck sitting together on a sofa, chatting about their plans for the evening.

"I have great news, ladies. I am ordered to join the Army of Tennessee as a corps commander."

"I suppose we must congratulate you, Sam, although we will hate to see you go," said Mrs. Chesnut.

"Yes, congratulations. When will you have to leave?" asked Buck.

"I'm not exactly sure. Soon, I expect." He turned to Mrs. Chesnut and said, "You know, when I'm gone it will be all over. I will not come back."

"Should you not be saying that to someone else?"

Hood laughed. "Do you think she'll care?"

"I have no idea," said Mary Chesnut, as she rose from the sofa and left the room.

Hood looked at Buck. "Will you care when I'm gone?"

"Of course I will. I have enjoyed our rides together these last few weeks."

"And is that the only reason you'll be sorry when I leave Richmond?"

Buck smiled and looked down at her clasped hands. "No, not entirely."

"Will you do something for me, Buck?"

"If I can."

"I'm going to buy a new hat to replace this old one that's so faded. Will you keep my diamond star and pin it on my new hat for me?"

"Yes, I will do that," said Buck, who had expected some other request, less easy to grant.

Mrs. Chesnut returned in time to say good-bye to Hood, and noticed his star was no longer on his hat. "Sam, where is your diamond star?"

"Oh, it's safe, Mrs. Chesnut."

When Hood had gone, Buck said, "I heard you ask Sam about his star. I have it. He wants me to pin it on his new hat."

"Oh?" said Mary Chesnut.

February came, and Hood was still in Richmond, still seeing Buck as often as possible. Even Tudie, who had found an opportunity to help at the hospital developed by Dr. James McCaw on the Chimborazo plateau and named for its site, and who spent as much time there as her mother would allow, commented that she could not turn around at home without seeing Sam Hood. He knew his time in Richmond was short, and he was determined to make the most of it.

As usual, the Chesnuts' home was a favorite gathering spot. One evening Hood arrived in his carriage with Buck, whose eyes were sparkling dangerously. Coming into the parlor, she said in a voice low and sweet, but distinct enough to be heard by Hood, though she was addressing Mary Chesnut. "I do not like General Hood."

"Why ever not, Buck?"

"You know how faithful his man Cy is, and helpful, and tonight Sam spoke so harshly to him as we got out of the carriage. I saw how he had hurt Cy's feelings, and I tried to soothe Cy's mortification."

"Cy nearly caused me to fall, and I shouted at him," said Hood, looking amused. "But she told him how good he was and how I couldn't do without him."

Buck retorted, "I hate a man who speaks roughly to those who dare not resent it."

"Oh, Buck, you are making too much of it. Cy knows me. I've said worse than that to him and he's not minded it."

Buck looked at him scornfully and moved away with Mary Chesnut to another part of the room. She said softly, "I have done something tonight I regret."

"What is that?"

"Coming over here, I told Sam that if Mama and Papa did not oppose it I could care for him, and now I realize it's not true."

"Good heavens, Buck! I wish Sam were out of Richmond and away from you for a while."

"So do I. I feel sorry for him, and then I say things I don't mean."

"Now, Buck, you know this has happened before. You've been kind and sympathetic, and Sam thinks it means more than it does, just like those other men you've been engaged, or almost engaged, to. Once you seem to commit yourself, you begin to reconsider and realize you've made a mistake. Your good sense tells you that, and then you try to get out of it."

"That is so unfair! I don't deceive men like that!"

"Perhaps you don't intend to, but the result is the same. I think you are unhappy about all those men who cared for you having been killed. You remember saying to me that it was odd Hood was always lucky until he fell in love with you? You may want to make him happy, but it seems to me you are playing games with him."

"How can you say that?"

"Because I hear from the girls what you say to them. They report on your affair as if it were a game of chess that has moves to be studied."

"If this were a game it would be backgammon, where a throw can be lucky or unlucky, all chance. But there are two things certain in this world. The first is that I will never love anybody as much as I do Willie, and the second is that I'll never disobey Mama and Papa."

"Very well, but if you are not playing a game with Sam don't go and take him away when some other girl sits down next to him, as if you had a right to him."

"I wish I knew what I should do," said Buck pensively.

"Nothing impulsive, please," said Mary Chesnut. "Now let's rejoin the others. They must be wondering what we've been talking about all this time."

"Don't tell them, please," Buck implored.

"Certainly not. But do think about what I've said," Mrs. Chesnut answered.

"I will. I promise." Buck patted her hair and shook her skirts out, and walked back to join her friends.

As the time for Hood's departure from Richmond drew nearer, he made up his mind that he would try once more to win Buck's consent to an engagement. His opportunity came one chilly evening in February as they rode in Hood's carriage to yet another party.

Turning to Buck he said, "This is the last chance I'll have to ask you to marry me, and this time your answer must be positively 'yes' or positively 'no'. I don't want to have to guess what you mean. You know I love you more than anything in this world and I want you for my wife, and before I go I must have your promise to marry me or your refusal."

He reached over and took both her hands in his, grasping them so firmly that try as she might she could not release them.

"Marry me, Buck. Say 'yes'. I'm not going to turn your hands loose till you do."

"You can't be serious, Sam. Let me go this instant."

"No, I won't. You must say you'll marry me or tell me once and for all you don't love me and I have no chance."

"You're hurting my hands. Please, let me go."

"No. You must say 'yes' or 'no'. You told me once that if your parents weren't opposed to it you could love me. Didn't you mean it?"

"Oh, I don't know what I meant." And Buck struggled to pull her hands out of Hood's grip. He laughed softly and tightened his hold.

"Say 'yes' and I'll let go your hands."

"If I say 'no' will you let go?"

"I will, but I believe you want to say 'yes'."

Buck sat quietly for a moment, thinking. She stole a glance at Hood's face, which had a look of utter determination. She wondered how long he would hold her hands imprisoned. Apparently he meant to have a firm answer and would not be satisfied with an equivocation. Perhaps it would be good to have someone take charge of her life and settle her doubts. Hood certainly did not lack decisiveness, and he had proclaimed his love for her often enough to persuade her that it was truly how he felt. Suddenly she thought, "Why shouldn't I agree to marry him? Mama and Papa will consent if I ask them to. Maybe it's better to marry someone who loves you more than you love them. I'll never, ever find anyone I love as much as Willie. And Rawlins—well, Rawlins must not love me as well as I thought he did. It's been such a long time since I've seen him. Sometimes I can't even remember his face."

Hood had waited patiently, watching the changing expressions on Buck's face. He was prepared to hold her hands until she came to a decision, one way or the other, no matter how long it took.

Finally, Buck sighed tremulously and said, "Yes, Sam, I will marry you."

Hood barely restrained himself from giving a yell like the one his troops had given at Chickamauga when the Yankees retreated before them. He relaxed his grasp on her hands, lifted them to his lips, and kissed them passionately. "You won't regret this, Buck. I'll make you happy, I promise."

Buck gave him a shy smile and said, "You mustn't tell anyone till you can speak to Papa."

"I'll see him tomorrow. Oh, Buck, I love you so much. Say you love me too."

"I think I do."

"When we are married you'll know you do."

"I don't believe Mama and Papa will consent to our marrying right away."

Hood was disappointed. "I had hoped we could be married before I leave Richmond."

"Oh no, Sam. I'm sure that wouldn't be possible."

"At least we can be engaged. Surely your parents will agree to that."

"We can see what Papa says, but he always has to talk to Mama and find out what she thinks."

Hood looked thoughtful. He knew Caroline Preston did not particularly approve of him, but he hoped to convince her of his devotion to Buck. At this moment, with Buck's hand in his and her promise to marry him, he felt there was no obstacle he could not surmount.

Later, after Hood left her at home, Buck slowly climbed the stairs to her room. She hoped Mamie and Tudie would be asleep, since she did not want to answer any questions about her evening. There would be questions enough tomorrow, when Hood came to call on her parents. She knew that she could persuade her father to accept her engagement, but she also knew that her mother would be bitterly disappointed. How many times had she told Buck that Sam Hood was not the right man for her, that he lacked refinement and culture, that he was, in short, not a gentleman. Buck had promised not to act on impulse, and now she would have to tell her mother and father that she had, really on the spur of the moment, accepted Sam's proposal.

Maria was waiting outside the girls' bedroom door to help Buck undress.

"I'm sorry to keep you waiting up so late, Maria. Just unhook my dress and hang it up, and I can manage the rest by myself. You go on to bed."

"Yes, Miss Buck. I believe Miss Mamie and Miss Tudie are asleep, and they put out the lamp."

"That's all right. I can see well enough to put on my nightgown. Good night."

"Good night, Miss Buck." Maria carried Buck's gray silk dress away over her arm to hang it in the small closet just off the hallway.

Buck opened the bedroom door carefully. Both her sisters were asleep. She took off her undergarments and put them on the chair at the foot of her bed, and then pulled her white flannel nightgown over her head. The room was cold, and she was glad to feel the softness of the flannel and the weight of her quilts and blankets as she snuggled into her bed. After the excitement of the evening she didn't expect to be able to fall asleep, but once in bed her eyelids could not stay open, and she slept.

Hood arrived on the Prestons' doorstep as early as possible. He would have come at dawn if he could, eager as he was to ask John Preston for his daughter's hand.

Fortunately for him, Colonel Preston was at home. William escorted Hood into the parlor where John Preston sat reading the Richmond *Examiner*. "General Hood to see you, sir."

Preston put down his paper and said, "Well, General Hood. What brings you here so early?"

"Sir, I have asked Buck to be my wife, and she has agreed. I hope you will give us your consent."

"What do you mean? I had no idea you and Buck were even thinking of such a thing."

"Colonel, I have been seeing her as often as I could for weeks now, and I have loved her from the moment I met her."

"Are you telling me that Buck says she loves you and wants to marry you?"

"Yes, sir, I am."

John Preston called out, "William, go ask Miss Buck to come to the parlor right away."

William, who had been standing outside the door listening to their conversation, said, "Yes sir, I'll go find her."

He went up the stairs and knocked at the girls' door. "Miss Buck, your papa wants you in the parlor right now."

"All right, William. I'll be there in a minute."

Buck's heart was pounding and her cheeks were flushed a delicate pink. She had heard Hood arrive, and she knew that he must have told her father that she had promised to marry him. Now she must confront her father, who had probably not been pleased to hear what she had done. But Buck never lacked courage, so she took a deep breath, stiffened her spine, and walked out the door and down the stairs to the parlor where her father and her lover were.

When she entered the room where the two men waited in silence, her father said, "Come in, Buck. General Hood has just told me that you have accepted his proposal. Is this true?"

"Yes, Papa, it is."

"Are you sure this is what you want?"

"Yes, I am," said Buck, as she walked across the room to Hood's side and took his hand.

"Buck, you haven't known this man very long. How can you be certain he is the one you want to spend your life with?"

"Well, Papa, I don't believe you and Mama knew each other all that long before you were married," Buck said, looking at her father with an impish smile.

"Your mother will be very upset about this, you know."

"Yes, I know, but you can talk to her and persuade her that this is what I want."

"I suppose you are old enough to make your own choices, but I will ask you not to announce your engagement just yet. Will you agree to that, and to wait to marry for at least a year?"

Hood, who had stood quietly holding Buck's hand while she and her father talked, broke in, "Colonel Preston, I must leave Richmond any day now. May I not tell my friends of our engagement and give Buck a ring?"

John Preston looked at his daughter's bright face. "Very well. You may do that, but there will be no formal announcement."

"Thank you, sir. You won't be sorry. I'll take care of Buck. It will be my life's work to keep her safe and happy."

Preston sighed heavily. "I must go speak to Mrs. Preston about all this. I think it would be as well if you were to leave now, General."

Hood nodded. He had accomplished far more than he had expected. "Good-bye, Buck. May I see you this evening?"

Buck looked at her father for approval. He said, "Perhaps tomorrow would be better. Yes, come tomorrow. Good-bye, General Hood."

"Good-bye. And thank you again. I am the luckiest man in the world." Hood turned to go, looking triumphantly contented.

William held the door for him, thinking, "I never see anyone that pleased with himself. But I wonder if Miss Buck know what she doing?"

John Preston sat down in the nearest chair and regarded his daughter with amazement. "Buck, how has all this come to be? I had not seen anything in your behavior which would lead me to believe you were seriously attracted to General Hood. Do you really love him?"

Buck came and sat on the floor by her father's chair and leaned against him, her head on his knee. "I wouldn't have said I'd marry him if I didn't love him, Papa."

Preston stroked her soft auburn hair abstractedly and said, "No, I don't suppose you would, honey. I just hope I've done the right thing, agreeing to an engagement. Your mother warned me something like this might happen, but I didn't expect it somehow."

"I hope Mama will understand. Shall I go and tell her?"

"No, let me talk to her first. Then I'm sure she'll want to speak to you."

"I expect she will," Buck agreed. "I'll be in the bedroom with Mamie and Tudie."

"Your sisters will be surprised to hear this news," her father commented.

"Perhaps not," murmured Buck under her breath as she rose gracefully from her place on the floor and left John Preston steeling himself to tell Caroline what he had done.

"You did what! I can't believe my ears! Surely you didn't agree to Buck's marrying that, that Texan! He is simply not a suitable match for her, not at all a gentleman!" Caroline stared aghast at her husband who had rather haltingly confessed that Hood had asked for his consent to marry their daughter, and that he had given it.

John had expected Caroline to be unhappy about his action, but he had not anticipated such vehemence. "Yes, my dear, I did. You know we agreed that our girls are old enough to marry and to make their own choices."

"You may have said that, but I most certainly did not agree with you. I told you it was up to us to see that our daughters married well."

"Well, Caroline, Buck seems very sure that she loves General Hood. . . ."

"Yes, and she has been sure that she loved several other eligible men, too, and then changed her mind. How could you let her do such a thing?"

"How could I stop her? I must admit, you were right about her becoming too involved with Hood, but I never dreamed she would actually agree to marry him. I thought she was more sensible than that."

"In wartime sense has very little to do with it. Everyone seems to think they must live for today because who knows what may happen tomorrow," said Caroline more calmly. She realized that John was right. How could he stop Buck from doing whatever she wanted? Everyone knew that Buck was his pet, and from childhood she had been able to wind her father around her little finger.

"I did say that we would not announce their engagement, and that they must wait at least a year before they marry," John said, hoping this would pacify his wife.

"Thank goodness for that! Perhaps Buck will come to realize her mistake in accepting that man. Very well. What's done is done. But I will not have him in this house every minute. Surely he will have to rejoin the army soon."

"Yes, I understand he'll be leaving to join the Army of Tennessee any day now."

"We will have to put the best face possible on this. I wonder what Mary Chesnut will say? She is so devoted to Buck."

"I'm sure she'll let you know what she thinks. She isn't slow to give her opinion," laughed John, relieved that Caroline had made up her mind to accept Buck's engagement, however reluctantly. "Buck is waiting to speak to you. Shall I call her?"

"Yes, do. We might as well have it all out."

John went to summon Buck, who peeped around the door and asked, "How did she take it?"

"Not well at first, but you know she loves you and only wants your happiness."

"I'll go to her and explain everything."

"I hope you can, my dear. I wish I understood 'everything' myself."

"You are my darling papa and I love you, and that's the important thing," said Buck, as she kissed her father's cheek and started down the hall to her mother's room, prepared to defend Hood and her sudden engagement to him.

※

The news of Buck's engagement to Sam Hood swept through Richmond. Buck had agreed that their engagement would be a secret, but Hood found it impossible to conceal his pride and happiness and told all and sundry.

Mary Chesnut, as usual, was the recipient of everyone's confidences. Buck came to see her a day or so after Hood had spoken to her father. "Mrs. Chesnut, Sam has asked Papa for my hand, and we are engaged. Now do you believe I love him?"

"No," said Mrs. Chesnut, but Buck had wandered over to look at the books on the nearest table and did not hear her answer.

"Tell me, Buck, what do your parents think of this?"

"Oh, they are not happy. Papa foresees all sorts of problems for us, and I can tell Mama is heartbroken. She had warned me so many times not to become involved with Sam, but he persisted in asking me to marry him and finally I said 'yes'."

"Is your engagement to be announced?"

"No, but I think Sam has told everyone. He wanted to be married right away, but Papa wouldn't allow it."

"No indeed, I should think not. But are you sure this is right for you? Not long ago you told me you didn't even like Sam, and now you claim you love him."

Before Buck could answer, Colonel Chesnut came into the room. "Well, miss, I have just heard that you are engaged to General Hood. A friend of mine assures me he learned this from the general himself. Is this true?"

"Yes, it is. Will you congratulate me?"

Colonel Chesnut kissed her cheek and said, "No, but I will congratulate General Hood when I see him. He is a fine soldier and deserves all the honors he has received."

At that moment, Hood himself entered the parlor, an unexpected guest.

James Chesnut offered his hand and said, "I must congratulate you, sir. You have stolen a march on half the young men in Richmond."

Sam Hood beamed. "Thank you, sir. I am the happiest man in the world."

He turned to Buck, who was wearing her hat with the pheasant wing tucked in the band. "You look mighty pretty in that hat. You wore it at the turnpike—where I surrendered at first sight."

She smiled and blushed. "I remember that day. You told John Darby I stood on my feet like a thoroughbred."

Colonel Chesnut broke in. "I have to go to the executive office. Will you all excuse me?"

"May I walk with you, Colonel?" asked Buck.

"Certainly, my dear. Come along."

Hood walked to the window and watched until Buck was no longer in sight.

"So persistence did pay off, Sam," said Mary Chesnut.

"Oh, yes. I knew it would. All this time I truly believed that she would accept me."

"Then you are convinced that she means to marry you?"

"If it weren't for her parents I think she would marry me tomorrow. Do you know, I can't understand them at all. Before we were engaged, they let me take her riding, driving, to parties, anywhere. I was invited to dinner, even to breakfast. But now that we are engaged, I never see her parents and I can never see Buck alone. There is always someone with us, her sisters or one of her friends. Does that seem fair?"

"Perhaps not, but I imagine you can find ways to see Buck by herself if she wants you to."

"There was a notice of our engagement in the *Charleston Mercury*. Mrs. Preston blames Buck, but I know she had nothing to do with it."

"Well, Sam, considering how many people have heard of it from you, I'm not surprised it appeared in some paper or other. If it was to be a secret you haven't kept it very well."

Hood tried to look remorseful, but failed utterly. "I know, but I was so proud she had said 'yes' I just couldn't resist telling it."

"I hope no one ever confides a military secret to you!"

"Surely you don't think I'd tell something like that, Mrs. Chesnut."

"No, not really. But perhaps that's why the Prestons aren't welcoming you with open arms."

"Well. I can't help it. I love her so much and I want everyone to know she's mine."

Mary Chesnut looked thoughtfully at him and said, "You know, this isn't the first time Buck's been engaged."

"I know, but it will be the last," Sam said confidently. "Now I must go. Please tell Colonel Chesnut how much I appreciate his congratulations."

"Good-bye, Sam. Come again." Mary Chesnut watched his slow progress down the street.

"I wonder what will come of this," she murmured to herself.

The days in Richmond passed too quickly for Hood. On the ninth of February he was ordered to join General Joseph Johnston's army in Georgia as a corps commander, but he delayed his departure until finally Johnston sent a telegram to the War Department on the eighteenth: "Lieutenant General Hood is much needed here". After that, Hood knew he had to go.

On his last evening in the capital, he called on Buck to tell her good-bye. For once, he found her alone in the drawing room, before the fire.

"Buck, I must leave tomorrow. General Johnston has wired that he needs me, and I have no choice but to go."

"Are you well enough to travel and to be in command again?" asked Buck.

"Yes, I believe so. Darby should be back from England soon with my artificial limbs and that should make things easier for me. But, darling girl, I can hardly bear to leave you."

Hood sat down in a chair next to the fireplace, where Buck stood warming her hands. "Will you write to me every day and tell me everything you're doing? Will you miss me?"

Buck gazed into the fire. Would she miss him? Yes—and yet in a way it would be a relief to have him away for a while.

When she did not answer him immediately, Hood reached out his hand and seized one of hers, pulling her down into his arms. "Oh, Buck, I love you more than life itself. Say you love me!" He kissed her hair, her throat, and finally her lips with a passion he could not control.

Buck struggled to free herself. Until this moment Sam had never done more than kiss her hands. She was shocked: somehow it had never occurred to her that he might expect more than that from his fiancée.

"Let me go! Let me go!" she gasped.

Seeing her distress, Hood regretted his impetuous action. "I'm sorry, Buck. Forgive me. Knowing this might be the last time I'll see you until who knows when, I couldn't help myself."

"I can't stay here with you. Your conduct makes it impossible."

"Please, Buck, say you forgive me," pleaded Hood, as he held her slim waist in his strong grasp, "You must stay until you forgive me. I thought, since we are engaged, that you would let me kiss you good-bye."

"Not like that," said Buck. "Now you must go. Mama and Papa may come in at any moment."

Hood slowly rose from his chair, balancing carefully on his crutches. "Good-bye, darling. Don't forget me. I love you."

As he picked up his hat and turned to go, he said, "I don't have an engagement ring for you yet, but will you wear my diamond star? Wear it, and think of me."

Buck gave him her hand and said, "Yes, I will."

He raised her hand to his lips and said, "I'll have a ring for you soon, and then you will be my own forever. Good-bye, my dearest."

"Good-bye, Sam. God keep you."

Buck watched him walk away from her, and into the darkness. She felt calmer now, but his behavior had given her a glimpse of what he might expect of her soon. She could not help but remember Rawlins Lowndes' kisses, which she had longed for. Sam's were so different, rough and urgent. He had made her feel defenseless. She needed time to consider what she had agreed to when she accepted Sam as her future husband. His departure would give her that time.

John and Caroline Preston were greatly relieved to know that Sam Hood had left the city. Caroline exclaimed, "Thank goodness that man is gone! I don't think I could have stood seeing him with Buck another minute."

John was not sorry to see Hood go, but he had come to respect him and to believe that he sincerely loved Buck. "Well, my dear, I'm sure he'll be back, if it's humanly possible. I've never seen a man more determined to succeed at any cost."

"I cannot like him, but you are right in that he loves Buck. I still question whether or not she loves him."

"She believes she does, and she's given him her word, so the result is the same," said John firmly.

"I suppose time will tell. I wonder when Doctor Darby will be back from England. Mamie has been very worried about him. If only Buck had found someone more like him, someone we could feel comfortable with, someone whose family we know."

Rawlins Lowndes, in Richmond on leave, decided it was time he visited his tailor. His uniform was definitely shabby, and before he called on his friends, particularly the Prestons, he hoped to be more presentable.

His first morning in the city he made his way to the tailor shop which had made other uniforms for him. He was greeted by Mr. Cox, who was gratified to see Colonel Lowndes.

"It is a pleasure to see you again, Colonel. How may I help you, sir?"

"As you see, I am in need of a new uniform. This one has seen better days. Have you any suitable cloth?"

"I'm sorry, but the only material I have just now has been promised to General Hood for his wedding."

"Oh? And who is the fortunate lady?" asked Lowndes.

"Miss Preston. Their engagement has not been announced, but everyone in Richmond has heard of it."

"Do you mean Miss Buck Preston?" Rawlins felt his heart sink as he asked the question.

"Yes sir. General Hood has been in Richmond for some time, recuperating from his wound at Chickamauga, and he has been seen everywhere with Miss Preston. Then just recently we heard that they were engaged. I understand that he is on his way to Georgia to join General Johnston."

Rawlins was able to control his voice and expression with some difficulty. "Indeed. Well, I must look elsewhere for a uniform. Thank you, Cox." He nodded to the tailor and left the shop.

As he walked down the steep street toward the Capitol, his mind was filled with jumbled thoughts. Buck engaged to General Hood? How could this be? It was true that his last meeting with her had not been a happy one, but he had had no idea that she was seriously interested in someone else. She had seemed so loving, so sincere in returning his kiss that night in the Hampton garden, when the war was just beginning and hopes were high that the South could win its independence. He knew that he would never love anyone as he loved Buck, and now she was to be John Bell Hood's wife. He had never felt such a sense of loss, such feelings of regret.

He found himself walking past St. Paul's, oblivious of the cold. He paused and entered the sanctuary, hoping to calm his racing thoughts. He walked down the side aisle and sat in the pew which he knew was occupied by General Lee when he was in the city. Perhaps something of Robert E. Lee's spirit lingered there and could give him the resolution to face the fact that Buck was lost to him. He drew a deep breath, and resolved to behave as a gentleman should, not showing the pain which racked his heart. At least he could write to Buck and offer his good wishes. He bowed his head in a brief prayer: "Oh, Lord, let Buck be happy with her choice, and give me the strength to accept it."

He rose, left the church, and went on to the Spottswood Hotel where he had taken a room. When he reached his room, he sat down at the desk and took out writing paper and a pen. After a brief pause for thought he wrote:

> My dear Buck,
>
> I have just learned of your engagement to General Hood. Your happiness is all I have ever wanted, and I hope this engagement will bring you the happiness you deserve.
>
> When I last saw you, I could not tell you what I longed to say, that I love you more than anything on this earth. So many terrible things had happened, the deaths of friends on the battlefield, the privations, the weariness in my very soul. I could not be as I was that night in the garden so long ago when we vowed our love.
>
> I love you more now that I have lost you than I did then. You will always be in my heart.
>
> My darling, I dare not hope that you still love me, but if ever you need a friend, I will be that friend.
>
> With all my love, forever,
> Rawlins

He folded the letter, placed it in an envelope, addressed it, and carried it down to the desk, where he asked the clerk to send someone to deliver it to the Prestons.

"Certainly, sir. Right away."

"Thank you."

As he turned toward the stairs to return to his room, he thought, "So this must be what death is like, a great emptiness."

Rawlins' letter was brought to the Prestons that afternoon. William carried it into the parlor where Buck sat, pensively regarding a stocking she was attempting to knit.

"A letter for you, Miss Buck," said William, as he handed it to her.

"Thank you, William," Buck said, gratefully putting aside her knitting.

As she reached for the letter, she recognized the handwriting. A letter from Rawlins—now, of all times! She tore it open and read it hastily. Then she read it again, slowly and painfully. She let the letter drop from her hand and sat staring at the wall, tears quietly rolling down her face.

General Hood reluctantly left Richmond, where he at last had achieved his heart's desire—Buck's promise to marry him. He had hoped to be a married man before returning to duty, but he was grateful for what he had gained, and prepared to wait for a while to attain his ultimate goal.

On his way to join General Joe Johnston in Dalton, Georgia, he stopped to visit his brother-in-law to be, Major William Preston, in camp. He was anxious to tell Willie of his engagement to his sister and to learn his reaction to the news, since other members of the Preston family had been less than enthusiastic.

As Willie reported his visit, in a letter to Buck, "As a general rule lieutenant generals don't call on majors of artillery, but this one did and said such nice things too. The outsiders who did not understand how the 'land lay' must have been amazed. General Hood seems a fine fellow and certainly devoted to you. I hope he will make you as happy as you deserve. He says if my company joins the Western Army, as we expect to do, he promises to look out for me. How he plans to do that I cannot imagine. We are all well here and expect to be moving out of camp soon."

Buck was delighted to have Willie's letter, and happy that he liked Sam Hood and seemed to wish them well. She valued his opinion more than anyone else's, and Willie's reassured her that she had not made a mistake in accepting Hood's proposal. Her reaction to the letter she had received from Rawlins Lowndes had frightened her. If she had done the right thing in becoming engaged to Sam, should she have been so upset by reading that Rawlins still loved her? Her moods changed almost daily, on one day confident in her love for Sam, and on the next bitterly regretting her engagement. She longed to see Willie face to face and discuss her confused feelings with him at length. Letters came at such irregular intervals, and it was hard to express oneself on a small piece of paper, especially since it might not reach the person for whom it was intended.

Hood, however, found it very easy to write to Buck, so easy in fact that his letters arrived almost every day. She felt overwhelmed by this flow of words—nothing in her past experience with Sam Hood led her to believe he would be such a diligent correspondent. She tried to reply to his letters, but found it more and more difficult. She and Sam had so little in common, and she could not write page after page expressing her love for him, as he did his for her. After a while, she wrote less and less frequently, which troubled Hood. He wrote, begging her to tell him if anything was wrong, but she could only pen letters telling of the daily round of life in Richmond, ending with 'As ever, Buck', which was not what he hoped to read. He felt that she was slipping away from him, but in his present circumstances he could do little or nothing about it.

In April, Hood was cheered by a visit from John Darby, safely returned from his trip to England. He had been given the position of medical director of the Army of the Confederate States in recognition of his superior talents as a physician and surgeon, which meant that he would no longer serve with Hood's corps. Nevertheless, he was able to bring the artificial limbs he had purchased for his friend, as well as the diamond ring Hood had requested.

Dr. Darby was welcomed enthusiastically by Hood. ""Well, John, it's been a long time. I'm very glad to see you again. We were all concerned for you. Was it difficult running the blockade?"

"No, not nearly as difficult as I expected. The blockade runners seem to know all the tricks, and we were never really in danger. I found what I believe is the best limb to replace the one you lost, and we'll try it out as soon as possible."

"Thank you, John," said Hood. "Now what about that other item I asked you to buy?"

"You mean the diamond ring?" asked Darby, as he pulled a small black velvet box out of his breast pocket.

"That's it. Let me see what you selected."

Darby opened the box, revealing a simple diamond solitaire set in yellow gold. "Here it is. It seemed the most suitable for the lady you wanted it for."

Hood looked at his friend with a twinkle in his eye. "So you guessed who it was?"

"Oh, it wasn't too hard. And I understand I am to congratulate you."

"Yes. It was a long campaign, but I won in the end."

"You are a fortunate man. And we will be brothers-in-law, since Mamie and I hope to marry in the fall."

"I had hoped that the Prestons would agree to my marrying Buck before I left Richmond, but no such luck."

"Perhaps they felt you and Buck needed to know each other better before you married. You haven't known her that long, after all."

"It seems like I've known her all my life. She is the most wonderful girl in the world."

"Nonsense, Sam. Mamie is," laughed Darby. "Come now, let's see about fitting this limb. At least it should make horseback riding easier for you."

Dr. Darby was right. Having the artificial limb helped Hood's balance in the saddle, but unfortunately did not give him that much assistance in walking. He still needed his crutches, which he had hoped to replace with a cane.

All too soon it was time for Darby to return to Richmond. Their last evening was spent in talking about their past experiences, and what the future might hold. Darby promised to give the diamond ring to Buck, with Sam's love. "You may even give her a kiss for me, but only on the tips of her fingers," said Hood, mock-seriously.

"I'll do that, and give her a report of your health as well. You seem to be getting along well, all things considered."

"Yes, I am, although the stump of my leg is rather painful at times. But my surgeon has given me morphine to take when I need it."

"I hope you don't need it too often. That can lead to trouble."

"I know. I'm careful."

Darby looked at Hood searchingly. "I wish I could be here to help you, Sam. Remember now, use as little of any opiate as possible."

Sam said, "Now, John, I'll be fine. Don't worry."

Back in Richmond, Darby called on the Prestons immediately and was greeted rapturously by Mamie, who threw her arms around his neck and exclaimed, "Oh, John! I've missed you so much. Welcome home!"

John returned her greeting with equal ardor. He looked at her happy face and said, "If I can have such a welcome every time I return from a journey, I'll want to go somewhere every day."

"Don't tease me, John. It's so good to see you again. Come and speak to the rest of the family. We all want to hear about your trip. Did you find Sam? How is he?"

John removed his hat, dropped it on a chair in the hall, and followed Mamie into the drawing room.

Buck was alone there, and rose from her chair, saying, "When did you arrive in Richmond, John? It's a pleasure to see you back with us."

"I've only been in town an hour or so. I couldn't wait to come and see you all."

Buck laughed, "You mean you couldn't wait to see Mamie."

"Well, I'm happy to see you, too. I have something for you."

"Oh? What is it?"

"Can't you guess? Something a certain person asked me to buy for him in England."

Buck blushed. "Perhaps I can guess."

Darby brought out the velvet box and handed it to Buck, who opened it and said, "Oh, John, it's lovely."

"I have instructions from Sam to put it on your finger, and he says I may even kiss the tips of your fingers. Put out your hand."

Buck extended her left hand, and John slipped the solitaire on her fourth finger. It fit perfectly.

She exclaimed, "How did you know the size?"

"Oh, we doctors have our methods."

"Yes," broke in Mamie, "he asked me. Let me see, Buck. It's a beautiful ring, almost as nice as mine."

Darby looked pleased. "I'm glad you ladies approve of my taste."

Buck smiled at him, with the look that had beguiled so many men, young and old. "I'll tell Mama and Papa you're here. They'll be glad to know you're back from Georgia."

After she left the room, John said, "I didn't want to say anything in front of Buck, but I'm concerned about Sam. The stump of his leg that was amputated is paining him, and he's begun to use morphine."

"Is that so bad, John? Everyone uses that, or opium, occasionally."

"I don't think it's serious now, but it's something that could become serious if he continues to take it. It's easy to come to depend on it, without realizing it. I've seen it happen before."

"What should we do? Do you think we should tell Papa about this?" asked Mamie.

"No, not yet. I've asked Dr. McGregor, who is a friend of mine, to watch Sam and make sure he doesn't use too much. Anyway, drugs are in such short supply now there's hardly enough morphine to give to the men who are gravely wounded and in pain. But enough about Sam. Tell me about you. What have you been doing? Have you missed me?"

"More than I ever thought possible. You have been missed every minute of every day. Having you here now is a dream come true."

"For me too, dearest Mamie," said John, as he bent to kiss her waiting lips.

With the coming of spring, the Confederacy faced a greater challenge. Major-General Ulysses S. Grant was promoted, commissioned a Lieutenant General by President Lincoln, and made supreme commander of all the Union armies, under the President. Grant's plan for the continuation of the war was simple: to put pressure on the main Confederate armies, Lee's Army of Northern Virginia and Joseph Johnston's Army of Tennessee.

By now, the Confederate forces were seriously depleted, with little hope of augmenting them. There were shortages of everything needed to wage war, guns, ammunition, cloth for uniforms, leather for shoes, food, iron for railroad tracks, horses and mules, even horseshoes and nails. But the Confederate soldiers fought on, in spite of the odds against them.

For the civilian population, life had become increasingly difficult. The blockade had strangled the South. Textile mills made cloth, but not enough for either the military or civilians. Women whose everyday clothes had worn out had little chance of replacing them. Dresses were mended, patched, and turned until they were in rags. Often women were reduced to wearing dresses meant for evening as their day dresses, if indeed they had such a thing. The simplest things, like bread flour, were frequently unobtainable, and, if available, were priced beyond the reach of ordinary citizens. Where Federal troops went, destruction and pillage followed. Small wonder then that there was not more food for the Union prisoners in the South, when there was little food for anyone, except in remote areas which had been untouched by the war.

In Richmond, even well-to-do ladies were obliged to sell their Paris gowns to buy black alpaca to make mourning dresses, since hardly a family was untouched by death.

Mary Chesnut, visiting Caroline Preston, reported that she had given five hundred dollars for a black dress, a bonnet, a crape veil, and gloves.

"My dear," she said indignantly to Caroline, "Before the blockade these things would not have been thought fit for a chambermaid, but I must have mourning. You know Mrs. Chesnut died on the fifteenth of March."

"Yes, I had heard that. I am so sorry. Is Colonel Chesnut very upset?"

"He is quite depressed. He adored his mother, and he regrets that he was not with her when she died. Her death was not unexpected—she had been a semi-invalid for years and was eighty-nine—but his father is even older, and James is anxious to return to Camden."

"But what will we do without you, Mary? The girls will feel quite bereft, as I will."

"You will not miss me nearly as much as I shall miss you and your family."

"We must see you as often as we can while you are here, then."

"Mrs. Davis has spoken to me about James being made commander of the South Carolina Reserves, but of course my husband would never mention it to the President himself."

"Perhaps it will happen anyway," said Caroline.

"Perhaps. Now let's talk of something else. Have you heard that Mrs. Davis may have to give up her horses and carriage? Money, paper money, has depreciated so much in value that she cannot afford to keep them."

"Surely something can be done to prevent that. It seems absurd that our president cannot maintain his own horses and carriage."

"The time may be coming when none of us will have either," said Mary Chesnut gloomily.

"Oh, come, Mary! Let's have a cup of tea to cheer you up. We depend on you to keep our spirits high in these dark days." Caroline rang the bell, and when Maria appeared, asked, "Maria, would you bring Mrs. Chesnut and me some tea, please?"

"Yes, ma'am, if there is any," said Maria.

"Oh, dear. Well, see what you can find. Anything hot will do."

"Yes, ma'am. I'll see what I can do."

"Thank you, Maria," said Caroline, and as Maria left the room she murmured, "It is so difficult to feed everyone these days. I think we will have to send some of the servants back to Columbia."

"We have sent Molly and Laurence home, and I am to have hired servants for the first time in my life. But as we are in mourning we will have no company."

The ladies sat together silently, their thoughts far away as they waited for Maria's return with "anything" hot.

Colonel Chesnut was made a brigadier general and given the command of the South Carolina Reserves, as Mrs. Davis had surmised. Plans were made to return to Camden as soon as they could. Mary Chesnut spent her last few days in Richmond with her friends.

Varina Davis, still in possession of her carriage, invited Mary Chesnut for a drive, with all the Davis children in attendance. The children, while sweet-natured and precocious, were completely undisciplined. Jefferson Davis believed it was wrong to correct or repress children in any way, and as a result they were as wild as untamed animals. In their large room in the White House they had toys and books and games to distract or entertain them, but in the limited space of a carrriage they had nothing but each other, and they fought and screamed and shrieked with laughter while their mother attempted, in vain, to calm them. It was a memorable drive.

Several days later, the Prestons gave a farewell dinner for Mrs. Chesnut, as it happened, on the twenty-fourth anniversary of her wedding. The pleasant evening was enlivened by Mary Chesnut's description of her drive with the Davises en masse. "You cannot imagine what it is like to be in a carriage with three small savages, each determined to outshriek the others. How Mrs. Davis can bear it, I do not know."

John Preston said, "President Davis is such an austere man. I am amazed he would condone such behavior in his children."

"Perhaps he does so because sometimes he would like to scream and kick himself," said Tudie.

The vision of Jefferson Davis kicking and screaming silenced the entire company.

Not long after the Chesnuts left for what Mary Chesnut called "that weary, dreary Camden," the Prestons found that they too would be returning to South Carolina.

President Davis asked John Preston to take on the task of expediting railroad shipments of troops and war materiel. He believed that Preston could be more useful in that capacity than as head of the Conscription Bureau. With inland rivers controlled by Union gunboats and harbors blockaded, the South was almost entirely dependent on the railroads to supply its armies. If the railroads were destroyed or captured, there would be no connection between the two main sections of the South. This would be a greater loss than the Union's gaining control of the Mississippi River. The position offered Preston an incredible challenge, and he had doubts of his ability to succeed, but he felt it was his duty to do his best for the Confederacy. He agreed to return to Columbia, where he would be near the important Atlanta terminus and the railroad line to Charleston as well.

By June, the Prestons were at home in Columbia. They were happy to see their friends there, but Mamie especially regretted the move since it took her farther away from John Darby, whose headquarters were in Richmond. Buck was closer to Sam Hood, but she had no expectation of seeing him, or indeed any wish to do so just now. Her thoughts were in turmoil, and she needed time to reflect.

When Hood had finally arrived in Dalton, he found that he commanded a corps of veterans, most of whom were from Georgia, Alabama, or Mississippi. This made it hard to hold them in winter quarters, since their homes were so near. Desertion was common. On the rolls, more than thirty-four thousand men were listed, but in actual fact Hood had about seventeen thousand in his corps. Their morale was surprisingly good, considering that their equipment was poor, their food supply undependable, and forage for their horses extremely scarce.

Typically, Hood was less concerned with practical matters like blankets, rifles, and bread, and more interested in the plans that had been devised in Richmond for joining Polk and Longstreet in an advance on Tennessee. Hood assured Johnston that he would have the support of the government and that General Lee himself approved of the campaign. Johnston, however, did not agree with this plan. He wanted Polk and Longstreet to join his army in Dalton, where they could move toward Tennessee or remain in Georgia, as the situation demanded.

From the beginning, Hood was corresponding with Jefferson Davis, against all military protocol, since he was going over the head of his superior, General Johnston, and reporting to the President and General Bragg, the president's adviser. Johnston and Hood had entirely different ideas of conducting a campaign, Hood wishing to take the offensive and Johnston convinced that defense was the best strategy. With Johnston in command and refusing to accept Richmond's plan, the result was that Longstreet rejoined Lee's army and Polk remained in Mississippi. Hood's Texans went with Longstreet, and Sam Hood never saw his division in action again. Johnston and Hood were left to face the Federal troops in Georgia without reinforcements.

The campaign for Atlanta began in May. General William Tecumseh Sherman was at the head of nearly one hundred thousand men, his armies twice the size of General Johnston's army. Sherman's plan was to attack constantly, while Johnston depended on strategic retreat, hoping to catch the enemy at a disadvantage.

There was great dissatisfaction with Johnston's actions among many Southerners, who felt that he was giving up his position in northern Georgia too easily. His retreat southeast had put him directly in Sherman's path to Atlanta. Hood, although still pressing for an offensive against Sherman, did not attack when he had opportunities to do so at Cassville and Pumpkin Vine Creek, and this harmed his reputation as a bold fighter.

On the twenty-second of June, near Kenesaw Mountain, General Joe Hooker's corps met skirmishers from Hood's corps, and, acting on his own initiative, Hood attacked. After numerous assaults on Hooker's position, Hood's troops were turned back, with about a thousand men lost. To replace these losses, Hood was given a division of Georgia home guard troops, three thousand old men and boys, without uniforms and without experience in combat.

By the end of June, Johnston and Jefferson Davis were at odds over the conduct of the Atlanta campaign. Johnston's tactics of retreat had been condemned by many in Richmond, and there was talk of replacing him, even at this crucial stage of the war.

The question of who might be Johnston's successor troubled the president. There was no outstanding candidate available, and in the end John Bell Hood was selected by default. Davis had asked Robert E. Lee's opinion, and Lee responded,

> It is a bad time to release the commander of an army situated as that of Tenn. We may lose Atlanta and the army too. . . . Hood is a good fighter, very industrious on the battlefield, careless off and I have had no opportunity of judging of his action when the whole responsibility rested on him. I have a high opinion of his gallantry, earnestness, and zeal.

Despite this generally favorable view of Hood, the president still waited to make a change in the command of the Army of Tennessee. Finally, in mid-July, after asking Johnston yet again what he proposed to do, and receiving the answer that Johnston "must be on the defensive", Davis acted. Hood received a wire from the Secretary of War on the seventeenth of July, naming him commander of the Army of Tennessee.

When the news reached Columbia, Buck was dismayed. "Poor Sam! He will have the responsibility for Johnston's mistakes. I have prayed that this would not happen. And I have asked the nuns at the convent to pray for him too."

Hood's advancement over other more senior officers was not popular. Since he was seen as President Davis' man, all those who were critical of Davis and his administration transferred their ire to Hood. Many felt that Hood was not qualified to command an entire army.

General John B. Gordon wrote, ". . . courage and dash are not the prime requisites of the commander of a great army." In the ranks, men of the Army of Tennessee shared these doubts of Hood's capabilities and resented his replacing Johnston.

Sherman, on the other hand, was delighted with the news. He knew that Hood was bold, even rash, and would fight in the open, not from breastworks and trenches, as Johnston had done.

And Hood lived up to his expectations. He did attack, but circumstances defeated him in the opening engagement of the battles for Atlanta, and his other plans failed in spite of heroic charges by his troops. His losses of men could not be replaced, as Sherman's could, and it was impossible to succeed by attacking as Hood wished to do.

An additional problem was caused by Sherman's shelling the city of Atlanta. Property was damaged, houses and other buildings burned, and roads were crowded with refugees. Trains were filled with people desperate to flee the threatened city.

Hood's third major attack on Sherman's troops failed as well, well-planned but poorly executed. This time Hood did not leave his headquarters in Atlanta to be on the field of battle, and gave his detractors another reason to criticize him. He blamed the defeat on his officers and men, but the true reason was simply Sherman's much larger and more experienced army.

Atlanta was finally lost, and realizing this, Hood left the city after ordering the destruction of ordnance and locomotives, and the explosion of much-needed ammunition, a useless and harmful act.

Along with the failure of his efforts against Sherman's forces, Hood had a more personal failure to regret. On the twentieth of July, Major William Preston had been killed, at the head of his artillery company. Hood could not forget that he had promised to look out for Willie, and he dreaded having to write and tell Buck what had happened. In his heart he knew he should never have made such a promise, but in the first flush of excitement over his engagement to Buck he was prepared to promise anything, however rash, that would please his fiancée. He could not find the words to tell her of Willie's death, and it was left to Dick Manning to take Willie's body home to Columbia and break the sad news to his family.

IX
Columbia, 1864

From his position on the front piazza, William could see two of the gardeners slowly pulling weeds in the border of boxwoods that surrounded the fountain and pool near the corner of the garden. It was a hot July afternoon, and the gardeners were grateful to be working in the shade. William thought about encouraging them to work faster and then reconsidered. It was just too warm to do anything fast. He had watched the young ladies walk toward Mrs. Chesnut's rented cottage a block or two away and continued to stand outside the front door, contemplating the dusty street before him.

As he looked toward town, he saw a ramshackle wagon pulled by two bony mules, driven by a dirty, shabby figure in gray, headed in his direction. He shaded his eyes with his hands and tried to see who might be driving such a wagon on a residential street where one might expect to see carriages drawn by high-bred horses instead.

The driver brought the mules to a halt directly in front of the house and climbed down from the wagon seat with an obvious effort. William walked down the steps and out to the gate, prepared to tell him to go around to the back of the house. As he drew closer, he suddenly recognized the driver of the wagon and exclaimed, "Mr. Dickie! Is that you?"

Dick Manning looked at William with tired, red-rimmed eyes and said, "Yes, William. I've come from Atlanta with Mr. Willie's body. He was killed in the battle there."

"Oh, Lord! You don't mean it! What will the General and Mrs. Preston do?"

"Are they in the house?"

"Yes, sir, they are."

"Go find Uncle John and tell him I'm here, but don't tell him why, and ask him to come out. And to come alone."

"Yes, sir, right away," and William hurried toward the house in search of General Preston, muttering to himself, "This will just about kill the whole family, much as they loved Mr. Willie."

John Preston was in his study, going over papers concerning shipments of materiel which had been delayed by the destruction of railroad tracks in Georgia. He had found the job of improving railroad service more difficult than he had expected. Every state seemed to believe that its manufactured goods or agricultural produce should be used only for its own troops, even when there was an abundance there and scarcity elsewhere. That attitude, combined with the loss of rolling stock and the tactics employed by generals such as Sherman, who had his troops burn the crossties and render the railroad tracks useless by heating them and twisting them around trees, made shipping by rail increasingly complicated. Preston wanted to justify President Davis' confidence in him, but he was becoming more and more discouraged by his task.

Hearing William's soft knock on the door, he looked up and said, "Well, what is it, William? I'm very busy just now."

"Yes, sir, General, but Mr. Dickie outside, and he say could you please come out and talk to him by yourself?"

John Preston pushed his papers aside and said, "Why didn't he come in? You should have brought him in the house."

"No, sir, he needs to talk to you outside."

"I don't understand this, William. Do you know what's the problem?"

"I do, sir, but Mr. Dickie want to tell you himself."

"Oh, very well, but I don't see why all the mystery," said John, as he rose from his chair and followed William to the front door and out onto the piazza.

Dick Manning sat slumped on the bottom step, leaning against the stair rail and looking utterly exhausted. His uncle went to him and said, "Dick, my boy, what's wrong? Why won't you come in?"

Dick looked up wearily and said, "I didn't want Aunt Caroline to see me yet. I have bad news for you. Willie was shot and killed outside Atlanta. I've brought his body home to be buried."

John Preston stared at his nephew in horror, hardly able to comprehend the words he had just heard. "What? Willie dead?"

"Yes, sir. He was bringing his battery into position when a shot tore out his heart. He died instantly. It happened on the twentieth."

"Oh, Dick. I can't believe it. My son, gone."

"I'm so sorry, Uncle John. It took me a while to find him and to get this wagon and mules to carry him. I came as fast as I could, but these are pretty sorry mules, and the roads are bad."

John said in a choked voice, "I'm grateful to you for bringing him home, Dick. It must have been a dreadful journey."

"It was."

"Is he in that wagon?"

"Yes, he's in a rough coffin, the best we could do."

"I understand. Now you must come in and have something to eat and rest. You must be completely worn out."

John turned to William, who had been standing nearby, waiting to receive his master's orders, and said, "Get one of the men from the stables to come and take care of these mules, but first let's move the wagon under the trees. I want to look at my son."

"Oh, Uncle John, I don't think you should," said Dick. "It's been five days since he was killed, and I really don't believe you want to remember him this way."

"I have to see him. Otherwise, I'll never be sure this is actually Willie."

"The coffin lid is nailed shut."

"William, find a carpenter and tell him to come here."

"Yes, sir, General Preston, right away," and William hurried off in search of a stablehand and a carpenter.

Caroline Preston had seen the wagon drive up and had wondered who could be coming to the front door in such a shabby turnout. She did not recognize her usually well-groomed nephew as the dirty and ragged driver who could barely sit upright. She called out, "Maria, go see who that is at the front of the house."

"Yes, ma'am." Maria went down the stairs and out to the piazza, where she could see General Preston standing next to the wagon.

"General Preston, sir, Miz Preston wants to know who that is with the wagon."

John Preston turned his head and looked at Maria, who was shocked by his pallor and his ravaged face. "It's Mr. Dickie, Maria. He's brought our Willie home to be buried."

Maria threw her hands up and said, "Oh, no! I can't tell Miss Caroline that!"

"I don't want you to. You stay here till I come back. I'll tell your mistress myself." John began walking slowly toward the house, trying to think how to break this dreadful news to his wife.

He met Caroline in the hallway. "John, who is that outside?" she asked.

"Come in the parlor, dear. I have something to tell you."

She looked at him. wondering why he seemed so distraught, and followed him into the room, where he sat down and reached for her hand. "Sit here beside me, Caroline. That is Dickie outside, with Willie." Before he could continue, Caroline rose abruptly and exclaimed, "Willie! Why didn't they come in? Let me go to them at once!"

"No, dearest. Dickie has brought Willie's body home to be buried. He was shot in the battle for Atlanta and died there."

Caroline stared at her husband in disbelief for a moment, and then, seeing his expression, realized that he was serious. She felt faint and dizzy. "Oh, no, John, not Willie—not Willie," she whispered.

"I'm afraid it is true. Dickie says he was killed on the twentieth, and he brought him back to us as soon as he could."

"And he's in that wagon?"

"Yes."

"I have to see him just once more."

"I don't think you should. Willie would want you to remember him as he was."

"But how can we be sure it's Willie? Perhaps there has been a mistake."

"Dickie would know his own cousin, Caroline. I will look, but you mustn't."

Caroline drew herself up and said firmly, "If you can bear it, I can too."

"Very well, but I must warn you it will not be a pleasant sight."

"Nevertheless, it is our son."

John held Caroline's arm in his as they walked down the steps to where the wagon stood. Isaiah, one of the carpenters, had arrived with his tools and had pried up the lid of the simple wooden coffin but had not raised it. Dick moved toward his aunt and uncle and said, "I am so sorry, Aunt Caroline. I don't know what to say."

Caroline took him in her arms and said, "Thank you for bringing Willie home to us."

She approached the wagon and ordered Isaiah to lift up the lid.

Isaiah looked at John Preston questioningly. John nodded. "Go ahead, do what Mrs. Preston tells you."

Isaiah reluctantly raised the coffin lid and then jumped down from the wagon. The Prestons, hand in hand, looked down into the coffin where Willie's body lay, pale and rigid, his uniform stained dark red with blood from the wound that had torn out his heart.

Caroline moaned softly, "Oh, God, it is Willie." She stumbled blindly away from the sight and collapsed in her husband's arms.

John had been equally appalled at the appearance of his son's body, but, exercising iron control, he supported Caroline's limp form and called, "Maria, come and help Mrs. Preston."

Maria ran to assist him, carefully not looking at the open coffin. "Yes, sir, I will. Give her to me. Come on now, Miss Caroline. Let me take you upstairs and you can rest."

Leaning heavily on Maria's shoulder, Caroline made her way up the steps to the piazza and into the hall. "Wait a minute, Maria. I need to sit down for a little while." She reached for the arm of the old leather sofa next to the parlor door and seated herself carefully. Maria stood beside her, patiently waiting until her mistress felt able to climb the stairs to her room. She knew what a blow Willie's death had been. Caroline had often spoken to her of her hopes and fears for Willie's safety. When Caroline conducted evening prayers for the household, there had been prayers for all the Preston and Manning and Hampton young men fighting in the war. Maria herself had known the pain of loss when her father died and she and her brothers were sold in South Carolina by their father's wife, far from their home and friends. She knew they were fortunate to have been bought by the Prestons, but nonetheless their lives were very different than when their father was living and they were treated as his children and not as his slaves. Maria could sympathize with the Prestons, but their conditions were very different.

Caroline leaned her head against the back of the sofa and thought, "How can I endure the rest of my life? My darling Willie gone forever, Jack and the others in danger. What will become of us?"

Maria said gently, "Miss Caroline, you ready to go upstairs?"

Caroline sighed. "Yes, Maria, I'm ready." Together they slowly ascended the staircase to the bedroom.

Maria helped her mistress remove her dress and corset, and held her dressing gown up so that she could put it on. Maria then closed the shutters and turned back the coverlet on the bed. "You lie down, Miss Caroline. I'll see to things. Me and William will tell the others."

Caroline turned her face away and said, "Thank you." Maria tiptoed out of the room and down the stairs to the kitchen where the other servants were gathered, waiting to hear what had happened.

After making sure that Dick Manning's needs were seen to, John called William to send some of the men to carry Willie's coffin to one of the storerooms, where it could remain until he was able to make arrangements with Dr. Shand for Willie's funeral and burial at Trinity.

By this time, all the servants had heard the news of Willie's death. He had been a favorite among the house servants, always cheerful and courteous to everyone, from the youngest boy who cleaned his boots to the oldest cook and housemaid. They mourned his passing, and as they sat together downstairs they recalled his boyhood days and his frequent visits to the kitchen for treats for himself and his friends. "Don't seem like any time since Mr. Willie be down here teasin' and beggin' for gingerbread for the chillun and bones for he dog. And now he dead." "Last time I seen him he say he miss us. He always have a good word for everbody." "Miss Buck, she gon' be wild when she hear 'bout this." "Yes, and Miss Caroline she near fell out when she seen Mr. Willie in he coffin." A shudder ran through the group at the thought of how Willie's body must have looked. "The funeral be soon, I reckon." "Yes, soon, soon." They fell silent, each with his own thoughts.

Mamie and Buck were visiting Mary Chesnut, who was just moving into the small cottage she and her husband were renting from Dr. Chisholm for their stay in Columbia.

Mrs. Chesnut met them at the front door, saying with a laugh, "Well, come in, come in! Everything is in complete disarray, but you all are always welcome. The servants are trying to put things in order, but there are no chairs in the parlor yet. Let's just sit on the mattresses in the front room. We can even lie on them if we want to."

Buck looked around at the boxes and bundles on the floor and said, "Perhaps we've come at a bad time."

"Oh, no, not at all. I'm glad to have a reason to sit down for a while."

The ladies settled themselves on the piled-up mattresses near the window, hoping for a breeze. The air was heavy with heat and dampness, as usual in Columbia in July. Even indoors or in the shade there was little relief from the oppressive warmth of midsummer.

Buck took her delicately carved ivory fan out of her reticule and waved it slowly back and forth. "I declare, I can't remember when we were cool. Every year seems to be hotter than the summer before."

"I do think it was cooler in Richmond, even though it's a river town too," said Mamie.

"Have you had any news from Richmond lately?" asked Mrs. Chesnut.

"Yes, Papa has had a letter from his friend, Mr. Wheaton, and he says that things are going very badly for us. So many people are saying that President Davis has made serious mistakes in his appointments, and there is a great deal of discontent in the army, particularly in Georgia."

Buck looked at her sister. "You mean the troops that Sam Hood is commanding now, don't you?"

"Well, yes, at least that's what Papa says. They don't feel confident with Hood in charge."

"I knew it would be wrong for him to take that command," declared Buck.

"How could you know that, Buck? Sam had had such success with his Texans. President Davis must have believed that he could be equally successful with the Western Army," said Mary Chesnut.

"Yes, but I've heard people talking about Sam. They say he doesn't know how to deal with the problems of a whole army. And he's too aggressive in his plans for meeting the enemy troops, even when he's outnumbered."

"Goodness knows General Johnston isn't aggressive. All he does is retreat and dig trenches."

"With so many troops in Georgia, something must be happening," said Mamie.

"And Willie is there with his company." Buck suddenly rose from her place on the mattresses and said, "Oh, it is hot in here. Mrs. Chesnut, I'm sorry, but I am suffocating. I must go home. Something has happened there—I can feel it. Come with me, Mamie."

"Perhaps we should go home," said Mamie. "We'll walk on the shady side of the street, and we can find something cool to drink in the kitchen. Good-bye, Mrs. Chesnut. We'll see you soon. I know Mama is expecting you for lunch tomorrow."

Mamie and Buck walked toward their home, more slowly than Buck would have preferred. As they reached the corner of the grounds where the seminary stood, they could see some of the men who worked in the garden surrounding their house carrying what looked like a large box toward one of the storehouses. The girls looked at each other, picked up their skirts, and ran as fast as they could, not stopping until they reached the front door, which stood wide open. William was just inside, and did not smile at them as he usually did when he saw them.

"What is it? What's happened?" asked Mamie breathlessly.

"Oh, Miss Mamie, Miss Buck, something awful."

"What, William? Tell us this minute!"

"Mr. Willie's dead. Killed at Atlanta, in the big battle there."

Buck tried to speak, but no sound issued from her throat. She felt as if she were caught in a horrible nightmare. She looked from William to Mamie, an anguished expression on her pale face. Surely she had misunderstood what William had said.

Mamie was as shocked as her sister, but she managed to ask, "Who told you that, William?"

"Mr. Dickie just come from Atlanta with Mr. Willie's body in a wagon. I seen the coffin. I went and told yo' papa they was here."

"Does Mama know?" asked Mamie.

"Yes, ma'am. She come down and seen him."

"Oh, poor Mama! Willie was her darling. We must go to her at once."

Buck said quietly, "He was my darling, too. How can he be dead? Sam promised me he'd look after Willie. There must be some mistake."

"No, Miss Buck. I see the coffin myself," said William mournfully.

"Come with me, Buck. Let's go find Papa first. He can tell us what happened, and then we must comfort Mama," said Mamie.

John Preston, sitting alone in his study, heard their voices in the hall and called out, "I'm in here, girls. Come in."

Mamie and Buck entered the room and rushed to their father. "Is it true, Papa? William says that Willie is dead and Dickie has brought him home."

"Yes, it's true. There was a terrible battle outside Atlanta and Willie was killed just as his battery was moving into position," John said, in a strange, muffled voice, unlike his usual firm speech.

Buck protested, "But Sam promised, he promised me that Willie would be safe. He gave me his word."

"Darling child, how could he keep such a promise? He couldn't know in the midst of a battle where Willie was. And Willie would certainly not expect to be protected from serving with his artillery company and doing his duty. Your brother was never a coward."

"Sam could have done something. And now it's too late." Buck dissolved in tears, her sobs shaking her whole body.

John held her in his arms, stroking her hair and saying helplessly, "There, there. Don't cry. Willie wouldn't want you to grieve so."

But Buck could not stop crying. Finally her father said, "Buck, you will make yourself ill. Please, for my sake, try to control yourself. Your mother and I need you girls to be strong now. I must go find Tudie. She's visiting the Gibbeses and I don't want her to hear this news away from home. And I must see Dr. Shand as well."

Buck gave one last sob, then wiped her eyes with the backs of her hands and sniffed a little. "I'm sorry, Papa. Go ahead. Mamie and I will take care of Mama."

John looked at both his daughters with a sorrowful smile and said, "I know you will. We'll get through this somehow. I'll be back as soon as I can. Maria took your mother up to her room to rest. Stay with her."

As Buck and Mamie neared the door to their parents' bedroom, they heard their mother sobbing, "Oh, God, what shall I do without my son? Why, why should Willie have to die?"

They had never known their mother to lose control of her emotions. She had always been calm in any emergency, and now to hear her in such a transport of grief left them feeling very young and helpless.

Mamie pushed open the door and went to kneel by Caroline's side. She patted her hands and said, "Mama, please don't cry so. I can't bear to see you like this."

Caroline looked at her as if she were a stranger. "Don't you know what's happened? Willie is dead."

"Yes, Mama, we know," said Buck. "But it's so hard to believe. Willie always told me the artillery was the safest division in the whole army."

"No one is safe in a battle. But I never expected. . . ." Caroline lay motionless, tears streaming down her face, which suddenly looked years older. "I hate this senseless war. It has taken my darling boy from me."

❧

On a sunny afternoon in early September Caroline and Mamie Preston drove out to Millwood to call on the Misses Hampton. Mamie had received a letter from Dr. Darby telling her that he had been able to get leave the last week in September and could come to Columbia then for their wedding. The Hampton ladies had offered to help with arrangements for the ceremony, and Mamie had persuaded her mother to go to Millwood to discuss their plans. This was one of the few times Caroline had left the house since Willie's funeral. She knew that Mamie depended on her, and she had forced herself to take an interest in the wedding despite her constant grief over Willie's untimely death. She remembered telling Buck, when she mourned Ransom Calhoun's death, that, in effect, it was wrong to neglect the living for the dead, and she could hardly say that to her daughter and do otherwise herself.

As they drove along the road to Millwood, the sky overhead was a deep, soft blue, with a few wispy clouds on the horizon. The hoofs of the carriage horses stirred up small puffs of dust, powdering the purple asters and goldenrod that grew beside the road. The live oaks that overhung some sections of the road were green, but a few yellow or red leaves had appeared on the swamp maples and chinaberry trees. Caroline looked around her and said, "I do hope the weather will be this pleasant on your wedding day. This is perfect, clear and not too warm."

"Yes, it is, Mama. And there should still be flowers in the garden for my bouquet and for the altar, perhaps even some late roses."

"I'm sure Kate will find some smilax and greenery at Millwood too. That always looks well in wedding decorations. Look, there she is, waiting for us on the porch."

Henry stopped the carriage at the front steps and then helped Mrs. Preston and Mamie to alight.

"Take the carriage around to the stables and unhitch the horses, Henry. I'll send word when Mrs. Preston is ready to leave," said Kate Hampton.

"Yes, ma'am, Miss Kate," Henry replied, and drove slowly around the driveway toward the stables.

"I am so glad to see you, Aunt Caroline, and you too, Mamie. How are you?"

"Better. You know it has been a difficult time for all of us these past few weeks, but Mamie has had some good news. Dr. Darby can be here in about three weeks, so we are proposing to have the wedding on the twenty-eighth."

"Oh, that is wonderful, Mamie. I am happy for you. I know you have looked forward to this for a long time."

"Yes, I have. I can hardly believe it's really happening."

"Come inside and we can talk. Ann and Caroline and Mary Fisher and I have been discussing what we could do, and we would like to give you the material for your wedding dress. It is hard to find any sort of cloth now, but we have something that we've had for years which should make a lovely dress. It's silk tulle, bought long ago when we thought. . . . But come in the parlor and let us show it to you."

Caroline and Mamie followed Kate into the wide entrance hall and on to the parlor where the other Hampton sisters sat. The three ladies rose and greeted them with sympathetic hugs and pats. They had felt the loss of Willie almost as much as the loss of their brother, Frank Hampton.

Kate said, "I've told Mamie what we'd like to do."

"Good," said Mary Fisher. "Come over here, Mamie, and look at this tulle. It was white when it was new, but it's turned cream-colored, even though it was wrapped in tissue paper."

Mamie crossed the room, and there on one of the rosewood tables lay yards and yards of delicate tulle, creamy white, and perfect for a wedding dress. "Oh!", she exclaimed. "It is beautiful! Are you all sure you want me to have it?"

"Yes, dear, we do," said Caroline Hampton. "We will never need it, and there is no use in our keeping something like this when you could use it."

"Thank you, all of you. I had expected to be married in one of my old dresses, but this will make a lovely wedding gown."

"And I know you will be a lovely bride," said Ann.

Caroline had watched Mamie's delight in the unexpected gift. She said, "You all are too kind. This will be such a help to us. I'll talk to Miss Tyler as soon as possible and see what patterns she has that would suit this beautiful tulle. She is an excellent seamstress, and I'm sure she'll do it justice."

Later, as the Prestons drove back to town, Mamie said, "Mama, I have always wondered why none of the Hamptons ever married. They are all pretty and clever and capable, and they must have had many suitors when they were young."

Caroline sighed. "It is a very sad story, and no one likes to discuss it. Years ago, something happened between the Hampton girls and their uncle, James Hammond. It was all hushed up, but there were rumors, and somehow all their suitors drifted away. I think the sisters have been content with their single lives, but I do wonder if they must sometimes regret that they have reared their brothers' children and not their own."

"Do you suppose this tulle might have been intended for a wedding dress for one of them?"

"That is quite possible. I believe there was someonce who once courted Mary Fisher, but he married another girl."

"That *is* sad. To think that they kept this material all these years. . . But I'm glad they did, and it was generous of them to give it to me."

"Yes, it was. It will make a beautiful wedding dress, and the blond lace they found to go with it will be perfect. We'll see what Miss Tyler suggests. That creamy white will be very becoming to you."

"Mama, I do appreciate what you are doing for me. I know it isn't easy."

Caroline patted her daughter's hand. "Life must go on, Mamie. Your brother would want you to have a happy wedding day."

"There is a great deal to do in the next few weeks. It will be good to be busy," said Mamie. "Buck especially needs to have something to take her mind off Willie and Sam Hood, if that's possible."

Caroline agreed. "I worry about Buck. She seems to blame General Hood for Willie's death, but of course that couldn't be possible."

"No," said Mamie, "but she says that Sam promised to take care of Willie, and he didn't."

"That was a promise he could not keep in the midst of battle."

"I'm surprised to hear you take Sam Hood's side, Mama. You seem to dislike him so much."

"It's true I don't care for him. I don't believe he's right for your sister. But one must be fair. Losing Willie will be an everlasting sorrow to me—to all of us—but in war we seem to lose our very best. No one can know who will live and who will die. We must believe all our dead are with God and we will meet them again someday."

"Yes, Mama," said Mamie. "I will try to remember that."

Miss Tyler found a pattern suited to the fragile tulle contributed by the Hampton sisters, and Mamie approved it. The dress was to be made with a full, tiered skirt, alternating bands of blond lace and tulle. The bodice would have long sleeves, gathered at the dropped shoulders and fastened at the wrists with tiny pearl buttons, a pointed waistline, and fine tucks from shoulder to waist to accentuate Mamie's slender figure. A veil of blond lace would complete the ensemble. Caroline had promised Mamie that she could wear her grandmother's pearl and diamond brooch, which Mary Cantey had worn on her own wedding day.

Buck tried to be happy for her sister and to show a cheerful countenance, but she found it quite difficult to see Mamie making ready for her wedding when her own future seemed so bleak. Her letters from Sam had become increasingly infrequent. Those she did receive had taken on a curious tone, not at all like the letters he had written when they were first engaged. While she realized Hood's situation was different now that he commanded the Army of Tennessee and not his Texas brigade and that he must be in constant pain from his leg, still she was puzzled by his letters. Her feelings toward him had changed since Willie's death, since she could not help blaming him for it, unreasonable though that might be. Having given her word, she could not break her engagement, but she now regretted her acceptance of his proposal. The letter she received from Rawlins Lowndes when he learned of her engagement had been a blow to her. To learn that he loved her after she accepted Hood was too painful to think about. If only she had waited! At least her parents had resisted Hood's wish to marry her before he left Richmond. She wondered how she had ever thought she could be happy with a man like Hood, so different from Rawlins or Ransom or the other men who had loved her. But as long as Sam was far away, facing unequal odds against the Federal armies, she could never give him any indication that her heart was no longer his. That would not be fair, and Buck had too much character to do such a thing. But, perhaps, one day, when the war was over. . . .

Plans went on for Mamie's wedding. Wedding cards were delivered by Caroline's friends to those who would be invited to attend the ceremony. And, at last, the twenty-eighth of September dawned, clear and cool, just as Caroline and Mamie had hoped. John Darby had arrived two days earlier, and he and Mamie were so happy that the family tried to put aside their sorrow and rejoice with them.

The morning of the wedding, the girls sat in their room, ready to help Mamie pack her things and dress. This was not a task to be left to the maids, eager as they were to help with the last-minute preparations. The door opened and Caroline came in. "Girls, if you are going to help Mamie get her things ready, you had better do so soon, or I will have to send Maria. Mamie, dear, have you met all the Darbys?"

"I think so, Mama. There are so many of them and they all keep talking about 'losing' John. I can't say that they are very agreeable company, but I suppose I must make the best of them. They are certainly nothing like John!"

"Well, he has had many advantages, and is perhaps more sophisticated, having traveled a great deal. But both his grandfather and father were doctors, and they are a fine family. Anyway, I doubt you will have to see much of them. I have never heard John say that he intended to practice in Orangeburg when the war is over. With his education and skill he could go almost anywhere. They are probably a bit jealous."

Tudie had been listening to all this, and when Caroline said 'the war is over' she could not help but think of her brother, who would not be back 'when the war is over'. "Oh, Mama," she exclaimed, "if only Willie were here!"

She had said the one thing the others had been carefully avoiding, and they all burst into tears.

Caroline was the first to pull herself together and said, "Girls, wash your faces and help Mamie. I must go see where your father is. When I came up here he was trying to entertain the Hampton cousins, and he needs to get dressed."

Friends had decorated the church with greenery and flowers, and a few precious candles had been saved for the altar.

General and Mrs. Chesnut arrived at the church a little before two o'clock and were ushered to a pew with the Fishers. The two ladies were seated side by side, and Mary Chesnut whispered, "The Wayside Hospital had a great deal to do with this wedding."

"I would like to take the credit, but I do believe Dr. Darby and Mamie fell in love when they first met. Didn't he come to Columbia in 1861 to join Hampton's Legion?"

"Yes, and General Hampton was fortunate to acquire such a fine surgeon. Not many doctors are as well-trained and conscientious. When I think of what I have suffered at the hands of some doctors! He will have a fine career when the war ends. I would like to be one of his first civilian patients."

Their husbands tried to hush the ladies, with little success.

"When I think of all the weddings I have seen and the beautiful parties we used to have, I could cry. Those suppers with turkey and chicken and ham, all those hot biscuits and egg bread, and pound cake, marble cake, spice cake, plum cake—remember how we used to have steeple cakes? Why, some were two feet high! My mother and the servants spent two weeks just making the cakes for my wedding. And the syllabub! I can almost taste it now."

"Mrs. Chesnut, please!" said her exasperated husband.

"I heard that the Hampton girls gave the tulle for Mamie's dress and the lace for the veil," said Mrs. Fisher. "Do you think one of them had been keeping it for her trousseau?"

"Perhaps, but how fortunate for Mamie. I do not believe there is any white cloth to be had in Columbia at any price. And of course every bride must have white since Queen Victoria wore it when she married Prince Albert. A nice dress of any color used to be good enough."

At that moment, a hush fell over the congregation as Mamie started down the aisle on her father's arm. Miss Tyler had outdone herself in making Mamie's dress, which looked as elegant as any bride could desire. Mrs. Preston followed with Dr. Darby, who was resplendent in a uniform which he had had tailored in London.

When Caroline reached the pew where the rest of the family was seated, in front of the Hamptons, who had come in from Millwood, she thought sadly of her mother. How proud Mrs. Hampton would have been today. She had always admired Dr. Darby, and Mamie was her namesake. She would have been pleased to see her own wedding brooch adorning Mamie's dress. As the young couple stood in front of Dr. Shand, tears filled Caroline's eyes.

Buck, seated beside her mother, was overcome by a most peculiar feeling. Looking at Mamie and John, she seemed to see herself and Rawlins Lowndes in their place. She imagined Rawlins' loving smile and look of pride as he gazed down at her, his happy bride. This was what her wedding should be like. How deeply she regretted her impulsive decision to accept Sam Hood. It was bitterly ironic that the news of her engagement had been the cause of Rawlins' letter to her, declaring his undying love. She looked at her engagement ring and shuddered.

Perhaps she could find an opportunity to talk to John Darby before he had to return to Richmond. He was Sam's friend. He might be able to explain the change in Sam she had noticed in his letters. She wondered if his feelings toward her had altered. If that were true, she might be able to end her engagement. Until she knew, she was committed to him, and she could not see any honorable way to change that.

She felt her mother's eyes upon her, and looked down at her prayer book as Dr. Shand began to read the collect: "O Eternal God, we humbly beseech thee favourably to behold these thy servants about to be joined in wedlock. . . ."

As John Preston took his seat beside Caroline, he felt a momentary sadness. He adored his daughters, and now he was giving one away. Well, he thought, at least she will be in good hands. He had great respect for his new son-in-law, both as a man and as a doctor, and he and Mamie truly loved each other. His eyes turned to Buck, and he wondered again if he had been right to consent to her engagement to General Hood. Caroline's violent opposition to the match had shaken him. She was usually correct in her judgments, but it was hard to refuse Buck. Of all the young men who had courted her, why had she chosen that one?

The house servants, seated in the balcony, had an excellent view of the nave and the congregation. Like others at Trinity, they remembered family weddings in the past, and they compared them, among themselves, to today's wedding. "Miss Mamie be a handsome bride, but not prettier than Miss Caroline." "Not so many folks here as when Mr. Jack married Miss Celestine." "Don't Miss Buck look nice? Wonder when she be walking down the aisle?" Even though this was said in whispers, William felt they were not upholding the honor of the Preston family by talking, and he looked at them sternly, saying softly but firmly, "Be quiet! You know better than talk in church!"

The younger maids giggled a little behind their hands. They knew William would like to comment himself but it was beneath his dignity to do so. But they sat quietly with the other servants as Dr. Shand read the beautiful, familiar words of the marriage service.

After the blessing, as Mamie and John Darby walked down the aisle as man and wife, there was a murmur from the balcony in spite of William's admonition to keep silent. "Oh, she look just as pretty as can be!" "Dr. Darby handsome too." One gentle voice said, "I be certain Miss Caroline thinking about Mr. Willie today." "Yes, yes, Lord." "Hush!" said William.

X
Georgia and Tennessee, 1864

In Georgia, after abandoning Atlanta, Hood consolidated his remaining forces. He desperately needed reinforcements but none were forthcoming. The troops he had lacked everything: food, shoes, uniforms, weapons, ammunition, and, above all, a time to rest. They had not been paid for months and were unable to send money to their families, whose needs were as great as their own.

Hood himself was exhausted, and his growing use of opiates was beginning to cloud his reason. At times he remembered John Darby's warnings, and Dr. McGregor often cautioned him, but he was unable to give up the drugs which gave him a measure of relief from pain.

He appealed to President Davis for more men, but there were none to send. He would have to depend on those he had where he was. He lost part of the men he had when the governor of Georgia, Joseph E. Brown, withdrew his state troops, claiming they needed the opportunity to harvest their crops and attend to private affairs. Governor Brown had opposed Jefferson Davis' selection as president of the Confederacy from the beginning, and was prepared to do anything he could to discredit his government, even if it meant crippling Hood's army.

To add to Sam Hood's problems, Sherman decided to move all civilians out of Atlanta. He wrote to Hood, informing him that he would take people and baggage south to Rough and Ready, but after that it would be Hood's responsibility. Hood protested, but to no avail.

Further exacerbating Hood's situation, President Davis paid a visit to Hood's army, and as he and Hood reviewed the troops, some brigades shouted "Give us General Johnston!", demonstrating the lack of unity in support of Hood's command of the Army of Tennessee.

Davis himself did not help matters. In a speech in Augusta, Georgia, where he had gone to confer with General Beauregard, who had been given command of the department including Hood's and General Richard Taylor's armies, the president announced that Hood's plan was to attack Sherman's communications and move into Tennessee. This was reported in Northern newspapers, and soon everyone, including General Sherman, knew what to expect. As Sherman remarked, "To be forewarned is to be forearmed."

Nevertheless, Hood went ahead with the plan, beginning to move his army toward Tennessee on the twenty-eighth of September, which, unknown to him, was Mamie Preston and John Darby's wedding day. By now he had about thirty-three thousand men, including infantry and artillery.

In a series of marches covering twelve to eighteen miles a day, moving north, Hood retraced the path the same army had used, heading south to Atlanta. Sherman pursued him, leaving only one corps in Atlanta. By the time Hood reached Cross Roads, near the Alabama line, he was ready to stand and fight, but his officers were very much against it, citing Sherman's much larger army. Hood reluctantly ordered his troops to move on, into Alabama. He met with General Beauregard in Gadsden on the twentieth of October, and the two men discussed Hood's plan to go to Tennessee, eventually moving into Kentucky. Beauregard finally consented to it, but with doubts.

To succeed, the plan depended on speed, since the weather would be a factor as the autumn days grew colder and wetter. But Hood, uncharacteristically, moved slowly and deliberately, looking for the best place to cross the Tennessee River. It was not until the thirteenth of November that the corps under Hood began to move across the river.

Sherman, having decided to leave Hood to General Thomas and General Schofield in Tennessee, returned to Atlanta, and on the sixteenth of November began his march to the sea through Georgia.

At last, the Army of Tennessee was on the march. Hood realized that if he could keep the Union forces under Thomas and Schofield apart, he had a chance for victory, and for moving on to the Ohio River and then to Virginia to join Robert E. Lee's Army of Northern Virginia. With the men in his command, he would defeat Schofield and then Thomas, and capture Nashville. His plan was simple. To carry it out was not.

In late November, the weather in Tennessee turned cold, with rain changing to sleet and then snow. The roads were muddy, with deep ruts. Despite these conditions, the army made steady progress. When Hood's forces reached Columbia on the twenty-seventh, they found Schofield's troops there, behind breastworks. Hood decided against attacking the breastworks, claiming he was not sure of the courage of his men in an attack on such a position. Instead, he ordered a flanking movement, ending in Spring Hill. Schofield, at the same time, sent General Stanley with five thousand men to Spring Hill.

Spring Hill was the beginning of the end for Hood. After some desultory skirmishing between the Confederate and Union armies, in the darkness of early evening both armies were in disarray. Schofield moved his troops out of Columbia and quietly marched them past the Confederate camps, down the Columbia Turnpike. Somehow, there was no one from Hood's army guarding the turnpike.

Sam Hood had retired to his tent, where he wearily removed his artificial leg and cautiously rubbed the place where his leg had been amputated. After days in the saddle, the pain there was almost insupportable. He reached for the small packet which contained his morphine powder. There was only a little of it left, but tonight he needed something to help him rest comfortably. Tomorrow he was sure that his troops could deal with General Stanley and his men. He tipped the white powder into a tin cup half-filled with brackish water, stirred it, and swallowed the mixture. He was very tired, and sleep came almost immediately after he lay down on his camp bed.

A short while later, he was roused from sleep by an excited soldier, a private, barefoot in the cold, saying, "Sir, sir, the Federal troops are passing on the turnpike!"

Struggling to sit up, Hood tried to collect his thoughts. "What do you mean, troops on the turnpike?"

"Sir, I've seen them. What looks like a whole army of Yanks is marching past us."

"Find Colonel Mason and send him to me," ordered Hood.

"Yes, sir, right away," and the private left Hood's tent in search of Colonel Mason, filled with a great sense of his own importance.

Colonel Mason reported to Hood, who said, "I've just had a report that there are Union troops on the turnpike."

"Yes, sir."

"I want you to go to General Cheatham and tell him to advance a line of skirmishers and confuse the enemy by firing into his columns."

"Yes, sir, I will." Colonel Mason left to carry out his orders, and Hood, feeling that he had done all that was necessary, returned to bed and was soon fast asleep.

Daylight brought a rude surprise. The Federal troops were gone. No one would admit that he had not done what was expected of him. No one checked to make sure that his subordinates carried out their orders. Hood was furious, but by then it was too late. An excellent opportunity to beat the Yankees had been lost, and the army was determined to make up for this fiasco, Hood most of all. He knew that his senses had been dulled by morphine, and that he had neglected his duty.

Schofield had marched all night, reaching Franklin at dawn. He had had time to have breastworks of logs built, and trenches dug along the bend of the river. These were defended by artillery and almost impregnable.

Hood pursued the Federal troops as rapidly as possible, with General Nathan Bedford Forrest's cavalry in the lead.

By three o'clock that afternoon, Hood's army faced Schofield's.

General Schofield and General Stanley could see, through their spyglasses, the Confederate Army forming in line as for battle. Both wondered: Would Hood attack?

After a brief consultation with his officers, all of whom opposed the idea of attacking such strong fortifications, Hood determined to attack at once. The cold, rainy weather had given way to Indian summer on this last day of November, as the Army of Tennessee assembled for its charge against the Federal lines. The armies faced each other across a plain, almost a mile apart. The Confederates, twenty thousand strong, marched in quick-step until they were within firing distance and then began a slow trot. The Federal skirmishers fired on the first line, and as they did, the Southerners charged, the rebel yell sounding as they plunged into the Union line. They gained an initial advantage, but were unable to sustain it, and gradually were beaten back. But they charged again and again in the face of shot and shell. Hundreds of men died in the bloody melee. Six Confederate generals were killed, including States Rights Gist, whose body was taken back to Columbia, South Carolina, and buried in the tree-shaded graveyard at Trinity, not far from the graves of Willie Preston and Frank Hampton, who had also died for the Cause.

The Battle of Franklin cost the Army of Tennessee nearly six thousand men, two thousand dead, and the rest wounded or captured. Hood could never again question the courage of his men in a frontal attack on breastworks.

He was confronted with a problem which had no viable solution. He could not obtain reinforcements, therefore with his present force it was unlikely that he could succeed against Thomas in Nashville. Since he had lost the Battle of Franklin he could not hope to attract recruits in Tennessee or Kentucky. He could not go south to challenge Sherman without more men. Presented with no practicable options, he chose to attack Thomas. This was a disastrous decision.

The December weather took its toll. The Army of Tennessee was ill-prepared for winter, lacking overcoats, boots, and even jackets in some cases. Rain froze as it fell, then was covered with snow. They could not dig trenches in the frozen ground and huddled in misery around their meager campfires.

On the fifteenth of December, after the ice began to melt, the armies were ready for battle. The struggle lasted two days, at the end of which the Army of Tennessee was in retreat. The Union Army broke the Confederate left, with a combined attack of infantry and cavalry, and the rout was on. A few units of cavalry and infantry fought a rear guard action. General Forrest, with five thousand men, protected the remnants of Hood's army for seventy-five miles, until they reached the Tennessee River, which they crossed during the three days after Christmas.

Hood, riding along with his troops, kept hearing snatches of a song. It sounded like "The Yellow Rose of Texas", but somehow the words seemed different. His army had a new version, which it sang lustily as it marched toward safety on frozen, bloody feet.

> And now I'm going southward
> For my heart is full of woe.
> I'm going back to Georgia,
> To find my Uncle Joe.
> You may talk about your Beauregard
> And sing of General Lee,
> But the gallant Hood of Texas
> Played hell in Tennessee.

What was left of the Army of Tennessee finally reached Tupelo, Mississippi in January of 1865, the same town to which they had retreated after Shiloh in April of 1862. Then they were still confident of beating the Yankees; now they looked at the shattered remains of a proud army and wondered.

Hood resigned as commander on the twenty-third of January, a resignation which was immediately accepted by General Beauregard. Sam Hood still believed he could serve the Confederacy, and he wired Jefferson Davis that he was certain he could raise additional troops across the Mississippi and would come to Richmond to explain his plan.

XI
Columbia and Richmond, 1865

John Bell Hood, a forlorn figure in gray, stood on the piazza of the Prestons' home in Columbia. He had traveled a long way, and now he hoped that when the door opened, Buck would be standing there to welcome him. He knocked and waited. He could hear footsteps approaching and then the door swung open. But it was not Buck he saw. Instead, her brother Jack looked at him in surprise. "Why, General Hood! I had no idea you were in South Carolina. I'm sorry the rest of the family isn't here. They are all back in Richmond. But come in, come in. How are you, sir?"

Hood stood in the hall, turning his broad-brimmed hat in his hands, and replied, "Well, Major Preston, you know about my problems in Tennessee, I expect, and my resignation. I left the army in Tupelo, Mississippi, and I'm on my way to Richmond to speak to the president about raising more troops across the Mississippi."

"We heard what happened at Franklin and Nashville. I'm very sorry, General. Please, come in the parlor and have a seat. May I get you something to eat and drink? You must be very tired."

"It's been a long trip. I find it hard to sleep at night. I keep seeing those men lying on the cold, muddy ground at Franklin, the wounded and the dead all mingled together. And the brave men who charged the breastworks, with soot and powder burns on their dead faces."

"But you did the best you could, sir. We all know that you were short of men and supplies. And the winter weather prevented you from moving as fast as you might under better conditions."

"That is true. No doubt we were outnumbered in every battle. But that doesn't excuse my failure at Spring Hill. We had General Stanley at our mercy, and he escaped. Down the turnpike, where I should have posted sentries."

"No one could have predicted such a turn of events, General Hood. You mustn't blame yourself."

Hood looked at Jack Preston ruefully and said, "Who else can I blame? It was my responsibility to see that our lines were secure and that there were pickets guarding them, and I failed. But, tell me, Major, how is it that your family is in Richmond again? I had understood that General Preston was in charge of improving shipments by rail, rather than the Conscription Bureau, now."

"He was, but in November President Davis asked him to resume his duties at the Bureau, and he and my mother and the girls returned to Richmond."

"I had hoped they would be here, in Columbia. It seems such a long time since I've seen Buck. You know your sister and I are engaged?"

"Yes, I know."

"Your parents don't approve of me. I know that. But I love Buck and I believe she loves me and I can make her happy if I have the chance."

Jack stood up and said, "Yes, sir, I'm sure that's true. Now I'm going to have the servants prepare a room for you. Perhaps you would like to rest before dinner."

Hood grasped the arms of his chair and pulled himself up. "Thank you, Major. I appreciate your letting me stay here."

"Delighted to have you, General. An old friend of yours from Richmond is in Columbia too. I'll send word to Mrs. Chesnut that you're here. I'm sure she'll want to see you."

"Mrs. Chesnut was very kind to me when I was last in Richmond. It seems so long ago now, and it was only last year. Buck accepted me on the eighth of February, the happiest day of my life. I had hoped to be in Richmond on that anniversary, but it may not happen."

The following day, Mary Chesnut appeared at the Prestons, accompanied by one of her young friends, Isabella Martin. William Walker was in Richmond with the Prestons, but Caleb was acting as butler in his place, and welcomed the ladies.

"Good morning, Miz Chesnut, Miss Martin. Please to come in."

"Thank you, Caleb. Is General Hood still here?" asked Mary Chesnut.

"Yes, ma'am, he in the parlor with Mr. Jack, I mean Major Preston."

"Then we'll go in and speak to them. Come, Isabella."

They found Sam Hood seated near the fireplace, his hands stretched out toward the blazing log fire. Since his failed campaign in Tennessee, he never seemed to be warm enough. The long days on the march in the freezing rain had chilled him to the bone, and even now he sought the warmth of a fire whenever he could.

When he saw the ladies he rose and went to meet them, holding out his hand. "Mrs. Chesnut! And Miss Martin! How good to see you both."

"Well. Sam, it's been a long time. I'm happy to see you again. We've been very worried about you," said Mrs. Chesnut, shaking his hand.

"Oh, nothing ever finishes off a tough old soldier like me. I'm one of the lucky ones," said Hood. "So many weren't lucky, but here I am. No army and no command, though."

"Yes, we read about your resignation. I'm sorry, Sam."

"Well, I had to resign. The army had lost confidence in me. That whole campaign in Tennessee was my fault. My plan was a failure from the start."

"But how could you succeed, given the odds against you? You were expected to work miracles, and no one could have done so under the circumstances."

"In my mind I know that, but then I see those soldiers of mine charging the breastworks at Franklin again and again, and each time with fewer men left to attack. And I should have found a better way to achieve my goal."

"Don't think about it, Sam. That's in the past. There is nothing you can do now to change it."

"You are right, and yet I cannot forget it."

Jack Preston, who had listened to all this, hoped to distract Sam Hood from his painful memories. He said to Isabella, "Miss Martin, you must have attended the Great Bazaar on the seventeenth of January. Tell me, was it a success?"

Isabella responded eagerly, "Oh, yes, Major Preston. It was immensely successful. You know it was held at the State House, which was beautifully decorated with bunting and banners. The columns were twined with smilax, and there was a sign in gold letters above the entrance that read "A Tribute to Our Sick and Wounded Soldiers". Each state had its own booth, in the shape of a tent, with the state coat of arms on it. Oh, it was lovely! The railroads provided free shipping for the goods that were sold at the Bazaar. I don't know when I've seen such food, and such beautiful things for sale, even silver and gold jewelry. They say the Bazaar raised over three hundred thousand dollars for our soldiers."

"Yes, in Confederate bills," commented Mrs. Chesnut. "And unemployed generals were as thick on the ground as acorns in the fall." Then she looked appalled and clapped her hands over her mouth. "Oh, Sam, I'm sorry. I'm as bad as Mary McDuffie, saying the most tactless thing possible.

Hood smiled but his eyes were sorrowful. "That's all right, Mrs. Chesnut. I am an unemployed general. But when I get to Richmond perhaps President Davis can find some use for me."

"Are you going to Richmond soon, General Hood?" asked Isabella.

"Yes, I'd like to start tomorrow. I'm anxious to see the president."

"And to see Buck, no doubt," teased Isabella.

"And to see Buck," Hood agreed.

"You will be married in Richmond? Don't let them keep putting it off," said Isabella.

Hood did not answer her immediately. Then he said firmly, "If it is at all possible, I'll be married in Richmond."

In Richmond the news of Hood's debacle in Tennessee caused consternation in some quarters and a reaction of "I told you so" in others. Hood's friends were distressed by the wave of criticism of his actions, since they were sure he had done the best he could with what he had. Those who had questioned his qualifications for command of the Army of Tennessee felt vindicated. The Hero of Chickamauga had become the Villain of Franklin.

Hood guessed what he might expect from governmental and political figures in the capital, but he hoped for a better reception from the Prestons, and especially from Buck. He longed for a reunion with her, the chance to see her smile and to hear her soft voice assuring him that all would yet be well. He had not received a letter from her in months, which was not surprising given his peregrinations through Georgia, Alabama, Tennessee, and at the last, Mississippi. He prayed that she had forgiven him for Willie's death and that she still loved him, but in his heart he feared otherwise.

The Prestons were settled again in Richmond. At the request of Jefferson Davis, John Preston had resumed his duties at the Conscription Bureau, where his services were even more essential than they had been at the beginning of the war.

The Confederacy was reduced to arming old men and boys. Even men who worked in the mills and armories and foundries were taken from their jobs to man the lines of defense around cities such as Richmond and Petersburg, which were constantly threatened by Union forces. They were needed as much in their civilian jobs as in the army, and President Davis hoped that General Preston could devise some way to keep the factories manned and still maintain an army for defense. Women were working in some factories, but there were tasks beyond their strength to perform. It had been suggested that Negroes might serve in the army, but this was strongly opposed in the Confederate Congress. All this presented a challenge for John Preston, and he accepted it, but with a heavy heart.

Buck was reluctant to leave her home, since so many things there brought fond memories of Willie. She found comfort in going to his old room where, holding his favorite jacket against her face, she could breathe in his familiar scent lingering in its fabric and dream of happier times when he had worn it.

Looking through the drawers in his bureau, she discovered the emerald and diamond studs he had worn in his dress shirt on very special occasions. She thought, "If I could have a ring made from one of these I'd have something of Willie's to cherish forever." She carried them to her parents' room, where she knew she would find her mother.

"Mama, look. I've found Willie's dress shirt studs in that leather box he bought in Florence. May I have one of them made into a ring?"

Caroline picked up one of the studs gently. She remembered the last time Willie had worn them, at the party they had given after returning from Europe, before the war began and wrecked so many lives.

"I think that would be a good thing to do, dear," she said. "I'll ask your father to take it to Mr. Edwards and see what sort of setting he can make for it."

"Thank you, Mama," said Buck, as she hugged her mother affectionately. "I'll treasure it more than any ring I have."

Caroline regarded her daughter thoughtfully. "More than your engagement ring?" she asked.

Buck looked down at the diamond ring John Darby had given her from Sam Hood. "That's different. Something that was Willie's is special to me. But I'll never forget him even if I don't have any tangible thing to remind me of him."

"I know," said her mother. "Willie will be a part of us and live in our hearts always. I'll speak to your father when he comes home. It shouldn't be too difficult to make a ring from one of these studs. Perhaps your sisters would like to have one also, since there are five studs."

"I know it's selfish, Mama, but I wish I could be the only one to have a ring."

Caroline nodded. "Perhaps Mamie and Tudie could have a brooch or a locket made from the studs, something unique for each of you. They loved Willie too."

"I know they did, just as you and Papa did."

"When Willie was killed, I thought my heart would break, but having your father and you girls and Jack to think of, as well as Jack's Celestine and Mamie's John, means that I, and all of us, must go on with our lives and do the best we can. Willie would want us to do that. He was the happiest child, and a happy young man. We were fortunate to have him as long as we did."

"Yes. we were," whispered Buck, as she brushed away the tears rolling down her cheeks.

Before the Prestons left for Richmond in November, Mr. Edwards had completed the ring for Buck. He had designed a simple setting, with the two emeralds and single diamond of the stud placed in gold wires and set diagonally on a gold band. Buck slid it onto her finger and felt that somehow Willie knew and approved. She could almost hear his voice saying, "Now, honey, take care of that—it's a gift from me to you, with love."

"I promise I'll keep it safe till I die, Willie," she said in her softest voice.

In Richmond, the Prestons were received warmly by all their friends and acquaintances who had missed them during the months they had been away. Buck and her sisters regretted that Mrs. Chesnut was still in Columbia. She had been such a good friend to them, and her house had been like a second home. Caroline Preston missed her most of all, as a friend and confidante. There were a great many things she would have liked to discuss with Mary Chesnut.

Everyone in Richmond had followed with interest the events in Georgia and Tennessee, and by January knew that John Bell Hood was on his way back to the capital. There was much speculation among the ladies as to the reception he would receive at the Preston home. Some murmured behind their fans, "Buck Preston will never marry him now. It's nearly a year since they were engaged, and I hear she's been seeing other men." Others were sympathetic to Hood and declared, "Poor man, he's suffered enough. Buck would never jilt him when he's been forced to resign and give up everything. She's far too kind-hearted."

When a weary Sam Hood arrived in Richmond, he took a hack to the Spottswood Hotel, the only hotel whose name he could remember. He was fortunate enough to secure a small room where he could rest and change from his travel clothes before setting off for the Capitol, where he hoped to be able to see Jefferson Davis. But when he made his way to Davis' office he was turned away. "Come back tomorrow," said the president's secretary. Hood realized that meeting with the president might not be as easy as he had imagined. He was no longer the popular general he had been after Gettysburg and Chickamauga. Doors which had opened for him then were closed now.

He resolved to find the Prestons' residence. Jack had given him their address, the same house they had rented for their previous stay in the capital. He found a hack outside the hotel and directed the driver to Cary Street.

After a brief, uncomfortable ride in the rickety hack, they stopped at the Prestons', where Hood told the driver to wait for him, then walked haltingly up the steps and knocked at the door. Just as in the past, William Walker opened the door and said, "Come in, sir. May I take your hat?"

"Hello, William," said Hood. "You don't seem surprised to see me."

"No, sir. Major Preston sent a wire saying you were coming. We looked to see you any time after that."

"Is Miss Buck in?"

"No, sir. She and Miss Tudie and Miss Mamie, Mrs. Darby I should say, are visiting Mrs. Davis."

"What time do you expect them back?"

"I don't rightly know, sir. They didn't say."

"Are General and Mrs. Preston here?"

"No, sir."

"Please tell them that I called and that I'll come back tomorrow."

"Yes, sir, but I don't think anyone will be here then."

"Well, when will they be at home?" asked Hood in exasperation.

"I couldn't say, sir. They've been away a great deal since we've been here."

"William, I want to see Miss Buck. I've waited a long time. Can't you tell me when she'll be home?"

William looked down, his brow wrinkled in thought. Then he said, "If you come early in the morning, General, you can catch her before she goes out."

"Thank you, William, thank you. I'll be here by eight o'clock." Hood smiled at the butler and turned away, content to know that tomorrow he would finally see his darling Buck.

The hack driver said, "Can I take you back to the Spottswood, sir?"

"Yes, take me back." Hood climbed slowly into the hired carriage and sat down, an expression of utter satisfaction on his face.

The next morning, Hood dressed in his best uniform and found the same hack driver. "Take me to the same address as yesterday."

"Yes, sir."

Hood sat in the carriage, impatiently waiting for their arrival at the Prestons. As soon as they reached the house, he alighted as quickly as possible and paid the driver.

He walked up the steps and knocked. William opened the door and said, "Why, General Hood. Good morning!"

"Good morning, William. Is Miss Buck in?"

"Yes, sir, I believe she just finishing breakfast."

"Tell her I'm here, please."

"Yes, sir."

William walked down the hall to the dining room where the family sat around the oval mahogany table. He said, "Excuse me, Miss Buck, but General Hood is here and would like to speak to you."

Buck half rose from her chair, her napkin clutched in her hand, and then sat back down. She looked at her mother and said, "Mama, I have to go to him."

Caroline was astonished that Hood would call at such an early hour but she said, "Very well, Buck. There is a fire in the back parlor. You may talk to him there."

"Thank you," said Buck in a strangled voice as she left the room.

As soon as she entered the hall Sam Hood advanced toward her. His face lit up, and he exclaimed, "Buck! Let me look at you. You are even more lovely than I remembered. Oh, darling girl, I have waited an eternity for this moment."

He reached out for her, ready to clasp her in his arms, but she put out her hand and said, "Sam. I can't believe you're here. Jack told us you were coming but I didn't expect you this soon."

"Aren't you glad to see me? It's been a long time, I know, but I love you, Buck. Nothing has changed for me. Have you changed your mind about me?"

"Oh, Sam, so much has happened since we saw each other. I feel as if we are strangers. I need time to know you again. Please don't rush me."

Hood took her hand in his and looked for his ring, but it was not on Buck's finger. Instead, she wore an emerald and diamond ring he had never seen before. He lifted her hand and asked, "Whose ring is that?"

"Mine," said Buck sharply. "Papa had it made for me from one of Willie's dress shirt studs."

"Oh." Hood said blankly. "I'm sorry, Buck. I didn't know that. I haven't had a chance to tell you how deeply I regret your brother's death. He was a fine soldier and a good man."

"Yes, he was."

"If I could have done anything to prevent. . . ."

Buck interrupted him. "Yes, I know. I can't talk about it."

"Buck, if you feel I'm a stranger, may I call on you so that we can become as we were before I left Richmond last year?"

Buck hesitated. "Yes, I suppose so. Right now I need to think about it."

"I understand. I'm going to try again today to see President Davis. May I call on you tomorrow?"

"Yes."

Hood looked at Buck wistfully. This was not the way he had envisioned their meeting after a year's absence. Nevertheless, he would not give up.

"Till tomorrow, then. Good-bye, Buck."

"Good-bye, Sam. William will show you out."

At the door, William handed Hood his hat and said, "Good-bye, sir."

"Thank you, William." Hood walked down to the street and stood on the sidewalk. He felt lonelier than he ever had in his whole life.

William closed the door and went to find his sister, Maria. "I tell you what, Miss Buck not marrying that man now or later. He lost his chance with her sure enough."

With the defeat of the Army of Tennessee under Hood, and the uncontested march to the sea of Sherman in Georgia, the Confederacy faced insurmountable problems in the lower South. In Virginia, Lee's army held the lines between the Chickahominy and Petersburg, the only defense Richmond had left, with the Confederates freezing and starving in the trenches they had dug with immense effort.

In the Confederate Congress, the question of enlisting slaves in the armies of the South was debated again. President Davis urged the purchase of forty thousand slaves to serve as army cooks and laborers, but there were objections to this idea from all sides. General Robert E. Lee believed that arming the slaves to fight for the Confederacy, with emancipation as a reward for their service, was the best possible measure, if it could be done without delay. However, no action was taken by the Congress until March, and even then emancipation was not included as part of the law.

A futile effort was made to control the cargoes of the blockade runners, who were bringing in luxuries instead of necessities, but in March the Confederate Congress removed all restrictions against the blockade runners, overruling Jefferson Davis' wishes. By the time this happened, there were no more ports in the South still open anyway.

A few men hoped to gain a peaceful settlement to the war. In Paris, Mr. Mason and Mr. Slidell endeavored to enlist the support of the Emperor Napoleon III by suggesting that the Confederacy might begin a program of emancipation of the slaves in return for recognition by France, but the emperor had no interest in that proposal. In the United States, there was a meeting of Confederate Commissioners and President Lincoln and Secretary of State Seward on board a ship at Hampton Roads, Virginia. President Lincoln refused to accept any terms except the disbanding of Confederate armies, restoration of Federal authority in all the seceded states, and enforcement of the Emancipation Proclamation. This was not acceptable to the Confederates, and hopes for a negotiated peace died.

In Richmond, John Bell Hood continued his attempts to see Jefferson Davis, but the president was too involved with his struggles with the Congress and the military leaders to be concerned with the plans of a failed lieutenant general.

Like Lee's Army of Northern Virginia, the inhabitants of Richmond faced starvation daily. Prices for the most common foods were at unheard of levels: fifty dollars for a bushel of cornmeal, seventy-five dollars for a bushel of beans. The Confederate dollars used to buy these goods were virtually worthless. There were dealers in goods which had been brought in through the blockade, sugar, coffee, flour, even soap and candles, but few could afford them.

Even the Prestons, despite their wealth, found life in the capital increasingly difficult. They had sent most of their servants home, keeping only Maria and William. The Preston ladies, like their friends, discovered that great ingenuity was required to keep their dresses clean and mended, and food on the table at mealtime.

With so many daily crises to cope with, Buck had little time to think about Sam Hood or anyone else.

Hood came to call on her frequently. At times he seemed disturbed or almost dazed, and Buck wondered if something more than his estrangement from President Davis and her family's cold reception of him was affecting him. She herself could hardly remember the feelings she had had when she accepted his proposal a year ago. How she wished that had never happened.

One day after a particularly unsettling interview she asked Mamie, "Does Sam seem very different to you? I find him acting sometimes as though he were not really speaking to me, as though he were in a daze."

"I expect that may have to do with the morphine he uses. John says it often has that effect."

"What do you mean? I know he takes a little now and then for the pain in his leg, but that wouldn't affect his behavior."

"Buck, I didn't want to mention it, but I believe he takes more than a little occasionally. John says there are rumors that that is the reason he lost all those battles."

"I don't believe it! John is cruel to say such a thing!"

"He also said that it will get worse, and you could not live with it."

"You are all against my marrying Sam and always have been!"

"I think you are against it too, but too stubborn to admit it."

"Oh!" said Buck, and ran out of the room, slamming the door behind her

Mamie was both sorry and relieved that it had all come out in the open. She slowly sat down by the fire and took up the sock she was knitting of coarse brownish-gray wool. She knew she was right, but could think of no way to help her sister. Buck's loyalty had been challenged, and she could not honorably break her engagement to Hood.

Just then a knock sounded at the front door, and she heard William say, "Good afternoon, General Hood. Come right in. I believe the ladies are in the parlor."

Hood entered the parlor, and seeing only Mamie seated near the fireplace said, "Oh, I thought Buck was here too."

"Good afternoon, General," said Mamie. "As you see, I am alone."

"You used to call me 'Sam', Miss Mamie."

"Yes, I did, once. But things have changed since then, haven't they?"

"Not for me. I thought you were my friends, you and John. I have never lost my regard for you, and you know I love your sister and hope to marry her."

Mamie set her knitting aside and said, "Please, sit down. I think you do love Buck, but I'm not sure you and she should marry. I don't believe you realize how much Willie's death has affected her. She still feels that you are to blame, much as she tries not to. How could she be happy, married to you and holding you responsible for Willie's being killed? And consider how little you have in common. You are older, and your background is so different from hers."

Hood stared at Mamie in dismay. Until this moment he had assumed that she was one of his supporters, particularly since her husband had been his friend for years, and the surgeon for his Texas brigade. What could have changed her opinion of him? He said, "You are very blunt, Mrs. Darby. What you say about my age and background is true, but surely Buck knows that I could not have prevented your brother's death, much as I wish that had been possible."

"Mama and Papa have never really approved of you, or of your marrying Buck."

"She has known that all along."

"The worst is your use of morphine!"

Hood's eyes blazed with anger. "Who told you that? John Darby, I suppose. Do you have any idea what my life has been like since my leg was amputated? Constant, unremitting pain, whether I walked, rode, sat, or stood. Yes, I do take morphine, but only when I could bear the pain no longer. How can you know what I suffered? I cannot believe your sister feels as you do. Please tell her I called." Hood rose abruptly and left the room, his whole body stiff with rage.

Mamie sat back in her chair, her face flushed and her hands gripped tightly together in her lap. "Well!" she exclaimed. "John was right. That man is certainly not refined or gentlemanly. I'm glad I told him what I thought of him, but what shall I tell Buck?"

When Buck came back downstairs later, she found her sister still sitting in the parlor, gazing into the dying embers of the coal fire which barely warmed the area nearest the fireplace.

"What are you doing, sitting here in the dusk, Mamie?"

Mamie was startled by the sound of Buck's voice. She had been going over her conversation with Sam Hood in her mind and had begun to have doubts of the propriety of expressing her opinion so strongly. She was sure that she was right, but perhaps it was wrong to say such hurtful things to a man who had indeed suffered greatly. After a moment's pause she said, "Oh, I've been thinking. . . ."

"About what? Are you worried about John? Have you heard something?"

"No, it's not that. Sam Hood was here this afternoon and I said some things to him that perhaps I shouldn't have."

"What in the world did you say?" asked Buck, as she stretched out her hands to the flickering fire.

"I told him that I didn't believe you and he were suited to each other and that you didn't have anything in common. And that you blamed him for Willie's death."

"And what did he say to that?"

"He agreed with me, but he said he loved you and thought you understood that he couldn't have prevented what happened to Willie."

"But he's heard all that before. You must have said something else."

Mamie hesitated, then plunged ahead. "Well, I did. I never told you, but when John came back from Georgia that time when he took the artificial limbs to Sam and brought back your engagement ring, he told me that Sam was taking morphine and that he was worried about him. And this afternoon I accused Sam of taking too much."

Buck collapsed into the nearest chair. "Oh, Mamie! You didn't!"

"Yes, I did," said Mamie defiantly. "And I'm not sorry, not a bit."

"But why? Why would you say such a hateful thing to Sam. I thought you liked him."

"I did. But John says he doesn't think it would be right for you to marry him, and I agree. So when he came and you weren't here, I just told him what I thought."

"You mean you told him what John thought. Poor Sam."

Mamie looked rather abashed but said, "John has known him longer than we have, and he must be right about him."

"Perhaps he is, but consider, Mamie. With all that has happened to Sam lately, how can I break our engagement? It would be heartless."

"It would be much worse if you married him when you didn't love him, and I don't think you do, truly."

"Oh, Mamie, I'm so tired and so worried. Every day seems to bring some new disaster. I just can't deal with my own problems right now. Things will work out somehow. I don't want to talk about Sam anymore. Let's find something to eat. Where's Mama?"

"Probably in the kitchen, trying to make an apple pie with no apples in it. She said she was going to try out the instructions in the Confederate Receipt Book she bought. It calls for using soaked crackers and spices instead of apples."

"I hope it's better than the potato pudding she tried last week. I do miss Harrison. What a shame he was sent home. It's hard to remember now what really good food tastes like."

Mamie agreed fervently, and the two left the dim parlor to find their mother and the apple pie without apples.

Richmond's defenses were stretched to the breaking point, but the situation in South Carolina was even more perilous for the soldiers and civilians there. Sherman met with little or no resistance in his march from Atlanta to Savannah. That city surrendered to him in December of 1864, and on the first of February he turned north and moved into South Carolina with sixty thousand men, all ready to make sure that the state which had been the first to secede would pay the price.

Most of the Confederate troops were in or near Charleston, at the insistence of Governor Magrath, who believed that if Charleston fell the Confederacy would be lost.

General Wade Hampton, more practical, declared that Branchville, where the railroads from Charleston, Augusta, and Columbia joined, was more vital to the Confederacy than Charleston, but his advice to concentrate troops there was not followed.

Sherman's army took Branchville and moved on to Columbia, General Hampton and the remnants of the Confederate cavalry moving out of the city as Sherman's guns shelled it from across the river. On the seventeenth of February, the Union Army marched into the state capital, which had been surrendered by its mayor, Dr. Goodwyn. Despite Sherman's promise to protect civilians and civilian property, the city was destroyed.

Some news of this appeared in the Richmond newspapers, but it was not until Caroline Preston received a letter from one of her friends in Columbia that the Prestons learned the true extent of the destruction. Caroline read the letter aloud to her shocked family:

> My dear Caroline,
> Be thankful you are in Richmond! We have experienced the horror of invasion by Sherman's dreaded forces and a devastating fire. The city is in ruins. From our unfinished statehouse to the river nothing is left but a few chimneys and charred trees.
> This has been such a terrible shock to us all. We had believed that we would be safe here. Indeed, there were refugees here from Charleston because they feared that their city would be the next target of Sherman's incendiaries. Who can forget the result of his army's occu-

pation of Atlanta? And the sixty mile wide path of destruction left in his wake from Atlanta to Savannah?

When General Sherman and the Yankee army appeared on the western side of the river and began shelling the city, our mayor, Dr. Goodwyn, no doubt remembering that Savannah was spared (the idea of Sherman presenting it to Lincoln as a Christmas gift!) went to Sherman and surrendered our city to him. Dr. Goodwyn asked at that time if our citizens would be safe, and the general assured him that no civilian or civilian property would be harmed. A cruel, false promise, for as soon as the Union troops entered Columbia, fires, looting, and drunken rioting broke out.

General Hampton and the cavalry left the city, moving north, as Sherman came in, leaving us defenseless and at the mercy of Sherman's brutal soldiery.

There were bales of cotton left on Richardson Street and set on fire to prevent their falling into Union hands. General Hampton had ordered the cotton fired, and then, realizing the danger, ordered it extinguished, but, alas, the high winds made it impossible to prevent the fires from spreading. No attempt was made by the heartless Yankees to control the fires that destroyed our old state house, which burned very rapidly, since, as you know, it was constructed of wood. The unfinished new capitol sustained some damage from the shells fired by the Federal guns, but being made of stone, it did not burn. I have heard that when the city's fire engines were attempting to pour water on the blaze, their fire hoses were cut by soldiers, who mocked their efforts.

The flames eventually reached the Ursuline convent and school and reduced the building to ashes. Even the church was not spared. Mother Superior Baptista Lynch, her nuns, and the girls who were students at the school were obliged to seek refuge in the cemetery, spending the cold February night huddled under water-soaked blankets to protect themselves from the fiery sparks that filled the air.

All this I learned the following day when we were able to venture out and see for ourselves what was left of our once lovely city.

Your home had been taken over by General John Logan for his headquarters. His soldiers occupied the house and picketed their horses in your mother's garden. You may imagine the result! As it was told to me, barrels of pitch had been placed in the basement in anticipation of setting fire to your home as soon as the soldiers left to continue their work of destruction elsewhere. But Baptista Lynch approached Sherman and asked for a home for the nuns and young girls left without shelter after the fire. That monster Sherman had the audacity to say that she might have any house in Columbia still standing! After the dreadful night of conflagrations there were many which were not. The Mother

Superior said that *yours* was the house she wanted. Your past kindnesses to the convent must have guided her to that choice.

General Logan was forced to remove the pitch and to abandon the house to more deserving occupants. When you return, you will find your home undamaged, except that many of your beautiful oil paintings and sculptures have been vandalized or stolen by the soldiers who stayed there.

Dr. Gibbes has lost everything except a small statue of his son. His vast library, his collections of fossils and Indian artifacts were all consumed by the flames which ravaged his home, deliberately set by the Yankees, who roamed the streets of Columbia in drunken bands. I can hardly credit it, but it must be true that the whiskey in the distillery was not destroyed before the Union troops arrived, as it should have been, and soldiers and slaves as well became intoxicated and lost all restraint.

I regret that I must tell you the sad news that Millwood is no more. A group of soldiers, bent on looting and burning, made their way out to that incomparable plantation and what they could not carry or drive away they wrecked and burned. Mercifully, the Misses Hampton had fled by then, having preserved what they could of their possessions by wrapping them in those rose colored curtains that adorned their drawing room and sending them to York County in the charge of Cato, who reportedly drove the wagon which contained them with such care that nothing was broken. That, and what few things they could carry with them, is all that is left of Millwood. They are safe in the Up Country, but oh, what agony they must feel to know that their home is naught but a burnt-out shell.

You remember that scandalous girl, Marie Boozer, and her disgraceful mother, Amelia Feaster, who was so friendly with those Yankee prisoners when General Preston was in charge of the prison camps? Well, they have left town with Sherman's army, in the Elmores' best carriage. They had the impudence to take that handsome black carriage and leave their own antiquated wreck in the Elmores' carriage house. We always knew that they were not ladies, and this surely confirms our opinion. I never thought Marie was all that beautiful either, no matter what some gentlemen claimed.

Trinity Church has been preserved, but, alas, Dr. Shand was accosted by a band of soldiers as he was attempting to carry away the church records and his sermons and all the communion silver. He was forced to relinquish the trunk in which he had placed them, and the soldiers took all the silver and cast the records and sermons to the winds. Later, Dr. Shand found some of his sermons, but that treasured silver is in some pillager's knapsack. I suppose we must be thankful that our church is still standing, when Christ Church is in ruins.

We hear that the Yankees intended to burn the First Baptist Church, as it was the site of the writing of the Ordinance of Secession, but when the pack of soldiers came in search of the sanctuary the sexton was standing on the steps of the building. When asked if this was the Baptist Church he supposedly indicated the Methodist Church a block away as being the church they sought. Conceive of the feelings of the Methodist congregation when they learned the reason their building was put to the torch!

I do not know how we can survive in this wilderness that our beloved city has become. Every material thing we treasured is gone. Only our faith in God and in our President and General Lee sustains us.

Dear friend, I long to see you again, but I rejoice that you and your family are in Virginia and far away from this scene of desolation and despair.

As ever, your friend,
Charlotte Simpson

There was a long silence as Caroline Preston finished reading Mrs. Simpson's lengthy letter. Finally, she said, "This is dreadful! I cannot believe that any army could behave in such a lawless and brutal manner. What a mercy that our home was saved, but to think that Millwood has been utterly destroyed. I wonder if Woodlands is still standing? And what of all our servants who were there in their quarters? Oh, I wish Charlotte had told me something about them."

The Prestons sat together quietly, their thoughts and prayers with their relatives and friends in South Carolina. After hearing of the disaster that had befallen Columbia, they could not help but wonder if and when Richmond might suffer the same fate.

They had not long to wait. As winter ended and spring began, the Union armies gained more and more ground in the Confederate States. Their forces by now greatly outnumbered the Confederate armies which were left. General Grant was prepared to make a supreme effort to end the war.

By late March, even Jefferson Davis was forced to realize that Richmond was in grave danger and no longer safe for his wife and children. Reluctantly, Varina Davis agreed to take the children and go south to Charlotte, which might prove to be a place of refuge for them. Before they left, Mrs. Davis sent a note to the Prestons, telling them that she and her family were to take the train south the next day and urging the Prestons to do the same.

John Preston had feared that it might come to this, and with the departure of the Davises and their servants he resolved to make arrangements for his own family to return to South Carolina. He called on President Davis, who urged him to leave Richmond at once.

"You can do no more here, General Preston. Your duty is to your wife and children. I release you from your position with the Conscription Bureau: there is no one left to recruit," Davis declared.

"I regret I could not accomplish all you had hoped for, sir. With your permission, I shall take my family home to South Carolina."

"Yes, go soon. Thank you for your services and your loyalty."

"Thank you, Mr. President," said Preston. "Good-bye."

"Good-bye, General. I wish you luck on your journey."

As soon as he left the president's office, Preston went to the train station and secured the only available space for his family and servants, a boxcar. When he returned home and told his wife they were to leave Richmond as soon as possible, Caroline was shocked at the sudden turn of events. She had not expected to leave Richmond so soon. She immediately began to think of what they should take and what could be left behind. John told her that unlike their other trips to Columbia, they would be traveling in a boxcar, and not only that, they would have others with them, including the Lawson Clays, Captain Rodgers, Mr. Portman, a friend of Wade Hampton III, and of course their various servants, men and women.

"Good heavens, John! Will there be room for all of us?" Caroline had asked, on hearing this.

"At this stage, with so many people desperate to leave Richmond, we are fortunate to have only this many people with us, my dear."

"You are right. I'll make sure we pack very carefully and only take what is absolutely necessary. But I do hope there will be room for my silver, if nothing else."

"Well, do the best you can. Will you be ready to leave in the morning?"

"Yes, I think so. I'll have Maria and William collect and pack the silver, and the girls and I will pack our clothes. We should be finished in a few hours."

There was no time to say good-bye to their friends in Richmond. Buck sent a brief note to Sam Hood, but by the time he received it, the Prestons had left the city. Mamie left a message for John Darby with a neighbor, who promised to tell him that the Prestons were on their way to South Carolina, probably to York.

With a last look at Richmond as the train pulled away from the station, the Prestons began their journey to York and, they hoped, safety from the advancing Union armies.

During the interminable train journey, the Preston sisters had occupied the time reliving their romances. Thinking of their beaux who had been killed or captured, they had become too sad to continue.

Their talk turned to Willie, and suddenly Buck knew with absolute certainty that she could never marry Sam Hood. She said nothing to the others, but moved slightly away and put her head down as though sleeping.

The thought of Willie, killed while under Sam's command, made marriage to him impossible. She could never forget the day she and Mamie had returned from a visit to Mrs. Chesnut to hear the terrible news from William and to find a stricken family. Of course it was not Sam's fault. She knew that, but she also knew that every time she looked at him she would see Willie's face, and she couldn't bear it.

The only person who even came near to Willie in her affections had been Rawlins Lowndes. Thinking of the letter he had written to her when he learned of her engagement, she shuddered in despair. How handsome he had looked the last time she saw him. He had been so formal and correct, taking leave of her parents when he and Cousin Wade had come to pay a farewell visit, months ago now. Her engagement had not been mentioned.

She had thought so much about what she should do. Her mother had been right from the beginning. If only her father had been firm and not indulged his favorite daughter as he usually did, she would never have become engaged to Sam in in the first place. "Oh, Buck, stop!" she told herself. "Stop blaming others for your own weakness. You wouldn't listen to anyone, and now you're sorry. It's happened over and over again. Just as Mrs. Chesnut told me, I'm playing at love-making and hurting others. It all begins and ends in vanity. But when I see Sam again I'm going to tell him the truth—that I can't marry him. And that I'm sorry I made him so unhappy. It is the right thing to do, I know, for both of us."

XII
York, 1865

Buck came slowly down the stairs at the McDonald house in York where the Preston family had found refuge. The McDonalds were friends of John and had kindly taken them in after a terrible journey from Richmond.

Buck had received word from Sam Hood several days previously that he was in Chester and, finding that she was in York, was coming to see her. She promptly sent word to Mary Chesnut, who was also in Chester and whom she knew Sam would see, to try to keep him there and stop his coming to York. To no avail, as he was now in the McDonalds' parlor waiting for her. Only God knew how she dreaded this meeting. She prayed He would give her strength to do what must be done and words to say what had to be said.

She opened the door to the parlor. Sam Hood, standing at the mantel, slowly turned. He knew at once that, as he had long feared, all his dreams were over. The look on her face was enough. He had been so angry in Chester when he heard someone refer to his "broken engagement", but even then he had a strange certainty that they were right. He had waited too long. Hoping to win over Mrs. Preston and allowing Buck's procrastinations to stand in the way, he had lost his chance. If only he had insisted on an immediate wedding in Richmond instead of agreeing to wait until the ceremony could take place in Columbia. His wedding clothes were now packed away in a trunk at the Preston home, where they had been for six months, unless they had gone up in Sherman's conflagration or were adorning some Yankee soldier. Why on earth was he thinking of wedding clothes now?

He looked sadly at her. "It's all over, isn't it my darling? It was too perfect for me and not perfect enough for you."

"Oh, Sam, I am so sorry. I never thought it would end this way." Slipping his ring off her finger, she handed it to him.

He, taking her hand in his, gently folded her fingers back over the ring, saying, "Keep the ring, my dear, in remembrance of me. No other woman can ever take your place in my heart, and I would never give it to anyone else."

"No, no. Someday you will find someone who will love you as you deserve," she said as she gave it back to him.

Reluctantly he tucked it in his watch pocket. "I am going back through Chester, and Mrs. Chesnut wants you and Miss Mamie to come to her. I will escort you if you wish."

"Sam, Sam, you are so kind. We will pack our things and go with you tomorrow, if Mama agrees."

"Please present my compliments to your parents. I do not feel quite equal to seeing them. I shall await your answer at the York Inn."

Buck went back up the stairs to find her mother. Caroline, who was writing a letter, looked inquiringly at her daughter. "Well, dear? I see General Hood has just left."

"Mama, do you remember that time when I refused Cousin Ransom and was so miserable because he said he would go out and get shot?"

"Indeed I do. That was a night I shall never forget!"

"Well, you told me then that I had done the right thing. That it would be far worse to marry someone I didn't really love; that it would cause a lot more pain later. I didn't understand exactly what you meant then, but now I do. I don't know what is the matter with me. I can't ever seem to decide something once and for all. Willie said it was my greatest fault and so did Mrs. Chesnut. I thought I loved Sam, but I can see now I was just flattered that he loved me so much and all the girls in Richmond were jealous. I should have listened to you."

"Have you told him that you don't love him?"

"I didn't have to. He seemed to know it already. We have spent so little time together, it was almost like talking to a stranger."

"What will he do now?"

"At least he didn't say he hoped he would get shot! He will probably go back to Texas and perhaps to Mexico. But Mama, he did say he would escort Mamie and me to Mrs. Chesnut in Chester tomorrow. She wants us to come stay with her very badly."

"That was certainly kind of him. I know he is devoted to Mary and she to him. I think he has behaved in a very gentlemanly manner. I can't pretend I'm sorry. I think you have acted wisely. You had too little in common for a happy marriage. I'm sure it will all turn out for the best. If you are going to leave tomorrow, you had better go tell Mamie and ask Maria to help you pack your things. I wish I could go with you."

"Thank you, Mama. Will you tell Papa for me?"

"Yes, indeed. I'm sure he will be very relieved."

The next day, Mamie and Buck, escorted by General Hood, made their way to Chester, on horseback. Mamie was unusually quiet. She, for once, could think of nothing to say. She was eager to discuss the whole situation with John and to hear his opinion, but since he was not here, she would have to wait and talk with Mrs. Chesnut. She doubted that this would come as a great surprise to that lady, who had hinted many times that, fond as she was of Sam, she thought it was a mésalliance.

Mary Chesnut was delighted to receive her guests. "You see I did bring the ladies to you, Mrs. Chesnut. They permitted me to accompany them, I suspect, because no one else was available," said Hood, as he helped Mamie and Buck dismount from their horses.

"Why, no, Sam, we are grateful to you for escorting us," Mamie replied.

"Yes, thank you, Sam," said Buck. "We would not have been able to come without your help."

"Let me call someone to take your horses," said Mary Chesnut.

"No, no, I'll take them around to the barn myself." Hood carefully remounted his horse, gathered the reins of the other two animals, and led them away to the barn behind the house.

"I am so glad to see you all again. How is your mother? And Tudie? Have you recovered from your trip from Richmond?" Mrs. Chesnut looked closely at Buck, who seemed unnaturally quiet. "Has something happened? Nothing is wrong in York, I hope."

Buck bowed her head and sighed softly. "It isn't that, Mrs. Chesnut. I have told Sam I can't marry him. I know it was the right thing to do, but still I feel guilty that I allowed him to hope for so long."

"Dear girl, I am sorry for Sam, but you were not suited to each other. Better to break it off now."

Mamie agreed. "John said months ago that he hoped Buck would give up the idea of marrying Sam."

"Everyone seems to have known what I should do except me," commented Buck.

"Do you mind that Sam is here in Chester?" asked Mrs. Chesnut.

"No. He has behaved in such a thoughtful way that he has made it easy for me to be in his company," Buck answered.

"Come in the house and we'll put your things away and have something to drink, even if it's only water. Do you remember the starvation parties we had in Richmond with nothing for refreshments but water from the 'Jeems'? All that seems a hundred years ago now," said Mary Chesnut, as she led the way into her rented quarters.

During the time Buck and Mamie were staying with Mrs. Chesnut, they saw a constant stream of refugees passing through Chester. Among them were Mrs. Davis and her children, in flight from Richmond. They had been in Charlotte, but were continuing southward in hope of reaching Florida, where they might be able to find a ship to take them abroad, to safety, away from the pursuing Federal troops. Coming into Chester at dawn, they were met by Mary Chesnut, Mamie and Buck, and Sam Hood. They were invited to dine at Mrs. Chesnut's, who did not hesitate to welcome the Davises, unlike others who feared retribution from the Yankees if they befriended the wife and family of the president of the Confederacy.

Louly Wigfall and her father also came through the small town on their way to Texas and then possibly Mexico. Hood called on them, as an old friend.

"Why not join us, Sam? We're going to Texas. You have friends there, and there's nothing left for any of us this side of the Mississippi," said Senator Wigfall.

"Yes, do, Sam. We would be so happy to have you go with us," added Louly. Despite all that had happened, she still felt a tenderness toward Hood. She had admired him, then loved him, and when he had chosen Buck Preston rather than herself she had tried to forget him. But now, seeing him older, defeated, unhappy, she wanted to comfort him, just as she had when he had been wounded at Gettysburg.

"Perhaps I should," mused Hood. "There is a chance that I might be able to raise more troops for the Confederacy in Texas. Let me think about it."

"Of course, of course. You realize that we must leave very soon, perhaps even tomorrow," said Louis Wigfall.

"Then go without me. I'll catch up to you if I can. And if not, thank you both for all your kindness to me. I shall never forget it." Hood shook hands with the senator, and lifted Louly's hand to his lips. "Goodbye. God be with you."

He walked to the door and out into the darkness. He thought, "I'll go to Texas. Maybe not with the Wigfalls, but to Texas. That's where I belong."

The next day he went to say farewell to Mrs. Chesnut, Mamie and

Buck. "It's time for me to leave you ladies. I'm going west, to Texas if I can make it that far. Maybe I can do some good there. Knowing you all has been one of the greatest joys of my life. Good-bye."

"Good-bye, Sam, good-bye." The women stood on the porch and watched as Hood mounted his horse, removed his hat, and did not restore it to his head until he was far down the road.

Life in Chester settled into a routine. Mrs. Chesnut, Mamie and Buck visited their friends, did what they could to help other refugees, and talked. They discussed the news of the surrender of General Lee and their fears for the future. They had been greatly relieved to learn that the Prestons' home in Columbia was safe, but they were shocked and saddened by the burning of Millwood and Woodlands, which left the Hamptons homeless. It was difficult to believe that those magnificent plantation houses were gone forever. Sooner or later they would return to Columbia and see the desolation there, but for now Buck and Mamie were content to be with their friend. In her small house she entertained the elite of the Confederacy. Soldiers came and went. At night beds were made up on the landings to accommodate them. The troops which had fought so gallantly with General Lee and General Hampton and the other Southern leaders were on their way home from the battlefields.

Late one afternoon, as the setting sun gilded the white blossoms of the dogwood trees, Buck was alone in the garden, idly swinging to and fro in the old hammock slung between two giant live oaks. She dreamed of times long past, when life seemed full of promise and every day brought some new joy. How happy she and her brothers and sisters had been, and how heedless of the future. Now Willie was gone, Jack and Mamie were married, and only she and Tudie were left at home with their parents. She sighed, and shifted her position in the hammock. As she did so, she saw a horseman approaching, by his uniform a Confederate officer. She thought, "Oh, my! Another soldier to make a place for. Where can we find room?"

The mounted figure paused, and then urged his horse forward more quickly. He drew up beside the hammock and said quietly, "Buck."

She looked up in surprise and saw Rawlins Lowndes smiling down at her. "Rawlins! Where did you come from?" she exclaimed.

"I was in York and saw your parents. They told me you and Mamie were here in Chester with Mrs. Chesnut. And they told me you had broken your engagement to General Hood."

Buck nodded. "Yes. I came to realize I had made a terrible mistake. Sam is a good man, but we were not suited to each other."

Rawlins dismounted and tied his horse to one of the branches of the live oak. He reached out his hands and said, "Come and walk with me, Buck. I have a great deal to say to you."

Buck put her hands in his and rose from the swinging hammock. Impulsively, Rawlins drew her into his arms. Buck resisted for an instant and then yielded to his embrace. He held her close and murmured, "You don't know how often I've dreamed of this moment, holding you in my arms again. Oh, Buck, I've missed you more than I can ever say!"

Buck stood in the circle of his arms, her head on his gray-clad shoulder. She felt that she had come home after a long and weary journey.

Rawlins laid his cheek on her hair, and said, "I love you. I've loved you from the moment we met. The war separated us but now we can begin again."

Buck lifted her head and smiled at him, her violet eyes glowing. "I love you too. More than ever."

"Kiss me so I'll know I'm not dreaming," whispered Rawlins.

Buck raised her arms, encircled his neck and turned her radiant face up to his. Their lips met in a passionate kiss that brought back memories of their first kiss in the moonlit garden so long ago. But this kiss was now and real and the beginning of a new life for both of them.

At the end of the week, Caroline Preston received a letter from her friend. She was surprised when Maria appeared saying, "Captain Chesnut brought this letter for you."

"Captain Chesnut! Where is he? Why didn't you show him in?"

"He say he is in a big hurry and just told his aunt he would bring you this letter. Must be important."

Caroline tore it open and read:

> My dear Caroline,
>
> You may know this already, but when Johnny told me he had business in York I determined to write to you. The dear girls arrived safely, escorted by Sam Hood. They all seemed quiet and restrained, but I put it down to all that has happened lately to upset us. But then Buck told me that her engagement to Sam was broken, which made the situation much clearer.
>
> Poor Sam, I can't help feeling sorry for him, being attacked by all

the other generals, and now this! But I must say, my dear, I do think it is for the best, and I know you and John must be relieved.

My sympathy for Sam had blinded me as to what would be best for Buck, though I did warn her in the beginning about him. I do not think it would have been a happy match. Everyone cannot be as fortunate as we have been, and dear Mamie.

And Sam has left, on his way to Texas, he said. He came to tell us good-bye, and as he rode off he held his hat in his hand all the while he was in sight of the house. I asked Buck why he had remained uncovered so long and she said quietly, "In honor of my being here." I fear he may be a long time recovering from his disappointment.

Well, I am rambling on and almost forgetting the most important thing—imagine who appeared yesterday and went riding off with Buck for nearly two hours? Rawlins Lowndes! How could he have known? Mamie and I were almost out of our minds with curiosity, but Buck would not say one word when she came back. Just sat on the porch rocking and smiling. I really do not blame her wanting to escape all those bores in the drawing room moaning about when the Yankees are coming. As if we could do anything about it!

Caroline, my dear, all I can say is "Le roi est mort. Vive le roi!" I hope I am correct in my assumption.

Your friend,
Mary

P.S. Mamie or Buck may have written to you, but I have not seen either one with a pen in her hand since they arrived.

MBC

The End

Epilogue

Immediately after the end of the war, in April 1865, John and Caroline Preston took the family to Europe for a year, but their funds were low and they had to return to Columbia. They were forced to sell their art collection to maintain their house; in 1873 they had to sell the house as well. They moved to a smaller house at 128 Gervais Street.

John entered the banking business and became president of the Central National Bank of Columbia. He became famous as a speaker, especially in defense of secession and the Lost Cause. He died in 1881 at age seventy-two. Caroline died a year later.

Buck Preston and Colonel Rawlins Lowndes were married in Columbia on March 10, 1868. The Reverend Dr. Peter Shand performed the ceremony at the family home. It was the last family wedding to be held there.

Buck and Rawlins lived at Oaklands, his family's rice plantation on the Combahee River, and at their Charleston home on East Bay Street. They had three children, a son and two daughters.

Buck died in 1880 at age thirty-eight in Columbia, following an operation, and was buried in Magnolia Cemetery in Charleston. Rawlins lived to be eighty-one. He married a second time. With the decline of rice planting, he moved permanently to Charleston and went into his father's insurance business.

Mamie and John Darby accompanied the Prestons to Europe in 1865. John served as a volunteer surgeon at a Red Cross hospital during the Austro-Prussian War, later becoming medical director of the Prussian Army. They returned to Columbia in 1870, where he was a professor of surgery at the Medical College.

In 1874, he and Mamie and their children moved to New York City, where he became a professor at the University of the City of New York and was the author of many papers on surgery. His promising career was cut short when he died of blood poisoning in 1879, at age forty-two.

Mamie and their three children returned to Columbia to live with her parents. She became a teacher at Isabella Martin's school, and may have taught briefly at the School for Girls established in her childhood home. Mamie died in 1891 at age fifty-one. She and John are buried in Trinity churchyard.

Tudie married Captain Henry William Frost, of a famous Charleston family, on January 14, 1879, in New York City, where she was visiting the Darbys.

She and her husband lived in Charleston, where he was a cotton broker. They had two daughters and a son. She died in 1905 at age sixty. Henry Frost later married her niece, Caroline (Miela) Darby. He died in 1926.

John Bell Hood was captured by Federal troops in Natchez, Mississippi, on his way to Texas, and was paroled the next day, May 31, 1865. He made his way down the Mississippi River to New Orleans, and from there to Houston and San Antonio, Texas, where he was enthusiastically welcomed.

He returned to New Orleans in 1866, where he went into business for himself. In 1869 he was made president of an insurance company, with a salary of $5,000 a year, more than he had ever made as a Confederate general.

On April 30, 1868, he married Anna Maria Hennen, a young woman of considerable beauty, charm, and talent, from a well-to-do Louisiana family. The Hoods had eleven children in ten years, three sets of twins and five singles.

His insurance company failed in 1879, ruining Hood financially. In the summer of 1879 they were unable to leave New Orleans when the yellow fever epidemic broke out, and Hood, his wife, and their ten-year-old daughter died. Hood was forty-eight.

His Texas Brigade was prepared to buy a house and provide a housemother for the ten Hood orphans, but it was decided to place the children in individual homes, and one by one they were adopted.

A former chaplain of the Army of Tennessee said of Hood: "I never looked into the face of General Hood but felt an inspiration coming from him upon me always to act out the true, the brave, the right thing."

At the end of the war, Mary and James Chesnut went to Mulberry Plantation in Camden. It had been heavily damaged, and they were deeply in debt. Though disenfranchised during the period following the War, James took an active part in the re-building of South Carolina, leaving Mary to manage the plantation, which she did very efficiently. She also found time to write a novel and to work on revisions of her journal.

Eventually, they were able to build a new house in Camden, and, in spite of poor health and many family responsibilities, Mary continued her writing.

In 1885 both her husband and her mother died, and she was reduced to poverty, since under the terms of his father's will the Chesnut lands went to James' family. She died in 1886—never to see the publication of her journal.